THE
FRENCH
ANTILLES

THE
FRENCH
ANTILLES

A. Gerald Gravette

HIPPOCRENE BOOKS
New York

The author wishes to acknowledge the following for photographic contributions:
French Tourist Board, 3M Scotch Film, St. Martin Tourist Board, 'Ateuers Esope Lyon,' Office Tourisme du des Antilles et de la Guyane Francaises, Air France, French West Indies Tourist Board, Air Guadeloupe, Office Departmental du Tourisme de la Guadeloupe, Office Departmental du Tourisme de la Martinique, Pullman International Hotels, Hatteras Yachts, Sibarth. Other photos by the author. Street plans, maps and illustrations by the author. Old maps and prints from the author's collection.

We hope that this new, revised edition of *The French Antilles* will be of increased interest to the vacationer and holidaymaker, and we welcome any new information, additions and/ or corrections from our readers.

For information address: Hippocrene Books, Inc.
171 Madison Avenue, New York, NY 10016.

Library of Congress Cataloging-in-Publication Data

Gravette, A. G. (Andrew Gerald)
    The French Antilles/A. Gerald Gravette.
        p. cm.
    ISBN 0-87052-737-1
    1. West Indies, French—Description and travel—1981-
    I. Title. F2152.G73 1989
917.297'604—dc20   89-19944
                                                      CIP

Printed in the United States of America.

Contents

Introduction

Somewhere between Europe and Asia, speculated scholars of the ancient world, lay an archipelago of islands they named "Antilia." Although mythical, these islands, later known as the Antilles, were more tangible than any vague indications portrayed by imaginative geographers on early charts. Between Europe and the lure of Japan and China, past the western sunset, a necklace of tropical islands awaited discovery, cupped between the land masses of North and South America—The Antilles of the Caribbean.

Far different from the Mediterranean islands, more exotic than the warm islands of the Canaries, the Antilles had evolved from quirks in the shifting of continental plates, from the erosion of wind and sea on volcanic peaks, and from the action over millions of years by coral-forming polyps. In places thick vegetation carpeted rugged slopes, lush forests swept down to crescents of golden coral sand, lapped by lagoons, or to cliffs pounded by angry surf. The southernmost islands of the chain became arid and desert-like under the relentless sun, while in the north the regularity of tropical downpours insured fertile soil and bountiful rivers.

To the north of the Antilles lie four large islands and, stretching across the seas, between the Caribbean and the Atlantic Ocean, as far as the South American coastline a myriad specks form an island chain. This curve is divided into the islands to the Leeward and those to the Windward.

Straddling the two groups seven heavenly islands comprise the French Antilles. Caressed by turquoise waters on their Caribbean shores and linked by deep blue channels of the tropical Atlantic, these islands have evolved into some of the most idyllic vacation destinations on earth. Benefitting from a convenient location, easy access from Europe or from the Americas, these "Overseas Départements of France" offer isolated solitude, the brash celebration of a *joie de vivre* typical of Paris, or a comfortable medium of sophisticated cafe society in a tropical atmosphere. Almost 350 years of French influence have perfected an alluring septet of magical retreats.

French elegance, the unspoiled tranquility of their natural surroundings and the local's genuine effervescence, combine to create a group of island paradises—with a tang of garlic! Church spires, at home in any provincial French town, compete with the clinking masts of yachts bobbing in azure harbors. Low-rise modern municipal facilities contrast with tiny pavement cafes reminiscent of Montmartre. Classical doorways open onto narrow lanes and the streets are crammed with markets and shops. The backdrop is verdant mountain and the odd volcano, which invites trekking into primeval forest. Around sun-lit shores relaxing visitors pick secluded arcs of white sand, or native fishermen hang nets alongside gaudy washing lines. Flamboyant costumes indicate the traditions that have evolved the typical local music, an extravaganza of dances and the patois known as Creole.

Although situated in and among either staunchly British or Dutch islands, the French Antilles have maintained their unmistakable French air. The aroma of fresh coffee, the fragrance of mellow French wine and the scent of the world's finest perfumes confirms the essence of a Francophone Département. However, the mingling balm of fresh tropical fruit, spices, sugarcane and coconut palm assures the visitor that the French ambiance is just a cloak draped around the tempting delights of tropical Caribbean isles.

With a background of smuggling and privateering, being drawn into the Revolution of its mother country and having endured the harshness of poverty years, the seven islands of the French Antilles have capitalized on their greatest assets, their vivacious mingling of races from many lands, and their enchanting surroundings. Tourism has brought an unprecedented influx of revenue and transformed the lot of the islands without undermining the natural beauty or affecting the distinctive local way of life.

CHAPTER I

Caribbean Jewels

As the French islands are positioned in the northern and center sector of the Antilles they enjoy a similar ambiance both in climate and vegetation. Only one of the seven islands (Martinique) is in the region defined by the Windward group. This puts it in a different nautical category. However, all the French Antilles are characteristic of the islands known as the Lesser Antilles. In total, they occupy an area of sea about 18,000 square miles. Land surface amounts to some 11,000 square miles and this includes the major islands of Guadeloupe, Martinique, Marie-Galante, Saint Martin, La Désirade, Saint Barthélémy and *Isles des Saintes* plus minor coral and volcanic archipelegos. Politically, however, only the first two of these islands are the dominant.

Lying between the Caribbean Sea and the Atlantic Ocean, the French Antilles—spread across 350 miles of sea—are two of the three volcanically active isles in the region. Apart from the inner, Caribbean, side of Guadeloupe and central/northern Martinique (which consist of tropical mountain forest), the islands are quite green,

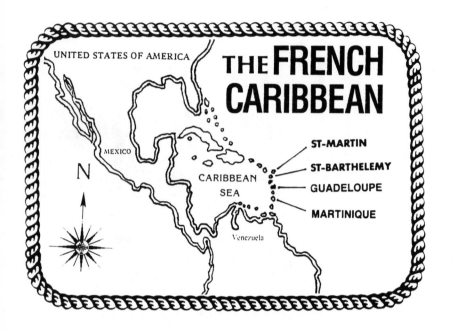

humid, and comparatively dry. Beaches are excellent for tourism and coves and bays are deep and prolific. The eastern section of Guadeloupe remains part of an arc of limestone isles and the western parts are a continuation of a volcanic link. Also in this chain, Martinique, the largest volcanic connection of the Windward islands, comprises three major peaks. Guadeloupe's volcano, Soufriere, is the highest peak in the Eastern Caribbean at nearly a mile in height.

Just the aboriginal names given to the main islands—"Karukera," Island of Beautiful Waters (Guadeloupe); and "Madinia" or "Madinina," Island of Flowers (Martinique) in the original Carib language, illustrate the very nature of these mystical isles. Even the half-island of St. Martin, shared with the Dutch Quarter (Sint Maarten), has a relatively fertile, forest-clad, hilly terrain compared to its southern counterpart. The smaller islands off Guadeloupe and the most northerly island of the French Antilles, St. Barthélémy, are arid, rocky, and with sparse, drought-loving vegetation. The limestone islands around Guadeloupe and the volcanic "Saintes" feature coral reefs and beautiful sandy beaches. Karst landscape on parts of Guadeloupe, Marie Galante and St. Barthélémy, together with the poor soil, generally restrict arable cultivation—far removed from the rich, watered lands of the main parts of Guadeloupe, Martinique and St. Martin.

Together, with the combined attributes of fertile soil, abundant seas, high forests, rainfall in some areas and aridity in others, plus all the requisites of the voracious tourist trade, the isles of the French Antilles have arrived at a happy balance of nature. Certainly these favored islands are among the most attractive and peaceful in the entire Caribbean region.

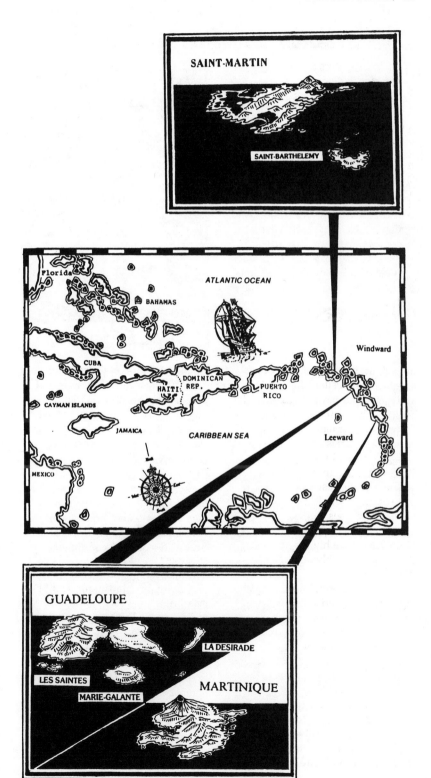

Amerindian Settlement

Before 200 A.D. Saloide Indians from the Orinoco Basin of South America had colonized the larger of the islands, Guadeloupe and Martinique. These primitive tribes, which left traces of their civilization in rock carvings, were driven from the islands by volcanic eruptions. Arawaks (Aruaks) followed these peace-loving tribes in their eighty-man canoes and, during this Neolithic period, a system of comparatively advanced culture existed. The occupation had lasted for nearly three thousand years until, in about 300 A.D., a more warlike people had pushed up through the southern islands of the Caribbean, first into Martinique and then Guadeloupe.

Slaughtering the Arawak male population and appropriating their women, fattening up children for the cooking pot and destroying fields and domestic structures, the cannibalistic Caribs carved a swathe of terror across the area that later was to be named after them. Carib means cannibal in the Arawak language and a remnant branch of Caribs, several families of the Salibia tribe, still exist on the island of Dominica (another reservation is located in Cuba); however, these survivors appear to have given up the grisly habits of their ancestors!

Prior to the advent of the Caribs, which caused the Arawak to flee toward the more northerly islands of the Antilles, a fairly well developed society had been established on Martinique and Guadeloupe. Remains of Arawak habitation can be seen in the northeast of Grande-Terre, on Guadeloupe and in museums. These, as well as artifacts unearthed in the region, testify to the achievement of the Arawak peoples. They had brought with them from the South

Early Arawak rock engravings on Guadeloupe.

American continent a wealth of produce important to their way of life—and now familiar to the world outside. Maize (Indian corn), potatoes, cotton, cassava, or manioc and tobacco, were all cultivated by the early tribes. The Arawak invented the hammock, the word "canoe" is theirs, as are "cigar" and the word "hurricane." Even "popcorn" was an Arawak discovery, as documented by Columbus's early accounts.

Games, popular in ancient times with the earliest inhabitants of the Caribbean, have been developed into the advanced sports of today—baseball, for example. Cave paintings throughout the Antillian region show that art was an important way of life in Arawak society as was the decoration of ceramic ware, found in many sites on the main islands. Petrographs and cave paintings on both islands endorse the theories of Arawak religious practices.

The Carib Indians, however, were

altogether more primitive, being obsessed with the capture of slaves and two-legged meals. Artifacts found that relate to the Carib tribes generally fall into the categories of weaponry or, in some cases, boneyards. Christopher Columbus, upon landing on Guadeloupe in 1493, found frightening evidence of their cannibal delictations in the still-warm cooking pots of a Carib village he happened to stumble on. Today, evidence of Carib habitation and culture is to be seen at the Beach of Skulls and Bones on Guadeloupe and on Martinique, and at Sainte-Luce where mysterious petrographs still baffle scientists. Columbus also encountered the Caribs in Martinique on his fourth (1502) voyage. The Great Admiral was earlier warned off by tales of the fierce tribes of Amazon women who were said to dwell there.

On St. Barthélémy and on St. Martin Columbus found resistance in the form of hails of Carib arrows and subsequently those islands were avoided.

Left to their own devices, the Carib tribes thrived on all the islands of the French Antilles except the most arid lands of Marie Galante, La Désirade and the Isles des Saintes. They defended their settlements most vehemently for many years after Columbus's first visitation. Even the Spanish conquistadors like Juan Ponce de Leon were dissuaded from erecting any permanent settlement, although they attempted a colonization on Guadeloupe in the early 1500s. Repeated sorties against the Caribs made little impact on the fierce tribe's tenacity until in 1604 the Spaniards abandoned Guadeloupe to its native fate.

Discovering the New World

The early settlers in these Caribbean islands were Arawaks on their migrations northward, followed closely by the bloodthirsty Caribs. For a little more than a thousand years the Caribs reigned supreme over the Lesser Antilles, disturbed only briefly by a curious visitation of strangely-dressed individuals from the other side of the world.

It was Christopher Columbus with his seventeen caravels, fresh out on his second voyage of discovery, who first sighted the lands later to become the French islands of the Caribbean. Late in October 1493, the Admiral noted the large island of Martinique south of Dominica. He was advised by Indians, captured on his previous voyage, that Martinique was inhabited by ferocious Amazons and therefore he pressed on northward.

Columbus named Marie Galante after his fleet's flagship; Isle des Saintes—Los Santos; La Desirade was reached by November 3rd as was the island of Guadeloupe itself. Columbus had made a promise to the monks at a Spanish monastery to carry their name to the New World, hence he named the large island "Santa Maria de Guadeloupe de Estramadura" after the religious order in Spain.

Sailing farther north, Columbus and his 1,500 crewmen came eventually to the island of Saint Barthélémy—named after his brother Bartholomeo. Landing on Saint Martin (after St. Martin's Day, November 13) the company was again surprised by fierce Carib Indians. With Columbus was his long-term associate and pilot, co-navigator and geographer,

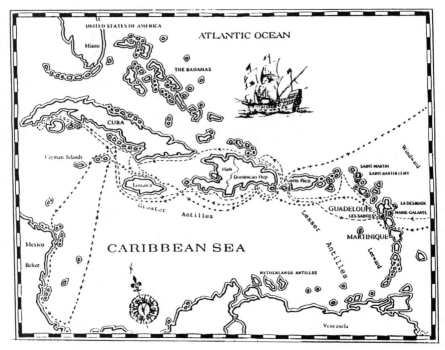

— — — route of Columbus in 1493-1496
+ + + route of Columbus in 1502-1504

Early Spanish map shows variations in the names of islands.

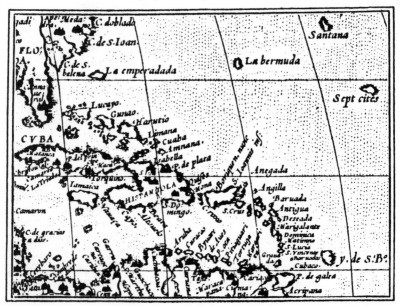

Juan de la Cosa. La Cosa compiled a map of their voyages showing the explorer's discoveries up until the end of his third (1498–1500) voyage, probably the earliest chart of the New World discoveries and the islands that make up the French Antilles. Returning on his fourth and last voyage, Columbus made his first landing in Martinique on June 15, 1502.

As fate would have it, Columbus's brother, Bartholomeo, in 1490 sought finance from France's King Charles VIII for their initial voyage of discovery to the Americas. If Charles had only entertained the Columbus proposals, the map of the Caribbean might be entirely different and France might have been the dominant power of the "New World"!

Juan Ponce de Leon had accompanied Columbus on his third exploration of the Caribbean and it was he who returned with a band of Spanish settlers in the late 1500s. It is supposed that as they attempted to establish a foothold on Guadeloupe the conquistadores had either considered that there was gold on the island or the Spanish Crown had insisted that—as Guadeloupe dominated the favored channel leading from the Atlantic, through the island chain, into the Caribbean—it should be Spanish-controlled at all costs. Whatever the reason, Spain's repeated efforts to capture Guadeloupe from the Caribs were abandoned by 1604, long after many other Caribbean islands had been over-run by British

Martinique is named "Asencion" on 1500 chart.

and Dutch counterparts or renegade groups of buccaneers.

It was not for thirty more years that any serious move to settle the French Antillian islands was attempted—and then it was made by the Dutch! In 1634 the island which was to later be divided between French and Dutch, was settled by colonists from Holland. This heralded the swift decline of the aboriginal population on Saint Martin (Sint Maarten). It did not take long for further islands to fall to the European invaders and, by around the mid-1600s almost the entire native inhabitants of St. Barthélémy, Guadeloupe and Martinique, were exterminated.

The Swashbuckling Years

Ever since Spanish explorers of the early sixteenth century began extracting gold and silver from the Caribbean, the West Indies became a free-for-all hunting ground for lawless

communities. With rich pickings to be made from lumbering Spanish galleons laden with spoils, it did not take long before other European powers began to muscle-in on the region.

Spain had already sealed its claim on all the lands to be found west of the Azores since Columbus's time but, noting the vast wealth of the "Indies" and conceding that there was more land for the taking both north and south of the Antilles, the Dutch and the English began to set up strategic fortresses throughout the island chain. Spain dominated the Greater Antilles, Cuba, Hispaniola, Jamaica and Puerto Rico and some of the less significant of the Lesser Antilles. Probably the major gains by foreign powers other than the Spanish Crown were the Cayman Islands in 1586, by the English seadog, Sir Francis Drake; his possession of the British Virgin Islands in 1595; and the English taking of Barbados and St. Lucia in 1605. By this time more than twenty-five Antillian islands and a myriad islets still remained either deserted, controlled by warlike Caribs, or haunted by pirates.

Between 1604 and 1609 both England and the Netherlands acknowledged Spain's dominance in the Caribbean as a result of the treaties of London and Antwerp. By 1621 the Dutch had set up their awesome West Indies Company to patrol the Spanish Main and to found and protect new acquisitions in the Caribbean. The race was on to find and settle the remaining West Indian islands, not to mention quashing any forces they might find on these tropical havens. Holland took possession of St. Croix in the Virgins, and the British, Tobago, in 1625; St. Eustatius fell to the Dutch in 1626 as did

Tortola, in the Virgins in 1627, the same year as the Spanish captured Curaçao; in the following year the English claimed Nevis and Barbuda. What, one may ask, was happening with the French forces?

As early as 1522 the French in the Caribbean were enlisting the aid of Florentine privateers in the capture of two rich Spanish galleons sailing out of the port of Havana, Cuba. In 1536 pirate Franceses—also, Jaques de Sores—attacked Havana and, from there on, Spain's Caribbean stronghold became a regular target for France's adventurers. Peg Leg Francois le Clerc and Jaques de Sores sacked both Havana and the country's second city, Santiago de Cuba, in 1544. Ten years later, de Sores raided Santiago and razed Havana City. In 1568, Richard, the French Corsair, plundered shipping all along Cuba's coastline. Another French pirate, Gilberto Giron, began attacking Spanish fleets in 1585 and a few

Pierre Belain d'Esnambuc on Martinique in 1635.

years later even captured the Bishop of Cuba, Fray Juan de las Cabezas Altamirano! In the troublesome period between 1600 and 1635, mayhem rode the waves of the Caribbean Sea and Frenchmen played no small part in the turmoil. The French, by then may not have established any permanent possessions in the West Indies but they were certainly, as corsairs and privateers, a force to be reckoned with.

In 1605 the Spanish abandoned their capital in Hispaniola, Santo Domingo, leaving the city to French pirates and opportunists. Frenchmen, either shipwrecked, marooned mariners, or fugitives, found a home among the fringe communities of "boucaniers" (from the method of meat preservation known as "boucan"—buccaneers). The French government enlisted many of these buccaneers as privateers, to systematically plunder and harass the Spanish. Many pirates were using the island of St. Kitts (St. Christopher) from which to raid Spanish treasure fleets. In 1623 this island was governed by the Norman aristocrat Belain d'Esnambuc and later it was owned both by the French and the English. The influential Cardinal Richelieu instigated colonization and sometimes financially supported the more noble French settlers in the seventeenth century.

As if to whet the appetite of the French back in Europe, those eager to commandeer vessels for privateering in the West Indies or anxious to escape from some felony in their mother country, a crew that was shipwrecked in 1624 on Martinique returned to their homeland with tales of tropical bliss. They were the first Frenchmen to spend any time at all, legitimately and documented, on any of the French Antilles. By this time pirates had adopted hundreds of islands, islets and coral atolls as their bases for sorties against navies and merchants alike. It was the time for a concerted effort by the French authorities to establish a foothold in the Antilles.

In 1635, the same year as the Dutch compounded their hold on the ABC group of Aruba, Bonaire and Curacao, France moved volunteers and indentured settlers into Martinique and Guadeloupe. Lienard de l'Olive and Jean Duplessis d'Ossonville were among the earliest settlers landing at Pointe-Allegre, Guadeloupe, June 28, 1635. Fort St. Pierre was established on Martinique by Belain d'Esnambuc in September of the same year.

French "je ne sais quoi" had enabled a foothold to be established on the English island of St. Kitts, which resulted in the division of this island over an 88-year period. St. Martin/Sint Maarten, already split between the French and Dutch, officially recognized its French section in 1648, also the year that French sovereignty was established on St. Barthélémy. Two years later France claimed St. Croix from the Dutch and also Grenada, in the southern Caribbean. French names on all these islands today testify to the hold French corsairs and their supportive Navy had over its territories.

Expert planning between freebooters (*filibusters*), privateers, pirates and the indentured population of the French Antilles, with special dispensation from Paris authorities, extended the French hold in the Indies. A governor of the French Northern Caribbean, one Bertrand d'Orégon, ceded parts of Hispaniola to the freebooters in 1655, as recounted by the chronicler Alexander Oliver Oexmelin, or Exquemelin. In the latter half of the seventeenth century Oexmelin wrote his famous essay "History of Outstanding Adventures in the Indies, with Life, Customs and Morals of the

Buccaneers." Oexmelin was an indentured servant in the West Indies and joined the buccaneers in 1669, once having sailed with the French West India Company. This was founded in 1664 but dissolved ten years later.

By 1664 the French had overrun the island of Montserrat, once a British colony. French settlers were already well established with the freebooters and Hispaniola, a legacy which was to last 42 years. By this time the ruthless pirate Francois L'Olonois was patrolling the Spanish Main attacking any ship in his path. The king of France, Louis XIV, in 1674 officially claimed the islands of Guadeloupe and Martinique for the Crown. In the 1680s "Le Chevalier de Grammont" began his privateering activities which culminated in a "Lettre de Marque" (letter of authority from the government to operate as a pirate) in his latter years. The Paris tribunal "Cour des Prises" endorsed these acts. The war between France and Spain in 1667 just accelerated the animosity in the Caribbean and spawned even more pirates. Even some commissioned naval personnel turned to a form of piracy, like Lieutenant Caraccioli, who, together with a Captain Mission, late of H.M.S. Winchester, after a bad encounter off Martinique supported the universal use of the "black flag" against the "brotherhood of pirates"! In the 1690s the respected Jesuit priest Père Labat, a noted writer of the day, played Father Confessor to rogues and filibusters, privateers and "men of the coast" who practically ran any society or township that did not fall within strict government administration. Familiar names include the pirate Jean Bart, Corsair René Duguay-Trouvin and Robert Surcouf. France certainly contributed a great number of rogue adventurers to the panoply of Carib-

Francois L'Olonois

bean romantics who haunted the Spanish Main. Forbin was well known as a pirate, as were Grammont and Pierre Gros.

By the first quarter of the seventeenth century the French began searching for permanent bases in the Caribbean. What better retreats for the French to adopt than those already commandeered by their own kinsmen, even if they were pirates, corsairs and buccaneers. It did not take long for this combination of organized French naval power and the cut-and-run expertise of the pirate element to instill even more fear into the European forces of Spain, England and the Netherlands. By this time both buccaneers and pirates had moved from St. Kitts to the island of Tortuga and it was not long before it had become an "official" French base from which to raid shipping.

With the advent of the war between the American colonies and Britain, the name Lafitte conjures up visions of smuggling and freebooting, a pastime also enjoyed by Victor Hugues. Born in Marseille and with an established privateering center in Pointe-à-Pitre, Guadeloupe, Hugues is said to have almost initiated the 1798 conflict between America and France. Victor Hugues's life was documented by the Cuban writer Alejo Carpentier. Another practitioner of the art of pirateering was the corsair Jean-Jaques Fourmentin, said to have captured 100 British ships off Guadeloupe between 1793 and 1814. The roll call of French pirates seems endless—Modesto Fuet, Petreas le Mulatto, Peg-Leg Langlois, Montbars the Exterminator, Pierre le Grand and Babord-Amure all had fearful *nom-de-plumes* but none so hideous as the pirate Louis le Golif. Golif's nickname was "Borgne-Fessé"; this was an undisguised comment about the part of his rear end lost in a battle by some unfortunate cutlass stroke!

The famous twenty-one French pirates brought to mind here are just the tip of an organized tropical iceberg that was designed to bring the Spanish, if not the English and Dutch navies, to their feet. However, France was not alone in its recruitment of renegade assistance in plundering and harrassment of trade. The British and the Dutch had their own privateers and a much larger force was represented by the combined independent pirates and filibusters, buccaneers and corsairs. Sir Francis Drake and John Hawkins could be added to this list, as could Captain Henry Low, Henry (Long Ben) Every, "Black Bart" Roberts, Howell Davis, Stede Bonnet and the notorious "Blackbeard"—all of whom were active off the coasts of France's Caribbean terrritories.

Many stories of buried treasure on desert isles, sunken galleons on lonely coral reefs, pirate forts and caches of loot in isolated island caves stem from those days of French activity during the two hundred and fifty years of piracy, smuggling and privateering around the waters of the Leewards and Windwards. It was these lawless actions that laid down the skeleton of island communities which eventually united into the French Antilles.

Typical early nineteenth century buccaneers.

Island Selection

The mêlée in the Caribbean, created by the major European powers of Spain, England, The Netherlands and France, was joined, as early as the mid-1600s, by the Baltic Province of Courland in the late seventeenth century; by the State of Brandenburg in 1733; by the Danes; and, finally, in 1784, by Swedish settlers. Although France had laid claim to Guadeloupe and Martinique in 1674, the British made their first sortie against Guadeloupe in 1691, and another, by 1703. French possessions again suffered badly at the hands of the British during the Seven Years War, 1756-1763. Throughout this period the French had been following the examples of the Spanish and English, particularly, in importing large quantities of black slaves from their colonies in West Africa. The proportion of black to white inhabitants on Martinique by 1745 was four-fifths slaves and one-fifth white "colons." The new labor force supported the island's plantation-based economy, but it had its own drawbacks. Unrest among the slaves resulted in frequent uprisings and the actual commodity of the slave trade itself became fair game for poaching black workers, either on sea or land. Not one French claim in the Caribbean escaped harrassment by some adversary or another. The British were the main contenders for takeovers and for commandeering French slave labor. Unrest at home on mainland France during the French Revolution also caused instability in the French colonies of the West Indies. The latter quarter of the eighteenth century was also a state of flux for the French, who were as yet comparatively unsettled in many of their Caribbean teritories. By as late as 1878, when Swedish occupants finally ceded

Above and opposite: Native costume.

Saint Barthelemy to the French government, France had won and lost six important islands including Hispaniola, St. Croix, St. Kitts, Montserrat, St. Vincent and Grenada. Some they had held for only a brief period but evident throughout the French involvement in the Caribbean territories, the British remained their toughest contenders. The seven properties that finally stayed in French hands represented some of the most strategic and important possessions of the Lesser Antilles.

From early experiments of importing volunteer settlers from Europe, adopting the services of unsavory pirates and privateers, squabbling with the British over a period of 250 years and negotiating with other foreign powers for rights to other Caribbean colonies, a pattern of islands was gradually emerging. Guadeloupe prospered from ..s earliest occupation. The economy of Martinique, however, fared less successfully and therefore a balance between the two islands had been established as far back as the mid-seventeenth century. From this stem the basis of French Caribbean possessions was formed. Today these two islands remain the nucleus of the French West Indies. In 1815 Martinique was returned to France for the last time and the following year, 1816, Guadeloupe was handed over to the French Crown. St. Barthélémy joined the union by 1877 and in 1946 all the seven properties in the Caribbean became Overseas Départements of the French Republic. In 1897 Martinique was issued its own, and only, coinage—showing the bust of an Indian woman. The Guadeloupe coin of 1903 depicted the head of an Indian man. Both as full Départements of the French mainland, and therefore as two of the Regions of France represented in the European Economic Community, the joint future of the islands is secure. The two larger islands, Guadeloupe and Martinique, are both administered by a prefect appointed by the minister of the interior in Paris. The prefects, in Guadeloupe, are assisted in their duties by two general secretaries who in turn are supported by two sous-prefects. The two sous-prefects represent Pointe-à-Pitre and St. Martin/St. Barthélémy. The administrative region is now divided into thirty-four communes and thirty-six cantons. Martinique is slightly different in its administrative framework. Three deputies and two senators support the prefect, while the populace elect conseil général and conseil régional. Each town on Martinique has its own mayor.

A Bountiful Economy

Even though early Arawak Indians cleared small plots of arable land on both Guadeloupe and Martinique, agriculture at that time could only be described as a subsistence economy. Maize, cotton, tobacco, cassava, yam and most native tropical fruits could be grown simply by preparing the land by the slash-and-burn method.

It was only when volunteer settlers and indentured labor from Europe came to the islands in about 1635 that the islands were able to demonstrate the fertility of their soil and the bounty of the surrounding seas. Martinique and Guadeloupe were settled more or less simultaneously. By the 1640s the sugar plantation industry was beginning. Sugar was introduced to Guadeloupe in 1644 and Martinique in 1650. Political turmoil and the importation of great numbers of black slaves from Africa swelled the labor force and each successive takeover on both islands. It also improved sugar production and the methods of harvest and extraction.

For a ten-year period from 1664 the Compagnie des Indes Occidentales was founded. (French West Indies Company founded in the reign of Louis XIV by one of his ministers, Colbert.) This oversaw the development of sugar production and other crops which were introduced at a later date. In the early 1700's indigo, cotton, cacao, tobacco and coffee were grown on the main islands and on Marie Galante. Fishing, salt extraction and some pastoral smallholding supported the outer islands of St. Barthélémy, St. Martin and Les Saintes. With the wholesale clearance of land for sugar cane plantations, both the islands of Guadeloupe and Martinique became rich and important French possessions, albeit plagued by regular political changes.

The real Golden Age of the French Antilles began around 1763.

At the height of the sugar trade more than half of each of the main island's land surface was devoted to agriculture. However, by 1848—late in world terms—slavery was abolished in the islands and a new source of labor was tapped in the East Indies and parts of Asia. The negro slaves, now freed, or demanding payment for their services, acquired plots of land for cultivation, and vanilla, banana, pineapple, plus a range of vegetables, gradually appeared as economically viable cash crops. By the late nineteenth century the value of sugar had declined on the market as sugar beet became popular in the purchasing countries. With the drop in the price of sugar, some islands built up their production of sugar-based rum—like Guadeloupe, which became a famous center for the liqueur, "Tafia," a product derived from sugar, different from pure rum, was a speciality of the French Antilles.

The abundant fish in the Caribbean and Atlantic waters gave each island a supplementary source of food and income. Even today, the trade in fish, shell-fish, exotic fruits and flowers, vanilla, rum and the ubiquitous sugar, forms the backbone of the French island's economy—subsidized to a certain extent by the Government of France. Oil refining and fertilizer manufacture also play a significant role. Not to be overlooked as an important contributor to the economy of all seven islands is the trade that thrives on the attributes nature has bestowed on them. Tourism, although still not exploited to its fullest degree, is one of the most profitable foreign currency earners. Sun, sand, sea, forested

Birds of the West Indies: 1. Yellow Oriole 2. Yellow-Winged Parrot 3. Black-Faced Grassquit 4. Gray Kingbird 5. Bannanaquit 6. Black-and-White Warbler 7. Pearly-Eyed Thrasher 8. Hooded Warbler 9. Prothonotary Warbler 10. Ruby-throated Hummingbird/Butterflies/Flamingo 11. Little Tern 12. Booby 13. Frigate (Man o' War) Bird 14. Goose 15. Caribbean Parakeet 16. Roseate Tern 17. Least Tern 18. Gull 19. Greater Caribbean Flamingo 20. Bahama Duck 21. Black-necked Stilt 22. Cormorant 23. Brown Pelican

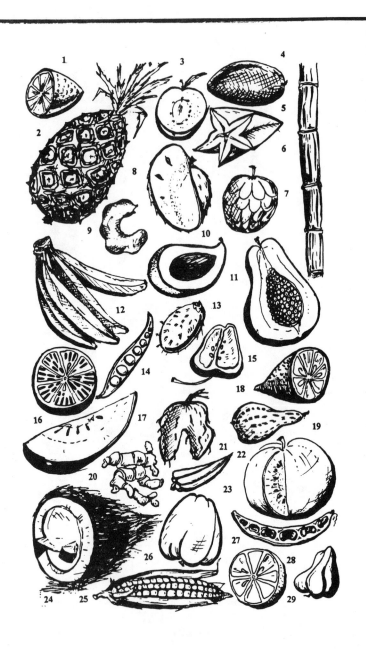

Fruits and Vegetables of the West Indies: 1. Lime 2. Pineapple 3. Guava 4. Sapodilla (Zapote) 5. Star Apple (Carambola) 6. Sugar Cane 7. Cherimoya 8. Sour-Sop (Guanabana) 9. Tamarind 10. Mango 11. Paw-Paw (Papaya) 12. Banana 13. Prickly Pear 14. Pigeon Pea (Gungar) 15. Capsicum (Red and Green Pepper) 16. Grapefruit 17. Water Melon 18. Lemon 19. Bottle Gourd 20. Ginger 21. Yam 22. Okra (Ladies' Finger) 23. Pumpkin 24. Coconut 25. Maize (Sweet Corn) 26. Chayote (Christophene) 27. Black-Eye Beans 28. Orange 29. Chili (Hot Pepper)

mountains, charming people and an intriguing historical background, rank these islands among the most desirable of all tourist destinations in the Caribbean. The future development of the tourist trade is expected to take an increasing priority in the economic structure of the islands. Fish may escape the nets, the price of sugar and sugar products may drop, but the sun and the lure of exotic scenery will remain to entice the discerning visitor and returning tourist.

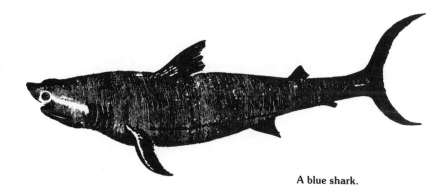

A blue shark.

CHAPTER II

The People, Their Customs and Faiths

Approximately 675,000 people live on the "Seven Sisters" of the French Antilles. Each island reflects a different phase in the panoply of history that has marched through this part of the Caribbean. Gone are the Asiatic features of the first Arawak or Carib Indians who tenaciously clung to their bountiful islands until the advent of the eighteenth century. Here, instead, are the ebony skins of Equatorial Africa, the saffron of Chinese origin and the blond of the Breton.

From as early as 1635, newcomers from European France settled either voluntarily or by convenience on Guadeloupe and Martinique and on the scattered attendant isles. Intermittant occupation by both the English and the Swedes added other elements to the initial French stock. Those adventurers, buccaneers and filibusters who first selected Spanish or Dutch-dominated islands as a temporary home introduced strains of Andalusia or the Netherlands.

The purest example of France's earliest colonization still is evident on Saint Barthélémy. It was here in 1660 that peasants from Normandy and Brittany established a colony replacing the earlier settlers from St. Christophe, who were of dubious descent. The seventeenth century dialect from northwestern mainland France still persists on this tiny, farthest-flung outpost of the French Antilles.

By the mid-seventeenth century a boom in the sugar trade and the extension of plantations across much of the arable land in the islands prompted the sugar barons to look abroad for sources of labor. The few Carib Indians that remained on Guadeloupe or Martinique had abandoned the islands by 1660 and black slaves, imported from the French West African colonies, swelled the population. Hundreds of thousands of blacks from Senegal, Dahomey, the Ivory Coast, Ghana, the Congo and Angola-Mandingo, Ibo, Nagoes and a host of tribes of different languages and practices were thrown together to work on the plantations. Interbreeding between white settlers and Negro slaves became so widespread in the West Indian islands that the king of France in 1694 imposed a levy of 2,000 lbs of sugar on anyone caught fathering a mulatto, or half-breed. Today almost 90 percent of the population of the French islands is either black or mulatto.

It was the French Revolution that in 1794 brought the "Reign of Terror" to the Caribbean, heralded the gradual decline in slavery and a new episode in the island's convoluted history. Guadeloupe had already experienced a short period under British rule when slavery had been abolished but the traditions of Madame Guillotine in ending the lives of several thousand Antillian plantation owners quickened the pace towards abolition. The Napoleonic Wars brought more instability to the sugar trade, upon which the isles were dependent. Slavery became a thing of the past in many adjacent islands and by 1848 the practice was abolished in the French territories. In Martinique alone on April 27 about

72,000 slaves were freed from forced labor on the sugar plantations. On Guadeloupe the figure was 87,500. Many blacks continued to work in their adopted occupation but the bottom was dropping out of the sugar market. The rises in production costs instigated an increase in the distillation of rum from the cane as a lucrative by-product and provided work for surplus labor.

At this point in the economy of the sugar trade, Asian Indians, also very cheap labor, began infiltrating the French islands from Calcutta and Pondicherry. Chinese began to take a part of the professional employment generated by changes in economic dependence.

In Guadeloupe today more than half the population are "Ti-moune," youngsters, of whom only about

2 percent are of European origin. In Martinique, the West Indian island most famed for the beauty of its women, the population is predominantly of mixed blood. The origins of Martiniquais can be identified on a scale diminishing in number from the mulattoes, generally lighter than the Guadeloupe equivalent; the pure blacks, second in numbers; the "Békés," Creoles, or "Blancs-Pays" (whites born on the island); those of Arab or Indian origin; and the "Blancs France," French whites who are generally visitors to the islands. The Emperor Napoleon, having selected his empress from among the Martiniquais, endorsed Lafcadio Hearn's observation on the island womanhood: "Straight as palms, supple and tall, with a dignified carriage and an easy elegance of movement."

For the character of the people one need go no further than the nearest carnival, folkloric demonstration or local dance. The ebullience of Africa, the elegance of France and the exuberance of the mulatto that mingles the two, has created an identity in the art of song and dance which is celebrated the world over. The beguine began before the advent of the gramophone. It began in the French isles with European settlers keeping the traditions of the mother countries. It began in Africa and traveled with the slaves to the plantation fields. It began with the mixing of a hundred different cultures and creeds, faiths, customs and dance skills. A dance like the beguine encapsulates the essence of French-Antillian rhythms and the particular variation of Caribbean music. It epitomizes the vivacity of these exotic island people. The "mazouk" is the Creole version of the mazurka and the evocative "calenda" stems from French and African roots. The "haute-taille" is a dance that emulates the quadrille, as is the dance known as the "bel-air." Music is omnipresent throughout the islands. In the olden days of slavery on the plantations it was the only way to alleviate the harsh conditions and futureless monotony of working in the cane fields. Today that same spirit runs through music and song, tempered with the prim graciousness of eighteenth-century French ballads and formal dances. One can detect a little of almost every European country's music in the sound of the isles. From steel oil drums the locals fashion a multitude of instruments based on those of more primitive times. The musical instruments like ping-pong, or pan, boom, cello pan and guitar pan figure in everyday celebrations as well as in folkloric exhibitions where

one can also see the mixed influence in the national costumes. Among the flamboyant displays are the kicking dance of the men known as the "laghia," the "grage," and the washer-women's dance called "le rose."

Early religious beliefs and customs prevail in some of the local practices of today's French Antillian cults. Indian and African religions can be noted in rural regions with their devotees sharing the same village. Little has survived of the ancient cult associated with voodoo, which early black elements introduced from nearby Haiti. In carnival, however, the mingling of pagan and Christian religions can be identified in such rituals as "La Fête de la Diablesse." "Obeh,"

the universal magic of the islands, still retains its dark secrets and ancient medicinal cures—dispensed by the local *quimboiseurs*—a word derived from the old tradition of curing known as "Tien Bois." Although the islands are predominantly Roman Catholic, Methodist and Evangelical, Hindu, Jewish and places of worship of several other dominations may also be found in the major towns.

Many of the island's traditional fetes and carnivals are based on religious observances like Christmas, Epiphany and Pentecost. Colorful and lively celebrations attend almost every episode in life, from birth to death, and each island has its own version of these festivities and pageants. There are special Indian fetes and days set aside for food fairs and fashion shows, sports days and those for the local cockfights or even the mongoose fer-de-lance serpent fights. Football and the ubiquitous French obsession with cycling is ever-present.

The peculiar and musical lilt of the Creole language is all-pervasive. In each island the variations differ but the origins and inflections go far back in Antillian history. It evolved from Old France, from sailors, from African tribal languages, from English, Dutch and Spanish. The evocative sound of Creole conjures up images of island color and vivacity. Although not easy to understand because of the transposition of certain word meanings, Creole is a patois and at the same time, almost a religion. Creole, as it refined on its passage through a hundred generations of time, must be one of the most "laid back" languages in the world—a language of easy grace and relaxed tones that reflects the everyday pattern of Antillian life. It is only the island of Barthelemy in the French Antilles that does not use this distinctive language. On St. Barthélémy, because of its location and past history, it has inherited a curious mixture of seventeenth-century Norman French tempered with some Brittany dialects.

Emerald Isles—Topaz Seas

". . . The best, the richest, the sweetest, the evenest, the most charming"—Christopher Columbus's comment on arriving in what is now the French Antilles. "Eleven marks out of ten for natural beauty"—quote taken from an international magazine. One can only follow that with language as flowery as the islands themselves!

Verdant and prolific as they are, there are a number of stars in the island's natural habitat that outshine those on other Caribbean islands for their exuberance, curiosity or flamboyance. The tropical rain forests of the French Antilles excel even the most ardent amateur botanist's ex-

pectations. Giant ferns shade poinsettia, croton, anthurium and hibiscus. Brilliant, iridescent hummingbirds hover and dart as though radio-controlled into the delicate lips of wild orchids sprouting from vines and lianas. In the height of the forest mahogany and gommier trees tower through damp, rich green foliage. Butterflies in a hundred hues and sizes swarm around oleander and bougainvillea flowers, while dappled sunlight imitates their play on the great curls of "archbishop ferns." Mammoth tree trunks create a catheral-like atmosphere with foot-wide bamboo doubling as organ pipes or the magnificent mahogany

(Acomat Batard) tree's thick boughs as massive arches. Steam from volcanic vents adds to the dank, sweet, exotic aroma on La Soufrière where songbirds like the mountain whistler trill with backdrops of tiger orchids and waterfalls. Heliconia and Bengal rose are pinpoints of color in the undergrowth below beautiful traveler's palms or the poisonous manchineel trees.

Red, black, white and button mangrove feature prominently on both Guadeloupe and Martinique, contrasting with the cactus and drought-loving plants on the Iles des Saintes. Pineapple and sugar cane are typical as are the coconut groves and bananas in these islands, which almost personify the tropical paradise of picture books. Gli-gli, pelican and frigate birds can be seen in the coastal areas while on the savannah and pasture lands the cattle ibis, turtle doves and tiny buntings follow grazing cows, coo incessantly or chirrup in the hedgerows.

A multitude of creatures live in the various habitats of mountain terrain, agricultural fields, dense jungle and the arid lands of some of the smaller islands. None of these is dangerous except the snake known as the fer-de-lance or pit viper. This venomous reptile lives only on Martinique and is the subject of an interesting ecological saga. During the days of the slave trade and forced labor on the sugar cane plantations many workers died from snakebite and overseers employed watchers to warn the cane cutters of the presence of these serpents. In 1893 a small foreign carnivore was introduced by way of the Indian laborers' migrations from Asia. It was the mongoose, one of the only rodents that delights in attacking any species of snake. Its skills went before it and soon the mongoose was one of the most common animals on the island. The mortality rate among field

Nineteenth-century sugar plantation house is a combination of Victorian, French and West Indian architectural styles.

workers dropped and the viper population decreased. Today the mongoose is part of the Martinique wildlife and, because of their taste for chicken meat, a pest in the eyes of the farmer and small-holder.

Other small mammals often seen in the French Antilles are rodents like the agouti—which sometimes finds itself dished up at table because of its delicate taste—and the possum, a frequent visitor at the outdoor breakfast table. The raccoon has successfully decimated the numbers of rats on Guadeloupe and is the symbol of the island's National Park. A bewildering variety of lizards and geckos live on the islands and one variety is known as "anolis." Frogs of every size and color make their presence known toward dusk when their calling may be anything from a croaking cacophony

to a shrill piping. On the island of La Désirade and on Les Saintes, iguanas, large lizards with direct geneology back to the dinosaurs, roam the rocky landscape and are a protected species. The iguana is the mascot of the Natural Park Authority.

As colorful and prolific as the Antilles birdlife and fauna might be, there is active competition below the topaz waters that surround the islands. From dolphins and whales on the Atlantic side to brilliant cromis and angelfish in the Caribbean shallows, from vivid corals and sponges along the reefs, to the gleaming lines of marlin and sailfish in the indigo deeps—the marine life around the islands is a study in itself. The gamut of the French West Indies flora and fauna is truly stunning in both its variety and its color.

CHAPTER III

Out and About

From the "fairytale land" of Saint Barthélémy to the jagged peaks of Guadeloupe and Martinique, from the arid "moonscape" of La Desirade to the green slopes of Les Saintes, and from the crescent bays of Saint Martin to the sombrero-shaped isle of Marie Galante, the choice of terrain and selection of environment in these delightful islands invites a plethora of activities.

Sun, sand, sea are the ingredients that provide dream conditions for the relaxing holidaymaker or the activity-oriented sportslover. Mountain crags, high rain-forest pathways, volcanic craters and clifftop walks attract the explorer and adventurer. Quaint red-roofed villages, historic fortresses and ancient churches supply ample targets for the sure-shot cameraman, as do out to sea, the ocean swells of the Caribbean or the great currents when the Atlantic yachts dip with billowing sails and the gamefisherman's line goes taut as the great billfish leaps through turquoise waves. Each sport and relaxation is catered for in the French Antillian islands. Whether a golfer or tennis enthusiast, scuba diver or just a sun-seeker, the opportunities are inexhaustible. Dip back into the past in lonely outposts where thatched villages have not changed since the time of Columbus. Peer into the future by calling on one of the local sorcerers with their ancient craft, which mixes the mysteries of African magic with France's famous tarot. Skirt the volcanic steam vents on twisting mountain paths with stupendous views and relax under a gaudy umbrella at a typically French pavement cafe.

Diving

Just to whet the appetite for diving, and as a cautionary note, by French law if a French person finds sunken treasure anywhere in the world, he or she is bound to forfeit it to the French government and, later, claim reimbursement for expenses as a reward. This snippet of French legalities came as a bombshell to the renowned diver Jacques-Yves Cousteau while he was hauling up finds from sunken Spanish treasure galleons in the Caribbean in the late 1960s. Cousteau, himself a frequent visitor to the French Antillian diving locations, regularly remarked on the fantastic coral and sponge formations in the Caribbean Sea which "was a constant source of astonishment" to him. Although the Caribbean boasts some of the most fascinating underwater scenery, and even the second longest living coral reef on earth, the waters around the islands of the French Antilles can claim some of the most accessible and convenient diving locations of the entire region. Cousteau once called Guadeloupe's Pigeon Island "one of the world's ten best scuba locations." St. Francois and Ilet du Gosier are among the best of the island's dive sites.

The temptation while swimming or gliding over vivid coral banks in a boat to slip under the surface and explore is almost irresistible. The warmth of the water and the heat of the sun almost confirm that the invitation to a cooler, submarine world is the most natural attraction and almost second-nature. Sea fans beckon and myriad varieties of fishes invite a game of "tag." The French name for bristle worms, playing hide-and-seek on the reefs, is "chénille de mer"—sea caterpillar. Queen, spade, jack and kingfish are names that conjour up the many species which inhabit the island's tropical waters. Clown fish, cardinals and sergeant majors can be found together nowhere but in the clear Caribbean seas. Trunkfish are known locally as "poisson coffre"—box fish. Pillar, brain and the colorful, but best avoided, fire coral form underwater jungles that beckon the snorkel or scuba enthusiast.

On Guadeloupe the Grande-Terre coasts to the west and the south offer guided dives and rentable equipment at most resort spots. Martinique has a number of dive shops and diving schools.

Recommended on the south coast are Cap Soloman and Diamond Rock. The latter particularly for the

abandoned cannon that litter the sea floor. Club Subaquatique Martinique offers dives off La Perle island, near a large rocky outcrop and a maze of underwater canyons and caverns. Also on the north coast is the popular dive site of Pointe La Mare near the town of Precheur, famed for its black coral.

St. Martin is an ideal amateur or experienced diver's paradise. Legend has it that in 1781 the Portugese treasure galleon "Santissimo Trinidade" sank off the eastern coast of St. Martin, carrying what must be now nearly a billion dollars worth of gold coins. The wreck has never been found because of the treacherous waters that swirl around this rocky coastline. However, it is not the lure of lost fortunes that attracts divers to the French Antilles. The absolute wonderland of nature's submarine life is the everlasting draw that brings divers from across the world to the Caribbean coves and bays, shallows and deeps. Jacques Cousteau selected Pigeon Island, off Basse-Terre, Guadeloupe, as one of his favorite spots for scuba diving and there are now about twenty dive

clubs throughout the islands. Hiring equipment is no problem at most hotels or organized resort beaches and instruction is offered at many poolsides. Boats can be rented at harbors and ports where guides will take divers out to selected dive locations and known submerged coral reefs or wrecks.

There are few dangers below the French Antillian seas except human carelessness of flaunting the laws of scuba and snorkling dives. Few creatures below the waves are harmful but one should take care to avoid the fire coral, which inflicts a nasty burn, the poisonous stone, scorpion and spiky porcupine fishes, the Portugese man'o war, and the spines of some sea urchins. Sunburn can be more of a danger than most sea creatures and adequate protection should be taken. Don't swim after dark and remember that shiny objects can attract the attention of shark or barracuda.

Deep Sea Sportsfishing

Forbidden on some Caribbean islands, the practice of spear fishing is a popular pastime in the French Antilles, but the real sport for the excitement of rod and line is game fishing. The waters around all West Indian islands abound in sportsfish and it is in the deeps off northeastern Guadeloupe, for example, that one finds the champion wahoo and kingfish, marlin and tuna.

Guadeloupe and Saint Martin offer the best selection of large, deep-seagoing, fishing craft for hire. Excursions go after kingfish and barracuda in the first quarter of the year—tuna, bonito and marlin (also dolphin, which is not the mammal) in the period from March to December. Most of the larger hotels can arrange fishing trips—anything from shark fishing to lobster-barbeque boat rides; from surf-casting, or spinning from the shore for jacks, yellowtails and tarpon, to crab and mussel-culling excursions in the mangrove regions.

Almost all fish caught off the coasts around each of the seven French islands are edible. Remember, the French are renowned for their fish dishes, such as boullabaisse. Grouper, snapper, parrotfish and the big game fish are regular items on the Antillian menus. Turtle meat, shark, sea urchins, the tiny "coulirou," eel, crawfish, "écrevisses" (a large river crayfish) and conch, are probably not so familiar to the short-term visitor on the islands. One word of warning, however; ask the locals about the fish you catch before cooking, as some, like some of the colorful, tropically vivid fish can cause a food poisoning known as "ciguatera."

Sailing, Yachting and Cruising

What more idyllic location for challenging the wind and waves with hull and sail than the French West Indies? Surely, as is often remarked since Columbus first named Marie Galante after one of his caravels, "these islands were created with the sailor in mind." Between Guadeloupe and Dominica, and the island of Martinique, is the channel which divides the Leewards from the Windwards, a passage that has been used by sailors coming from the east since 1493. The importance of this Martinique Passage has made the islands both to the north and the south famous among the sailing fraternity.

Martinique boasts no less than twelve internationally recognized yacht harbors and anchorages. St. Pierre on the northwest coast is most popular and the island has anchorages around its south coast: Anse des Cocotiers, Les Anses d'Arlet, Cul-de-Sac du Marin, the large harbor of Fort-de-France, Ilet-à-Ramiers, Pointe du-Bout (with its marina), Port Cohoe and the exquisite retreat at Trois-Ilets. On the east (Atlantic) coastline is the Havre du Robert, Marina du Francois and Pointe Brunet. Yacht charters and any craft from catamaran, sunfish, Hobie cat, schooner bareboat hire, motor boat, or even rental of flying spinnaker equipment is available at most yacht harbors, resorts or marinas. Glass-bottom boat cruises are a favorite as is the excursion now offered by the "Aquascope" from the St. Anne pier.

On Guadeloupe there are similar facilities for hiring marine sports equipment and yacht charter. There are seven anchorages on Grande Terre—the harbor of Pointe-à-Pitre,

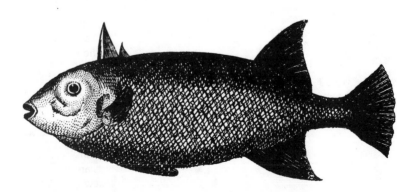

Le Petit Havre, Grand Cul-de-Sac Marin, Ste-Anne and St. Francois with almost 300 berths. On Basse-Terre the four recommended anchorages include Basse-Terre harbor itself, Anse-à-la-Barque, Baie Deshaies and Ste-Marie. An 80-foot ketch available for hire on Guadeloupe once belonged to King Farouk of Egypt. The Port de Plaisance Marina at Bas-du-Fort now offers more than 600 berths and a large marina is located at Carenage. Out on Les Saintes is a favorite haven known as Bourg des Saintes.

Another anchorage can be found on Marie Galante but the rocky coastline of La Désirade is not recommended for safe mooring. The harbor of Saint Martin is a classic example of the appreciation the French have for things maritime. Excursions to other islands are a speciality of the main harbor, Marigot and all manner of craft can be hired at either the port itself or the smaller piers or jettys at many of the coastal resorts. The Grand Etang is a favourite for sail craft enthusiasts. Each spring the whole island seems preoccupied with sailing during the annual regatta. Charters are available also at St. Barthélémy's three harbors and anchorages. Gustavia is the capital and it sports a fine harbor tucked into the lee of the island. Other mooring facilities are provided at Anse du Colombier and Baie de St-Jean and, farther out, the Ile de la Fourche offers safe anchorage for yachts.

Oceangoing liners and island cruisers ply the waters between the Antilles. Most notable among the shipping lines are Chandris, Cunard, Holland America, Norwegian Caribbean, Princess and Royal Caribbean Lines. Major ports of call are Pointe-à-Pitre, Les Saintes and Fort-de-France. Local craft and ferries add Gustavia, Basse-Terre and St. Pierre to their list of ports.

Walks and Special Excursions

Living up to its reputation as one of the most spectacular series of trail-hiking paths in the Caribbean, Basse-Terre's Parc Naturel, on Guadeloupe, offers some of the region's most fantastic scenery. Waterfalls, rain forest and mountain pools in secluded grottos contrast with the fumeroles, sulphur vents and lava-strewn landscape of La Soufrière. Horseback riding on Guadeloupe is an added attraction, but it is on the southern part of Martinique that this activity is still used as a means of transport. Horses, with or without guides, can be rented from clubs or ranches. Popular hiking excursions on Martinique are those in the Parc Naturel and on the peninsula known as La Caravelle. Trails are indicated on Mt. Pelée, where one can visit the volcanic disaster site of St. Pierre. Other treks include those to Le Prêcheur and Grande-Rivière.

Cycling is ever popular on these French islands and particularly on St. Martin. Here there are numerous trails and walks either along the fabulous coastline or up to the highest point on the island, Pic du Paradis. On St. Barthélémy the picturesque villages and hamlets invite strolling and, from the Petit Morne or the higher Montagne du Vitet, one can enjoy some stunning views of the island and out to the far islets off the northeast coast.

In Marie Galante the coastline offers amazing cliff walks that include natural arches in the rocky terrain. On La Désirade the views from the Grande Montagne are spectacular and one can hike across a landscape more reminiscent of Western movies or Mexico than the tropical lushness expected of islands in the middle of the Antilles. Les Saintes' beautiful, green, hilly islands are a casual walker's ideal as few walks can take more than two hours. The Morne du Chameau—"Camel Mountain"— commands some of the best views in the entire island chain.

Don't forget that the French Antilles are famed for their golf clubs and golf courses, among the best in the Caribbean. Tennis and watersports are provided at most resort hotels. Try your hand at traditional French sports such as lacrosse, or play "boulle" and "pelote" on the beach. All the islands of the French West Indies are health and sports-oriented and one is never far away from a workout, gymnasium, pool, sauna, people taking daily exercises or just soaking up the invigorating rays of the sun!

Very "F.W.I." are the cockfights, which are still an accepted part of island life. With lively gambling on the winners, the sport is an integral part of the entertainment of the islands as can be noted in the fact that Martinique alone has at least four recognized "cock pits" that operate on weekdays as well as weekends. Mongoose and snake fights are a similar pastime confined to Martinique. Horse racing is also a popular sport of the islands. The regattas— "yole" racing and "goelette" racing— with colorful local sailing craft is an experience not to be missed. There is even a flying school on Martinique for those who have taken their fill of the land and sea and wish to take to the air!

Traveling Tips

Health

Visitors require vaccination certificates only when entering the islands from an endemic area. Hospitals, medical and dental services are of a generally excellent standard. There are more than fifty hospitals and clinics throughout the French Caribbean islands. Basic first-aid attention is available in every resort and hotel.

Apart from unforeseeable instances the few times visitors to the islands require any form of medical attention is either due to the irritation caused by the sandflies found in some regions or from undue exposure to the deceptively strong rays of the sun. Several sea-dwellers, such as the stonefish, fire coral, or sea urchin can inflict severe pain which invariably calls for immediate treatment. It is highly unlikely that visitors may encounter the venomous Fer-de-Lance viper in the wild. The snake inhabits only the more desolate regions of Martinique and, even here, the mongoose has kept the serpent population to a minimum.

Packing a small first-aid kit may be no insurance against harm, but can be invaluable at times. Kits should include: antiseptic cream, adhesive tape bandages, aspirin, calamine lotion, diarrhea treatment, cotton, eye lotion, gauze dressing, tablets for indigestion, insect repellent, safety pins, scissors, thermometer, throat lozenges, travel sickness pills, paper tissues, surgical tape, tweezers and a pen, pencil and notepad. It is wise to pack one of the little pocket first-aid booklets which include advice on the "Kiss of Life," artificial respiration, and other emergency procedures.

Most everyday medical preparations can be purchased at the modern drugstores and pharmacies. There are five modern hospitals on Guadeloupe and more than twenty-three clinics. On Martinique there are about twenty hospitals and clinics.

The more precautious visitor may want to pack proprietary medicines for gastroenteritis, aspirin, elastic plasters and children's medicines. Individual prescriptions should not be forgotten and women should pack personal requirements. Taking out short-term insurance is a good policy.

Make a mental note of the nearest medical attention available on tour although guides, tour operator representatives or agents generally know where to find first-aid, a doctor or the nearest hospital. Most medical problems occurring on vacation are minor. Health in the tropics is more a case of common sense and taking slightly more precautions than one would normally in a cooler climate. Some exponents say: "Don't eat fish where you can't see the water and don't eat meat where you cannot see the beast!" Take ample liquids, preferably water, and keep cool! A beach wrap, one of those local straw hats and sunblock cream for ankles, nose and ears help to prevent problems of overexposure in the sun. Sand, water, the deck of a boat, or any reflective surface can increase the potency of the sun by nearly a third. A long-sleeved shirt or blouse makes sense when the sun becomes unbearable—particularly on boat rides. Remember sunglasses to prevent dazzle, especially on or by water. Headaches and migraine can be brought on by glare.

The water on the islands is not only most palatable but, on the Leewards, where it is distilled from the sea, it is considered some of the purest and most beneficial of waters in the Caribbean. Curaçao's Amstel beer is also the only beer in the world brewed from distilled sea water.

Zoos

Zoological gardens, game reserves, wildlife parks and sanctuaries all provide ideal or near ideal conditions for wild creatures. Unfortunately, these include the unwelcome creatures as well as invited guests, and visitors to these areas should be prepared for midges and mosquitoes and other biting or stinging insects. The worst places are swamps, mangrove marshes and crocodile breeding farms!

Climate and Dress

The French Antilles lie between 920 and 1,170 miles north of the Equator and, for this reason, and their special climatic conditions, are always pleasantly hot. Trade winds constantly cool the islands' climate to an average 77 degrees F (25 degrees C). It is wettest around May to November when showers can be frequent but typically short and sharp. The squally months of tropical showers produce an average of 45 inches of rainfull annually.

Between the seven islands of the Antilles some of the more enjoyable and pleasant climatic variations can be experienced more than anywhere else in the world. Balmy evenings and baking days for basking in the sun; waters which can vary in temperature from 72 degrees–80 degress F (22 degress–27 degrees C)—ideal for snorkeling and swimming; cooling mountain breezes, damp, musky rain forests and desert scapes for exploring. Choose them all for your vacation or select the climate you feel suits you best; you will never be far from the sun, the invigorating waters and the fresh trade zephyrs.

Clothing, as with health, is a matter of personal preference but, again, a matter for common sense. The evenings can get quite cool after the burning rays of the afternoon sun and, therefore, women would be well advised to take a wrap of some sort. Lightweight tropical clothing (cotton is best) is par for the day and a light jacket for evening wear can keep out the occasional chill of the night air. Clubs sometimes insist on men wearing jackets, although the casual Caribbean wear is evident in casinos. Don't forget your beachwear and any beach sports equipment you may require. Sunglasses are almost a must because of the glare off the sea and sand. A sun hat can also be a useful addition to the holiday wardrobe. Comfortable walking shoes are invaluable as are a stout pair of beach shoes or sandals for walking on hot sand or coral outcrops. Business visitors should remember that neckties are the custom but, whatever your requirements, the shops on each island offer excellent bargains and haute couture garments at most competitive prices.

Transport

All foreign driving licenses are recognized on the French islands and temporary permits can be issued to those drivers wishing to hire transport. Taxis are plentiful but buses are preferred because the fares are inexpensive: no buses operate on St. Barts, Marie-Galante and La Désirade; minibuses and taxis do run on Les Saintes. Collective taxis, popular particularly on Martinique, allow the visitor to mingle with local people. Scooter or moped hire are two of the most popular ways of getting around the islands and cars can also be rented at most garages, hotels and at the airports.

Bicyle rental is fine for the fit but remember that some islands have very steep roads and the combination of pedalling and the hot sun can be most exhausting. Walking tours are organized on almost all the islands, both in the towns and in the countryside. Bring stout shoes and be prepared for the rugged terrain of

volcanic mountain slopes. Horseback riding trips can get you out to places which you might otherwise have missed although the most comfortable method of sightseeing might be by the special coach trips organized in the main islands. A boat excursion from any of the French isles to secluded bays, coral reefs or just between islands, is a rewarding experience and sea travel is at its best in this part of the Caribbean. Try a sailing excursion or a romantic, moonlight barbeque outing.

Air connections are almost as natural on the islands as road or sea links—sometimes more regular! From New York the flying time is not more than four hours, and from Europe (London-Paris) eight hours. Major airlines linking the French Antilles with the rest of the world include: Air France, American Airlines, Air Canada, Pan American and Minerve. In the Caribbean region the main airlines are Air Guadeloupe, Air Martinique, BWIA and Liat. Air Saint-Barth, Caraibes Air Tourisme (Heli France) and Safari Tours also run air excursions.

Guidelines on air times between islands give Marie Galante, Les Saintes and La Désirade from Guadeloupe as fifteen minutes, St. Martin and St. Barthelemy from Guadeloupe as fifty minutes. Martinique is about one hour and ten minutes flying time from St. Martin and therefore around one half-hour from Guadeloupe.

Communications

All the islands of the French Caribbean lie along the same time zone and are Greenwich Mean Time minus four hours. From Paris they are five hours behind in winter and six hours behind in summer. Local time is the same as in New York.

Modern radio communications link the islands, and the French West Indies have their own television channel. Many English radio stations can be received, such as the BBC World Service and some American broadcasting stations. French radio stations for each of the main islands keep one in touch with local and international events.

For the visitor, reading matter on a daily basis is limited and the most regular newspaper in English is the *International Herald Tribune*. Tourist publications, both in French and English, range from the *Discover* magazine of Saint Martin and St. Bart's Vendome Guide, to *Guadeloupe Bonjour* or the Martinique equivalent. Many international journals and magazines are on sale throughout the islands and they publish their own daily newspaper, *France-Antilles*. There is no shortage of paperback and other reading matter in various languages in the main duty-free centers of Guadeloupe, Martinique and St. Martin.

Telephone and telex information plus details of individual island's communications, post and radio telephone systems may be found under the appropriate island chapters. Telegraph offices, post offices and hotels have facilities to arrange long-distance communications.

Hints on Holiday

Few diversions can be more beneficial for mind and body than the delight of traveling in foreign parts. The French-speaking countries of the Caribbean are among the selective islands where the locals go out of their way to welcome and make-at-home the tourist and visitor. Traveling in countries where the people are hospitable and friendly enhances the experience, and the beauty of these islands just completes the picture by placing the visitor in an idyllic setting for enjoying the experience that much more.

Above all, the traveler should remember that the local people are your gracious hosts while visiting their country. They are not subjects in a "cage" as some photographers seem to believe! The best way to get to know their land is to talk with them and then so much more can be learned about their home and way of life.

You are visiting, just as they would be if they traveled to your own country. Their goodwill is to be valued and their homeland and environment respected. Disturbing their wildlife, creating litter, unnecessary exposure in areas plainly not designated nude sectors, or taking the country for granted is only selfish—and you will never get so much out of your vacation as one who has respect and interest for the country.

The world may be your oyster while on vacation but these six islands are the real pearls of the tropics. A little conversation, a little demonstration of interest can go a long way. Why not try a few words in French or attempt the intriguing patois called Créole—you never know where it may get you! Certainly the local people will warm to you for your efforts and may even show you what makes their islands into pearls.

On Tropical Location with the Camera

First, load the film properly. Composition makes the difference between a snapshot and a photograph. Frame the subject in the viewfinder. Imagine the oblong "picture window" of your view is divided into nine squares and position your subject—a boat in a seascape; a house in a country setting; a figure in a landscape—on one of the intersecting "crosses." Your shot will then conform to a millenium-old picture design called the Golden Rule, which artists and photographers have confidently utilized in their masterpieces through the ages.

Try different angles and unusual perspectives. For groups and portraits, get in close, really fill the frame. Look for details of architecture, fruits, fishing boats, flowers, and get in close. A macro lens can be useful for single flowers, insects or minute details.

Buy a few postcards of the local attractions that give you some idea of how a photographer familiar with the subject has tackled the scene already; try to improve on this with a different angle. Use boats, buildings or trees to frame your subject. Remember, people in a landscape or on the beach, looking at the picture subject or watching an event make a photograph more interesting and alive. Remember also that both dawn and dusk last less than half an hour in the tropics and for at least an hour each side of midday the light makes photography, especially in color, almost impossible. A slight overcast sky is ideal. Focus carefully. Some autofocus cameras will home in on your subject frame—like surrounding palm leaves etc. If they are nearer to the lens, compensate for this. If the subject is nervous, pretend to take the photo and, when the subject relaxes, press the shutter. You have already had the time to focus!

For good photos of famous buildings, churches, fortresses, tourist postcards often give the best angles or at least ideas for fine shots. Archways, gun ports, battlements or palm trees make good frames for static structures and focus the eye, as do some added interest in the picture like individuals or groups of local people. A telephoto lens tends to compress the scenery and can produce effective compositions with groups of buildings or city streets.

Illuminated tableaux or pageants can be photographed without a tripod but it is best to use a high-speed film like an ASA 400 and to open the aperture to its largest at around ⅛th second exposure.

The following checklist may also be useful:—

Documents. Travelers checks, currency, passport, visas, tickets, insurance policies, checkbook, credit cards, driving license, maps, reservation confirmations and addresses, letters of introduction, vaccination certificates if required, dictionary or phrase book.

Equipment. Photographic equipment, binoculars, tape recorder, traveling iron, flashlight, Swiss Army-style pocket-knife.

Clothing. Beachwear, jacket, slacks, shirts, blouses, sandals, shorts, underwear, socks, footwear, ties, T-shirts, nightwear, dresses, jewelry, handkerchiefs, small umbrella and something warm if returning to a cold climate! A plastic raincoat can be useful during sudden squalls.

Accessories. Sunglasses, clock, razor, adapter, toothbrush, toothpaste, soap, scissors, first-aid items, brush, comb, needle and thread, bottle or can opener, towels, lotions (remember, pressurized containers should not be taken in the aircraft), hair dryer, nail-file, makeup, keys.

Personal. Diary, medicines, children's requirements, female essentials, tissues, wallet, handbag, pens and pencils, address book, name and address of next of kin, watch, small gifts like sweets, gum, pens, any sporting gear. If you might travel on boats, seasickness pills are recommended.

Miscellaneous. Stationery requirements, a small notepad and envelopes are useful. Only at the top hotels can typewriters be hired; visitors with tape recorders should bring ample tapes. At least one replacement battery should be brought for battery-operated appliances (remember, many cameras require the power from a battery, as do flash units). The humidity can often affect the performance of batteries. Cleaning cloths for camera lenses are essential. Take great care with film also because of the climate and, both entering the country and leaving, carry all exposed and unexposed film in hand luggage and request that it should be examined at any airport (this means worldwide) by hand and not by being put through the X-ray machines. Recording tape should also be carried in hand luggage. Conventional 35mm film is generally available in duty-free shops and in the main hotels, but it is wise to bring sufficient for your visit. Also bring enough flash bulbs and filters—a skylight filter is a wise addition, as is any other photographic equipment such as tripod, etc.

Currency. Throughout the French Caribbean the French franc is the official currency. Denominations of the franc are the same as on mainland, continental France—coins are 5, 10, 20, 50 centimes and 1, 2, 5 and 10 francs. Banknotes are issued in 10, 20, 50, 100, 200 and 500 francs. Exchange rates can be found at any bank. World and both local and French international banks are to be found throughout the islands. Hours of banking vary from place to place but generally opening hours are from 8 a.m. in the morning until 1 p.m. and from 2 p.m. until 4 p.m.

The U.S. or Canadian dollar is widely accepted, as are most international credit cards.

Customs. Customs regulations are indicated at all points of entry and departure and information is available in leaflet form. One brochure suggests that the islands have no customs officials; however, the duty-free temptations of the most celebrated tax-free shopping zones in the Caribbean can seduce one into being quite rash with one's purchases, only considering the penalties and dues when one nears one's homeward destination. Check allowances—imports of goods for personal use are entirely free in the French West Indies. Departure taxes range from about $5.00. Amounts of more than 5,000 francs, or equivalent in foreign currency, are not allowed out of the islands.

Electricity. Maintaining the European standards, the French islands keep to a 208–220 V (50 cycles) electrical current. Some hotels provide converters because so many people travel with portable equipment. Carrying your own universally adaptable power plug is a sensible move, especially if you intend visiting other Caribbean islands.

Tipping. It is the advent of tourism that has recently introduced this practice into the Antilles. Many islanders still look on a tip as a bit of an insult although those working closely with visitors have adapted to the idea. Taxis in the French West Indies are quite expensive and a tip is not generally expected. Use your guidelines of common sense and tip where the service has been particularly attentive. Tipping is a matter of discretion for general services such as portering or nightclub tipping.

Common sense also should be employed over personal security and the protection of belongings. Hotels provide safety deposit boxes and, provided you don't flaunt the basic guidelines of protecting personal items, the islands are among the safest and most crime-free in the West. Most islanders until quite recently found no need to lock their car doors or even secure home doors. Any loss of possessions, especially documents like passports, should immediately be reported to the authorities.

Food and Drink. The islands of the tropics exude a thousand aromas of nature's bountiful selection of fruit and vegetables, nuts and berries. Not only do the islands provide ideal conditions for the cultivation of a wide variety of foods but the social changes in the Caribbean region have attracted races with tastes as varied as those from Africa, the Far East and Europe.

Before the advent of the European, the Arawak and Caribs thrived on native vegetation, fish, shellfish, a few wildfowl and local meats like the iguana, the hutia and lizards. Avocado, arrowroot, beans, cocoa, maize, malanga, manioc, pineapple, pimiento, sweet potato and vanilla were all indigenous to the islands. From the mainland the Indians brought with them papaya, quantities of herbs and spices and the tobacco plant.

Sugar was introduced by Christopher Columbus. Friar Tomas de Berlanga brought the banana to the Caribbean; the cherimoya came from the Incas during Spanish expeditions as did the grapefruit, lime, melon, several varieties of vegetables and more herbs and spices. However, it was really the slave trade, used to build up the sugar production, that opened the route for a wealth of imports from the African continent. Captain Bligh, of "Bounty" fame, introduced the Akee, a tree whose fruit resembles egg in taste; he also brought the breadfruit, an important staple diet. Coffee, ginger, coconut, nutmeg, taro, yam, rice, plantain and mango flooded into the region from foreign climes. In some areas millet and sorghum were introduced—these are known as 'caffercorn' in the Dutch Indies. Other plants were imported, such as flowers and trees either to be cultivated or left to grow wild. In a few hundred years the Caribbean had become a botanical garden for the world's exotic fruits and vegetables. Add to the vegetarian diet the meats of cattle, pig, goat, sheep, chicken, rabbit, fowl (including peacock) and the bountiful produce of the seas, and even the most average chef is in a wonderland of natural produce—ingredients for a million meals fit for a thousand kings!

The Negro slaves brought with them their pungent recipes; the Chinese and those from the Indian continent brought the formulae for their curries and cookies; South and Central Americans imparted knowledge on Mexican and Brazilian culinary skills; and the North Americans introduced their homebaked recipes together with the cumulative cookery expertise of the European settlers there. It was from the countries that dominated the Caribbean scene that most influence was to come. The Spanish copied their counterparts back home by introducing paella and bouillabaisse; the English maintained their taste for roasts; the French brought menus including court boullion de poisson, chateaubriand and excellent wines. Each nationality also contributed a certain soupçon from the countries which they had previously colonized.

The heritages and traditions of France arrived in the Caribbean in typically flamboyant style. The opulence of Colonial dining halls of eighteenth-century French plantation owners in pre-Revolution Caribbean demanded the compliment of French cuisine. Grandiose furnishings and treasured Sevres plates, gilt cutlery and engraved goblets could be enhanced only by the artistry of traditional Parisian dishes and therefore the aristocracy brought these to their West Indies chefs from the kitchens of high-society Orleans or the chateau kitchens of Tours. Accustomed to the temperate climate, vegetables and fruits of northern France, the master cooks were in their element when confronted with the exotica of the Antilles. Preservable foods were imported, together with Gallic wines and brandies and the chefs had a field day combining the produce of the tropics with that of Brittany or Bordeaux.

One would have to be exiled for many months on the islands to appreciate all the wonderful selections the French Antillian kitchens have to offer—what a glorious sentence! In a matter of a few weeks any visitor's palate will have been spoiled for any but the genuine Creole cooking of the French West Indies. In these few islands fate has brought together the best of the East and of the West, it has taken the Carib's homeland as the scene for its superlative blending and now serves the enticing results at the tables of the rich and famous as well as those honeymooners and vacationers who have already been lured by sun, sea and the hospitable people of the French Antilles. Once there, try some specialties like Accra, deep-fried cod minced in a batter; soudin, small clam-like shellfish with a sweet taste; langoust, clawless lobster; oursin, sea urchin; chatrou, octopus—all cooked in a variety of special ways that surprise, if not elevate, the humble fish dish to the level of a "piece de resistance."

Whether it be a Basque-type fish stew or a Normandy pâte, the piquancy of the tropics hints at the exotic. Names for various foods are part French and part patois Créole:

the small clams can be known variously as soudin or palourdes; burgot is the local name for sea snail; anguille is the much-sought-after eel; cigale de mer is the sea cricket (like a shrimp); and requin, shark. Cooking terms leave no doubt about the French origins of dishes like poisson cru, thin sliced raw fish; anguillettes de canard, breast of duck; tourte de fruit de pain, breadfruit stew; ragout de raie, stew with skate; and haricot dombre, red beans and gnocchi. Colombes, ragouts and blaffs are the mainstay of the Créole table and, naturally, the sea provides a large percentage of the French West Indies diet.

As with the magical French herbs and allspice, the intrinsic ingredient of "boucann'd" meat, the local chef looks no further than his own kitchen garden for vegetables and fruit. Tropical savories include the ackee, a fruit that can be poisonous if plucked at the wrong time but if mature cooks like scrambled eggs and is often mixed with fried codfish as the traditional Caribbean breakfast.

Most other savory produce are well-known vegetables familiar in both temperate and tropical climes. Artichoke; a variety of beans, from lima to string, pigeon to soya; beets; cucumbers; cauliflower; cabbages and marrow, all figure in the vegetable plots of the French West Indies. Less familiar to the visitor are the aubergine, sweet potato, cassava and kohlrabi. Other produce are used in stews and soups as accompaniment to curry or blaff. Bananas are now used in cooking the world over and, thanks to modern refrigeration methods, plantain (the savory version) are available in Northern markets as are chritsophene, particularly good when its milk-white meat is stuffed with kingfish or tuna; okra, or ladies fingers, a regular addition to Indian-style meals; tannia, or to use its Carib name, taia, or its local name, malanga, the leaves of which provide the spinach-like callaloo and which is a starchy root vegetable, similar to dasheen; eddoe, taro, yautia, yam and yucca. Maize, thanks to the Aztecs and Mayas of the New York, is a common ingredient in meals from Austria to Australia and no new addition to the French Caribbean menu.

Tropical fruit, even in the corner shops of more temperate regions, always seems to exude the musty tang of the Caribbean. Even more exotic than the first bite of an imported mango is the exhilaration of picking and eating a pawpaw or papaya, straight from the tree. In the French Indies most fruits grow wild as well as being cultivated for the table and for export, like Guadeloupe's bananas, vanilla and cocoa, or Martinique's sugar cane. All manner of luxurious fruits compliment the savory produce of the Caribbean kitchen and none more important than the limes used so much in the serving of fish dishes like red snapper, swordfish, grouper, marlin or even flying fish. Guadeloupe is sometimes known as "The Pineapple Island" as this was where Christopher Columbus and his mariners first tasted the fruit. Less familiar, especially to European palates, are island fruit like the carambola, sapodilla, star apple and grenadilla. Oranges and lemons, picked fresh, should be a touch on the green side and would be regarded as unripe away from the tropics but, under the rays of the French West Indies sun, even avocado and grapefruit feel warm as they are harvested from tree or bush.

Herbs and spices hold the secrets of the West Indian cook's sorcery. Comfrey, parsley and mint, thyme, rosemary and pimento (allspice), each draw out the flavor of the French delicacies. Naturally, garlic

rates high on the list of ingredients, which often reads like a fisherman's guidebook: sailfish, dorado, barracuda and yellowtail, as well as freshwater trout and bass. Coriander and saffron tinge those dishes with a more Indian flavor and Chinese influence comes in the guise of spices such as cinnamon, ginger and mace. Garden plots, found all over the islands, are often a riot of color and the flowers of sage, tarragon and two-colored peppers often contribute to the brilliance of passion flowers, anthuriums and oleander blossom.

Not only do the Antillian kitchens benefit from the wealth of tropical fruit, vegetables, spices and herbs—the abundance of seafood and fish that were discovered in the Caribbean made the cod, halibut, plaice and sole of Northern France look tame. Nuts and pods of varying shapes and sizes have also been found to be useful in both savory and sweet dishes; for example, pistachio, coconut, peanut, carob, and vanilla. The African slaves on French West Indies plantations had brought a

number of their jealously-guarded root and herb concoctions with them to the cane fields and their cultivation added another dimension to the ingredients available to the French settler's cooks.

As more labor was needed to raise the sugar crops on the West Indian islands, Chinese and East Indians flocked to the thriving communities throughout the Caribbean. With them they introduced recipes like cur-

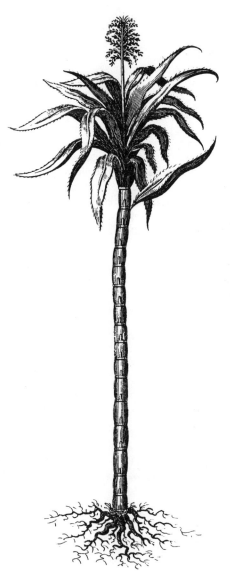

ries and stir-fry methods that were assimilated into the already varied menu of the French colonists. Rice particularly became a favorite, brought, by tradition, from the Far East. Coconuts were introduced, as were the hotter spices and herbs of the exotic East, and the tables of the rich groaned under a bewildering assortment of delights from the African cooking pots and the clay ovens of India. Still, the mainstream French, the colons, cleaved to their mother-country menus as they did to their mother tongue. Bouillabaisse, Provence's special fish soup, and garbure paysanne, the thick, country stew of Southern France, ratatouille and gâteau dominated the staunchly French cuisine. The lower down the scale, the nearer to the slave workers the settlers were, the more adventurous they became and the more they sampled the tastes of those indentured or enslaved races.

Gradually the melting pot of recipes from across the world, from Europe, Africa, China and India, mingled and the catholic tastes of the French aristocracy mellowed and accepted the peppery cooking of black slaves and the spicy rice dishes of yellow coolies. This trend was accentuated by the ruthless persecution during the French Revolution period when many aristocrats, wealthy landowners and rich merchants were introduced to "Madame Guillotine." "Chop," coincidentally, was the African slaves' word for their meagre diet consisting of a great pot into which everything edible was thrown and to which was added a generous portion of peppers to disguise the resultant aroma! Today the dish has been refined and its ingredients proportioned into a more or less definite recipe, pepper pot soup, an original slave delicacy now "de rigueur" through the black West Indies. Today French, African, Créole and East Indian Béké cookery has fused and blended into one of the most exotic tastes on earth. The especial subtlety and characteristic artistry of French cuisine remains dominant. However, behind each dish tasted in the exquisite surroundings of a French-style café or sumptuous Louis-style dining room, the unmistakable tang of tropical Caribbean, musky Africa and spicy India wafts through to endow the recipes with an incomparable mystical quality. Add to this the finest fragrance of the best French wines, Gallic liqueurs and Cognac, France's particularly dark variety of coffee, and its own unmistakable confectionery and confitures, no gourmet could help but wax lyrical over the culinary delights of the French Antilles.

Introduction to the exotic recipes of Guadeloupe or Martinique through these pages can be only a faint attempt at exciting the palate of the reader but rest assured once the merest miasma of their aromas has courted one's olfactory nerves, the conquest to Créole cuisine becomes a foregone conclusion! Just the very names on the French West Indies diverse menu of creations such as Harengs fumés à la Creole, hot pepper sauce poured over herring flambéed in rum (or, in French, *rhum*); soupe de tortue, turtle soup; matété de crabes, onion and pepper seasoning with sautéed Caribbean crabs; colombo, curried goat, fish or mutton served with spiced rice; blaff, or court-boullion of tropical fish with a hint of laurel, thyme, garlic, chives and pepper; feroce, avocado and salt codfish salad with manioc flour and a hot, local pepper sauce; migan de porc, a coarsely mashed vegetable puree (made with the traditional *baton lélé*, a stirring switch with three to five branches) served with delicious pieces of salt pork; ragoût de chatou (check this out with your waiter!); ouassous, really a *crevisse*,

or crayfish, but the enormous river variety, served with spicy sauces; and not forgetting the ever-popular Caribbean dish, lambi, conch (pronounced "conk"), presented in many ways, either boiled, sauteed, in a ragoût or baked. The variety is breathtaking, as are some of the hot Créole sauces!

Take a short quotation from a waiter suggesting a selection: ". . . *peut-être séduire par des fruits de mer, goûter au cochon, curry très pimentée, des crustacés ou un calalou* (vegetable soup made with local leaves similar to spinach with crab or pork meat added, the original pepper pot soup), *savoureuse soupe aux herbes parfumées.*" "Seduced with perfumed herbs," the words spell out the experience awaiting taste buds that have not yet sampled the paté en pot, rich vegetable soup with capers, cognac and mutton chitterlings; boudin Créole, a spicy black pudding (not the dessert type!); viandes boucannées, meats cooked in the traditional style of the old buccaneers, with preserving spices and peppers; soupe d'habitant, exotic vegetable soup prepared in a traditional way; potage à la crème de coco served in half-coconut shell, this is the real cream of coconut soup; or crabes farcis, devilled land-crab in breadcrumbs and seasoning.

Still with magical herbs and spices, the tamarind, fabled healer and essential ingredient of a cooling drink, grows in stately grace along roadsides and sometimes as the revered tree of outlying villages. The pith of the tamarind pods can be eaten like candy but in order to produce the soothing exhilarating Mauby drink, the Mauby tree's bark must be steeped for many months in a specially prepared concoction. Camomile also can be used to produce a beverage like tea, and more alcoholic infusions can be exhorted from the coconut or the fruit of some palms. Coconut, in many forms, crops up in the Caribbean cookbook variously as oil, dessicated or fresh, shredded or diced, meat, as a utensil for eating, or as a cup for drinking.

Coconut, guava, banana, mango and a host of fruit are used to make an astounding variety of juices and liqueurs. A planter's *(les planteurs)* punch is as familiar in New York as in Marie Gallante but unless you've sipped the freshly prepared recipe under a Martinique moon fanned by the fronds of a surfside palm, you will never have the reminiscences the more adventurous traveler can conjure. Rum, or *rhum* here on the Francaphone Antilles, is synonymous with the Caribbean and the French West Indies especially. It would be impossible to list all the favorite brews and local preparations of rum through the seven isles. The twelve-year-old Bally or Clément of Martinique, classic *vieux* or old rums, Charles Simonet and Montebello of Guadeloupe, favorite *jeune* or young rums, all have their various adaptions into a range of cocktails from a daiquiri to a pina colada. Trader Vic's 1947 *Bartender's Guide* lists at least fifty rum cocktails! Just as a taster, he describes the ingredients of a Martinique Swizzle thus: 2 oz Martinique dark rum, 2 dashes Angostura bitters, ½ oz. of lemon juice, 1 teaspoonful of French West Indies sugar, 1 dash of Pernod or Herbsaint. Trader Vic says also that the word swizzle comes from the West Indian twig traditionally used to stir or "swizzle" the cocktail. He also describes Martinique rums in particular as "heavy in body, coffee-colored and often, although faintly, with the dry burned flavor of the Demeraras." Is he, one wonders, just describing the rums?

Rums, like the legendary punch-making Trois Rivieres and La Mauny of Martinique, or the *agricole* rum of Guadeloupe, are used in the preparation of some famous culinary desserts. A dash of rum added to anything from the celebrated pepper pot soup to *grande anse pilau,* lends that special Caribbean twang to a good main dish but the soft rums of the French West Indies, having derived from the waving feathery stems of ripe sugar cane, impart a nonpareil flavor to such sweet delicacies as blanc manger coco (Coconut Pudding), or banana flambee. Remember that, traditionally, a typical French West Indian meal starts and finishes with the "produce of the cane"— rum. A *décollage* or tot of old, spicy rum often starts the first course with a mellow take-off. At the end of the meal a snort of old fine rum, quite like a cognac, accompanies the tiny cup of dark, strong coffee usually completing desserts. It seems that any time, any occasion and any excuse can rustle up a "Ti Punch," literally a Créole way of saying a little or "Petit Punch." The Ti Punch generally consists of a large finger of rum with a dash of cane syrup and a spot, or a slice, of lime or lime juice. Be warned. A meal in the French Antilles is a meal never forgot!

A short vocabulary of the Créole words for some of the native produce includes *banane jaune* for the plantain, a sort of vegetable banana; *christofine*—the delicious, creamy christophine with its shiny yellow or green skin; *dasheen* is the name for the violet-colored Chinese cabbage; *igames* is the word for the starchy yam, an important potato-like root crop; *fruit à pain* gets you the breadfruit, which can be boiled or baked; *gumbo* is okra, or ladies fingers, the soft, pod-like vegetable; *calaloo* is the spinach-like leafy green and *piment* is the name for hot peppers—beware!

CHAPTER IV

Seven Sisters

Split by the geographical division of Leeward and Windward islands, and intentionally divided by Columbus when he discovered the natural course of sailing ships from Europe into the Caribbean Sea was between Guadeloupe and Dominica, Martinique is separated from the other isles of the French Antilles and is their southernmost outpost. Martinique is, as politically defined, the farthest south of any state or country of the European Economic Community. As such, she commands a special position in the French West Indies and plays her Gallic role between the British islands of Dominica and St. Lucia. No less isolated from the main administrative island of Guadeloupe, is tiny Saint Barthélémy, over 150 miles from Basse-Terre, the capital of Guadeloupe. Saint Martin and Saint Barthélémy lie in the northern part of the Leewards.

Nuttall's Encyclopedia of 1900 lists Guadeloupe as being "subject to earthquakes"—no mention of seismic activity at all under the listing for Martinique but in May, two years after publication, Mt. Pelée erupted with tremendous force, wiping out

Martinique's capital city, St. Pierre. Each island of the seven French Antilles differs in terrain and individual aspects. Even the main island, Guadeloupe, really consists of twin islets of contrasting landscapes linked by a small land bridge. Guadeloupe is really an archipelago and for administrative purposes consists of the local islets of Les Saintes, Le Désirade, Marie Galante and the further island of St. Barthélémy as well as the half-French half-Dutch island of St. Martin. Therefore, the French West Indies definitively are made up of the one island of Martinique and the six islands which comprise Guadeloupe.

Today the French islands epitomize all those images of Caribbean resorts and West Indian hideaways. Beaches vary from brilliant white to sparkling black sand. Mountains, clad in forest, jungle and bush jut up to volcanic peaks. Palms and the ubiquitous hibiscus creep into the camera lens everywhere on the islands and period plantation mansions share the landscape with quaint, fretworked colonial shops and arcades straight out of the streets of Paris. The musical lilt of the Créole language lends a pleasant hum to the colorful marketplaces and vibrant fishing villages. Pirate forts sporting ancient cannon look out over golden, crescent-shaped beaches or wild, craggy cliffs with surf pounding on the coral reefs. Brochure photographs can only hint at the exhilaration of reeling in a giant marlin, or sailing waters where the Atlantic Ocean meets the Caribbean Sea. Although the islands themselves need no distractions, the availability of numerous diversions like golfing, tennis, diving, horseback riding and even cock-fighting just enhance the variety of these colorful and variegated islands.

A Necklet of Isles

Shopping in the Aladdin's cave of boutiques on St. Martin; sailing out from Gustavia's tiny, picturesque harbor; climbing rugged volcanic slopes on Martinique; diving for sunken treasure off Les Saintes or bathing in the sparkling waterfalls of Guadeloupe; the enjoyment of these island gems is limitless. Only by using a thesaurus of superlatives can one adequately describe the raging Antillian sunsets, the whisper of trade winds through feathery palm leaves, the riotous clash of colors in traditional costumes, or the hiss of effervescent spray against the gleaming hull of a catamaran. As different as each island might be, all share the same tropical sun and the warm, friendly people who must be among the most hospitable anywhere in the Caribbean. Whatever your purpose for visiting the islands, be it the attractions of their romantic history, or the magnetic beaches and inviting sea, the French Antillian islands cater to every taste and their people specialize in creating a festive atmosphere throughout the year.

Cast like a handful of gems on the limpid blue waters between the Atlantic Ocean and the Caribbean Sea, the French islands mingle among those of the English Antilles like neighborhood Antigua, Dominica and Anguilla, and even the Dutch isles of St. Eustatius, Saba and the half-island of Sint Maarten, Fifty special things to do in the islands might include:

1. Bathe beneath the 300-ft. waterfall of Les Chutes du Carbet on Guadeloupe.
2. Wander through the remains of Pompeii-like St. Pierre, destroyed by Martinique's volcano, Mount Pelée.
3. Photograph a portrait of old France in St. Barthélémy where Breton-style bonnets are still worn.
4. Trace the route of the Frenchman on St. Martin who claimed a slice more of the island from the gin-loving Dutch.
5. See the famous Dominican priest's early eighteenth-century tower at Père Labat's hideaway in Baillif, on Guadeloupe.
6. Take a gommier boat ride out to the site of one of the Caribbean's greatest sea encounters, the Battle of Les Saintes, 1782.
7. Visit the slave's "giant punchbowl" near the Pirogue distillery on Marie Galante, then taste its exquisite rum.
8. Visit the most feared island in the Caribbean, the former leper colony of La Désirade.
9. Hike through dank, primeval rainforests searching for the famous tiger orchids on Guadeloupe.

10. Make a visit to the birthplace of Napoleon's Empress Josephine at La Pagerie, on Martinique.

11. Dive on a natural barrier reef off St. Martin.

12. Mingle with the people of the Caribbean's only island to have been settled by Swedish colonists on St. Barthélémy.

13. Discover the past in the nineteenth-century Fort Napoleon constructed on the site of a seventeenth-century fortress, Fort La Reine, on Les Saintes.

14. Paddle in the underground lake of the Devil's Hole grotto on Marie Galante.

15. Watch as seabirds skim around the spectacular Gate of Hell on La Désirade.

16. Play a round on the Caribbean's finest golf course, the St. François on Guadeloupe.

17. Take a trip out to H.M.S. Diamond Rock and hear its history on the fabulous 6½-mile-long La Diamant Beach on Martinique.

18. Search for the fabled millions in gold cruzados, lost in the wreck of the Portuguese galleon, "Santissimo Trinidade," off St. Martin.

19. Buy some traditional palm-woven souvenirs in Corossol on the island affectionately known as St. Barts.

20. Marvel at the sight of the *Gueule Grand Gouffre,* Giant Chasm's Mouth, a natural sea-hewn arch in the cliffs on Marie Galante.

21. Play catch-as-catch-can with the fearsome-looking iguanas on La Désirade.

22. Wonder at the variety of fascinatingly colorful fish fresh from the nets and gaily decorated fishing pirogues of Les Saintes.

23. Play for high stakes at any of the many casinos on Guadeloupe.

24. Trek to the very top of a volcano on the Mount Pelée trail, Martinique.

25. Make terrific savings on purchases of the finest French haute couture and Paris perfumes in the shops in Marigot, St. Martin.

26. Explore the four ancient fort sites that used to defend St. Barthélémy from pirates in days of yore.

27. Visit the attractive beaches of the islands known as "Mini Rio," Les Saintes.

28. Attempt to decipher the petrographs that have puzzled centuries of scientists at the Rock Engraving Park on Guadeloupe. Are they Carib or, perhaps, more ancient Arawak?

29. Marvel at the colorful celebrations in traditional Indian style on Martinique where live sacrifices are part of the festivities.

30. Try to count the number of sugar-cane windmills on Marie Galante.

31. Imagine being in the deserts of Western films with only the *têtes-a-l'anglaise,* "Englishmen's Heads," cacti for company on La Désirade.

32. Trace the ancient Carib rock paintings in the Grotto Caribe at Trois Rivières on Guadeloupe.

33. Photograph "the most beautiful women in the world" in their madras headdresses and inquire about the significance of the knots, on Martinique.

34. Hike to the top of Paradise Peak, *Pic du Paradis,* for stunning views of French Saint Martin and Dutch Sint Maarten.

35. Sunbathe on a secluded beach consisting entirely of shells, on St. Barthélémy.

36. Take a ride on a traditional West Indian oxcart across the sugar cane fields of Marie Galante.

37. Search for the elusive, guinea pig-like *ajouti* on the table mountain summit of La Désirade.

38. Snorkel over some of the most fantastic coral gardens in the Caribbean from the shores of Les Saintes islands.
39. Watch a speciality of the French Antilles: cock-fighting on Guadeloupe.
40. Even more rare, try to get to see the traditional fight between mongoose and pit viper on Martinique.
41. Take a visit to "instant Holland" by driving across St. Martin's border into Dutch Sint Maarten.
42. Visit a genuine pirates' cove on St. Barthélémy at La Fourche.
43. Explore the ruins of one of the West Indies' finest colonial plantation mansions, Habitation Murat, on Marie Galante.
44. Tour the fascinating rugged coastline of the first island sighted by Columbus on his second voyage, La Désirade.
45. Take a photograph of your friends wearing the curious traditional hat worn on Les Saintes, the *salako*.
46. Enjoy a rare delight of bathing from beaches of fine black sand on Bassterre, Guadeloupe.
47. Join in the burning of King Carnival, Vaval, at Martinique's annual celebration, which lasts a full twenty-four hours.
48. Visit ancient Fort Saint Louis, a seventeenth-century bastion overlooking the beautiful Marigot Bay.
49. Try to locate the islands of La Désirade, Antigua and even Monserrat from the lookout cliffs of Grande Vigie on Guadeloupe.
50. Sail the entire seven islands on a bareboat charter from one of the finest marinas in the Western Hemisphere, on Guadeloupe.

CHAPTER V

Guadeloupe "Island of Beautiful Waters"

Size and Location

Shaped rather like the two wings of an exotic butterfly, the twin isles that make up the main island of Guadaloupe cover a land area of approximately 530 square miles. Basse-Terre (the lowland) lies to the west and is about 312 square miles in all and, across the narrow, Rivière-Salée (Salt River), of 3½ miles in length, the eastern isle of Grande-Terre is about 218 square miles in total area. The Rivière Salée is the only river connecting the Caribbean with the Atlantic Ocean. The major island's sisters of La Désirade, Marie Galante and Les Saintes, are treated separately in this book although, officially, are part-and-parcel of the dominant island. Each of the "wings" of Guadeloupe compliment each other by both having a long coastline in two different seas. Basse-Terre dips its wing in the waters of the Caribbean Sea while Grande-Terre has its shores in the Atlantic Ocean. The tip of Basse-Terre just touches the latitude of 16 degrees North and the northerly tip of Grande-Terre reaches about 35 miles towards its nearest neighbor, Antigua, 65 miles away. To the south of Guadeloupe is the island of Dominica, in the Windward islands, just 73 miles south. Martinique, its "big sister" lies 121 miles south of the island, about the same distance as Saint Barthélémy in the north. St. Martin is a little farther north, about 140 miles.

In the old sailing days the ideal spot to head for when journeying from Europe to the Caribbean, taking advantage of the fair winds, was the isle of Guadeloupe with its two passages into the Caribbean Sea, the Dominica Passage in the south and the Guadeloupe Passage to the north. Being the farthest island south in the Leeward chain, Guadeloupe is favored for its central position in the arc of Antillian islands.

Physical

To say that Guadeloupe's twin islands were as "different as chalk and cheese" would almost be correct in a geological sense. Grande-Terre is certainly composed of a shattered, limestone outcrop with karstic hills known locally as *montagnes russes*— "switchback hills" or *mornes*. Low plains known as *fonds* reach out to white, sandy beaches and spectacular rocky cliffs along its coast. Called Basse-Terre mainly because of its geographical (south) position, the twin isle across the Riviere Salee is totally different. Mountains caused by volcanic disturbances run the length of Basse-Terre. From low flat plains in the east, near the Salée River, the landscape rises sharply to high peaks and steep ravines in the island's center. Here, many important mountains, like the still-active volcano Mount Soufrière (the Lesser Antilles' highest point at 4,813 feet) and several others of about 2,000 feet high puncture the skyline carved by deep gorges and clad in tropical rain forest.

The terrain for the most part on Basse-Terre is wild, with cascading waterfalls and mountain streams. Its mountain range is the source of the Grande Rivière Goyaves, the island's longest river at nearly twenty miles in length. Many inlets with black, volcanic-sanded beaches lie on the south and southeast coast of the island and Basse-Terre's west coast is particularly rugged. This island is much larger and higher than its twin and the entire island of Guadeloupe is the Lesser Antilles' second largest island by area.

Climate

Guadeloupe enjoys a typically tropical climate tempered by the northeast trade winds for most of the year. These cooling, damp-carrying winds are generally no more than breezes, *Les Alizes*. Hurricanes have occurred in 1928, 1956, 1966 and 1979, mostly in August or September; however, the irregularity of these unusual conditions has never deterred anyone from enjoying the island's prevailingly idyllic climate.

Average temperatures range from 72 degrees to 86 degrees F (22–30 degrees C") on the coast, to inland variations of between 66 and 81 degrees F (19–27 degrees C). In mountain areas the temperature can drop to most untropical levels and showers can necessitate the use of raincoats. The seas are always warm and November through the end of May is the island's dry season. Special discounted tours are usually available from mid-April to mid-December. This is the time of year when hotels, shops and restaurants make special offers and concessions—the Guadeloupe Fête des Cuisinieres occurs during this period, in August, so it makes economical sense to travel during the less dry season.

Population

About 337,000 people live in the archipelago of Guadeloupe, almost 50 percent of whom are under twenty years of age. Most of the population are black, or mulatto, and are descendants of the thousands of African slaves brought during the eighteenth and nineteenth centuries to work on the sugar-cane fields of Guadeloupe. A percentage of the people are descendants of early settlers, "Békés," and also of Indian indentured workers brought to the country after emancipation.

Tourism and administration provide work for nearly half of the total populace and agricultural activities occupy more than another quarter of the islanders. Industry accounts for a large proportion of Guadeloupe's wage-earners.

Language

Primarily, and officially, the language in Guadeloupe is French. Creole, however, is the language of the people—once banned from educational establishments—now a proud demonstration of individualism and ethnic "belonging." Real Creole patois seems to be a language spoken by a people who celebrate the fact that they cannot make up their minds between a mixture of African languages, Spanish, French, English, and Carib Indian! It is also one of the world's only languages which seems to be invented for song. In Guadeloupe many of the staff at tourist resorts and in most of the hotels speak a fair amount of English but French dominates throughout. A phrase book is certainly recommended.

Holidays and Festivals

Although any excuse for celebration brings the people of Guadeloupe out onto the streets with their bands, dancers and revelers, the star attraction is the Carnival of Mardi Gras. From the first Sunday after Epiphany to Ash Wednesday the capital, Pointe-à-Pitre, and all major towns are a mass of color and sound as the people involve themselves in competitions, music contests, beauty shows, and local "vides," or exuberant demonstrations of rhythm, passion and entertainment. Carnival means, literally, carné vale, Latin for "a farewell to meat." Stemmed in ancient, distant paganism, Carnival in the Antilles wears the cloak of Christianity and the mask of Bacchus. The highlight of the feasts and processions, the dramatic masquerades and raucous dancing is the parading of King Vaval's effigy through the streets of the capital to its cremation at the stake as a token of cleansing. Carnival in Pointe-à-Pitre rates as one of the most spectacular festivals anywhere in the Western Hemisphere. As if in response, the "meat producers"—cooks, chefs and gourmets—have a celebration all their own. It is known as the Fête des Cuisinieres" and renowned worldwide as possibly the most colorful food festival anywhere. For the patron of cooks, St. Laurent, women chefs dress in traditional costumes and parade the most mouth-watering delicacies from the kitchens of the island through the city streets to the cathedral, accompanied by bands, dancing and a good deal of revelry. The nearest Saturday to August 11 is the date of this Guild Celebration and other fetes include Les Fêtes Indiennes "Bon Dieu Cooli"; Jour de l'An (New Year's Day); Pâques (Easter); Pentecost; Fête du Travail (Labor Day); French National Day, July 14; Schoelcher, July 21; Assumption, August 15; Toussaint (All Saint's procession with candles), November 1; All Soul's Day; The Festival of the Holy Family, November 4; St. Cecilia, November 22; Christ-Roi; and Christmas. In local areas the Fêtes Communales (Community Festivals) occur during July to October and, in Basse-Terre, the Fête du Carmel. A modern celebration is that of the ten-day "Tour de la Guadeloupe," the mid-August bicycle race around the island.

History

The earliest occupants of Guadeloupe arrived from the South American continent around A.D. 100. They were known as Saloides Indians and originated from the basin of the Orinoco River in what is now Venezuela. Little is known of their sojourn on the island but they were superseded within a few hundred years by a more famous race. These, the Arawak Indians, also from the same region in South America, established fishing and crop-harvesting communities throughout much of the Antilles chain of islands.

From around A.D. 300 the Arawaks thrived in areas such as Roches Gravees near Trois-Rivieres and around Basse-Terre. Petrographs in these areas date from 1,600 years ago and are attributed to the peaceful Arawaks. Other artifacts, such as pottery and crude tools, have been found on Guadeloupe testifying to the Arawaks' 500-year occupation of the island.

In about A.D. 800 the life of the Arawaks was shattered by the invasion of a race from a similar area of South America as themselves. The Caribs were ferocious warriors and cannibals to boot. Indeed, the name Carib means cannibal and the race more or less ate its way through the islands now named after them! In a very short time the Caribs had decimated the Arawak population on Guadeloupe and acquired the country for themselves. They had named the island "Karukera" or "Island of Beautiful Waters." The Caribs held sway on the island for an uninterrupted 700 years. Only toward the end of this reign of terror was the savage existence disrupted.

In 1493, nine years before he discovered the neighboring island of Martinique, Christopher Columbus happened upon the island he named after a monastery in Spain—Guadeloupe. In honor of Santa Maria de la Guadeloupe de Estremadura, Columbus christened the island in keeping with a promise he had made before his second voyage to the New World. Coincidentally, way back in the Moorish history of Spain, the name Guad-al-Upe derives from the Arab words for "River of Love"—

Oued-el-Houb. It was November 4 and not only was it the rainy season but Columbus's landing-party was met with a hail of arrows from the aggressive Caribs. The motley Spanish boat crew was driven from the beach at Ste. Marie on the east side of Basse-Terre, and at Grande Anse the fleet anchored to marvel at the waterfalls and take on provisions. So attractive and lush was the countryside that the landing sailors found that at least one band was lost in the forests for several days.

After the exploration by Columbus of a tiny portion of the coast and acknowledging his reports that the island appeared not to be rich in minerals or precious stones, subsequent Spanish attempts at discovering wealth on the island failed. The Carib warriors played their part in driving off most adventurous explorers as they had Columbus, and the island remained strictly in their hands for another 140 years. Scattered bands of pirates, buccaneers and renegades tried establishing themselves on secluded outposts of Guadeloupe but the harrassment of the Carib natives proved too much until, in 1635, it was decided by Cardinal Richlieu to formally colonize the island.

Belain d'Esnambuc, Governor of St. Christopher (St. Kitts), instigated the first landing by the Frenchmen Liénard de l'Olive and Jean Duplessis d'Ossonville. Indentured laborers and missionaries joined the French nobles' expedition and eventually established a thriving community at Poite-Allègre. Battles with the Caribs were to continue even when in 1644 a settler named Charles Houël cleared acres of land in order to start planting sugar cane. Under the auspices of nearby Martinique the farming community grew and slaves began to be imported to work the fields. The rich soil of Guadeloupe proved to be ideal for the cultivation of sugar cane and thousands more black slaves were imported from Africa and from neighboring islands in order to maintain the growing sugar production. By 1674 the island came directly under the control of Couronne de France. Numerous skirmishes over the control of Guadeloupe added an extra dimension to the lives of the planters and settlers on the island and English attacks on the small enclaves persevered through the latter half of the seventeenth and the early part of the eighteenth centuries. Père Labat, explorer-priest, led a revolt against the British assault in 1703.

By the mid-1700s there were more than five times as many slaves on Guadeloupe as there were white occupants and these workers required protection from the regular invasions from English forces as they had done in 1691 and 1703. Many slaves were abducted from Guadeloupe by maurauding British troops during the first half of the eighteenth century and, by 1759, during the Seven Years' War, the English occupied the island. For more than four years the control of Guadeloupe came under British rule and during that period the number of slaves on the island was increased to more than 150,000. Under the English the port of Pointe-a-Pitre was established and new methods of processing cane were introduced.

Throughout this turbulent period there were many cases of revenge attacks, pirate forays and sieges of lonely settlements. Off the island in 1666, on August 14, a great sea battle raged and twelve French ships were sunk by the British who lost only two, fatefully enough, just a few days later; a hurricane sank the remaining fifteen British warships! Several years later French privateers began salvage operations on three Spanish treasure ships sunk off the coast in 1603 and another sank in 1636, the "San Salvador." By the mid-1600s the "governor" of the French lands had established an organized filibuster network throughout the islands and privateers thrived along all the French coastlines. Blackbeard, Edward Teach and the pirate Stede Bonnet plundered and razed a settlement on Guadeloupe and sank at least one French ship in 1718. The "brotherhood of the sea" was not the only maritime peril. A disastrous hurricane on September 6, 1776, off Pointe-à-Pitre sank more than one hundred ships of a Dutch/French convoy. So active were the pirates of the French island that by 1798 America declared war against French shipping only to aggravate the pirate Jean-Jacques Fourmenin into venting his anger against any vessel that came in his path. Basing himself in Pointe-à-Pitre, he was said to have claimed at least 150 ships (most of them British) in little more than twenty years from 1793. A leading exponent, and participant, in sea warfare was the legendary Victor Hugues, commissaire of the French Revolutionery Convention. His established base was the Fort Fleur d'Epée, which he captured at the head of a band of 1,150 men.

General Richepance reestablished a semistate of emancipation imposed by the French Revolution on August 5, 1802. Although the British occupation lasted about 78 years, it was erratic since, in 1763, the territory had been returned to France in exchange for Canada. Again, the English occupied the island in 1794 and again in a number of short intervals between 1810 and 1815. In 1813, by some quirk of fate, the island of Guadeloupe fell into Swedish hands. It was only when Napoleon was permanently retired to St. Helena that the English finally relinquished the island to the French.

In 1847 one of the founding fathers of colonial Sene-Gambia, Louis Faidherbe, was posted to Guadeloupe. He supported Victor Schoelcher in his aims for emancipation making him an unpopular French officer.

In 1848 slavery in Guadeloupe was abolished and one of the French West Indies' most famous heros, Victor Schoelcher, who had been fighting slavery since 1833, drafted the laws of emancipation. Approximately 87,000 slaves were freed in the island during 1848 and the event marked the decline of the rich sugar-wealth of Guadeloupe. Only one instance temporarily delayed the eventual reduction of sugar production on the island. During the mid-1800s a great many Hindus from the Indian continent and some Chinese began to arrive in Guadeloupe and, for a time, supplemented the labor situation in conjunction with those black slaves who, being freed, elected to continue in their work on the sugar cane plantations. Although indentured to work the plantations for only five years, 45,000 Hindus supported the vast sugar industry and the "liquid gold"—rum—created a new and important sideline to the industry.

It was during the mid-part of the nineteenth century that the true "colons" or colonists acquired their name and many more *metropolitain* settlers arrived from Mother France. Faidherbe, in Senegal, fought against sending indentured African labor to the island in 1858. Almost a century later, with the advent of the Second World War, Guadeloupe sided with the Committee of National Liberation after several years supporting the Vichy regime. The island became a true overseas Département of France in 1946 and in 1974, after a series of incidents of unrest, became a fully-fledged Region of mainland France. Since 1970 the island has benefited increasingly from the growing tourist trade, which has really put Guadeloupe on the map.

French and Creole mix in the West Indies.

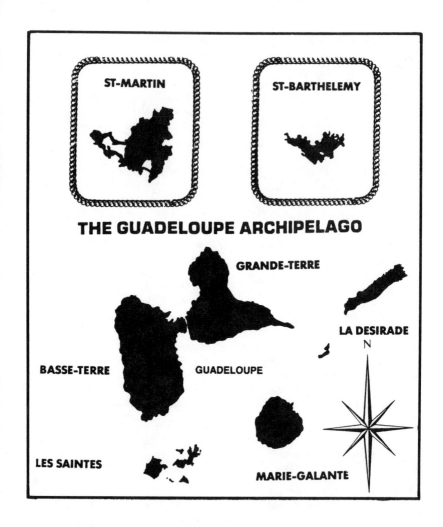

ST-MARTIN

ST-BARTHELEMY

THE GUADELOUPE ARCHIPELAGO

GRANDE-TERRE

LA DESIRADE

N

BASSE-TERRE

GUADELOUPE

LES SAINTES

MARIE-GALANTE

Trade, Industry and Economy

It is no coincidence that the coat of arms of Guadeloupe displays the radiant sun, struck through by two stalks of sugar cane. Guadeloupe is first and foremost an agricultural island and its cultivated life started when the first settlements were erected after volunteers and indentured pioneers landed in 1635. Initially just subsistance crops such as vegetables and fruit were grown but by 1644 the crop that was to change the island's future arrived. Sugar cane thrived in Guadeloupe's rich, volcanic soil and for the next 300 years molded the destiny of the island and its people. The five hundred original planters and farmers swelled as the sugar crop marched across the landscape. Many thousands of slaves from Africa and, later, indentured workers from Asia and numerous entrepreneurs from the French mainland changed the social structure of the island almost annually and sugar production snow-balled.

Other crops were grown side by side with sugar cane such as vegetables, fruit (especially bananas) and cocoa. Nothing, however, could compete with "King Sugar." New machinery was developed to speed up production which by 1650, just sixteen years after the introduction of sugar to the island, was dominating the lower Caribbean market in the commodity. The Dominican Friary Père Labat, in the early eighteenth century, developed new techniques for sugar production and the molasses and rum industry. By this time other crops contributed to the wealth of the island and some planters added indigo, cotton, coffee and tobacco to their harvest of sugar cane. No minerals of any significance were found on the island but the "white gold" of sugar compensated handsomely for the lack of minerals.

Sugar wealth attracted unwanted attention from enemy powers in the Caribbean and the island changed hands between the English and the French four or five times officially and many more times unofficially. Indeed, at one time, the island was practically governed by pirate hordes! With the abolition of slavery, temporarily declared by Hugues in 1794, many white planters were put to "Madame Guillotine" and hundreds of others sought refuge in various parts of the Caribbean and the Americas. During this short-lived period until 1802, the sugar plantations went into a steep decline only to revive for forty-six more years until the final emancipation of slaves in 1848. Again the industry dipped in production until supported by an influx of Asian workers during the second half of the nineteenth century.

Sugar today, together with the by-products of molasses and rum, still constitutes the major currency-earner of the island. Traditional ox-carts drawing wagons loaded with sugar cane stalks can still be seen throughout the French West Indies. Industrial alcohol and products from the "bagasse," or waste from crushed cane, add to the importance of sugar as the major crop. Banana cultivation, although regularly ravaged by hurricanes, constitutes another important segment of the export trade and, in Guadeloupe, three varieties are grown: *poyo'* for export; *figue* the dessert species; and *légume,* the vegetable grown for local consumption. Aubergines and vegetables add to the trade volume as do the immense quantity of flowers that are grown for export from this verdant island. Meat is produced in some quantity on Guadeloupe but much still has to be imported. Fish, on the other hand, are plentiful and in order to improve the employment situation about thirty new industrial enterprises have been established, many for the processing of such resources as timber, foods for canning and soft drinks from local fruits.

In the more heavyweight sector of industry, a number of factories have been erected and the country has a cement plant and a large electric power station. Shops and trading establishments employ a moderate section of the population but the real growth industry is tourism which, together with more diverse industrial development, is expected to be the saving grace of Guadeloupe's economy over the next few decades. Although there are indications of a trend for complete independence, the more realistic of Guadeloupeans suggest that the finance and support from the European Community as a Region of France, might give more reason to remain linked to Europe for the time being. There is certainly an indication that tourism to the main island and its five satellites is almost

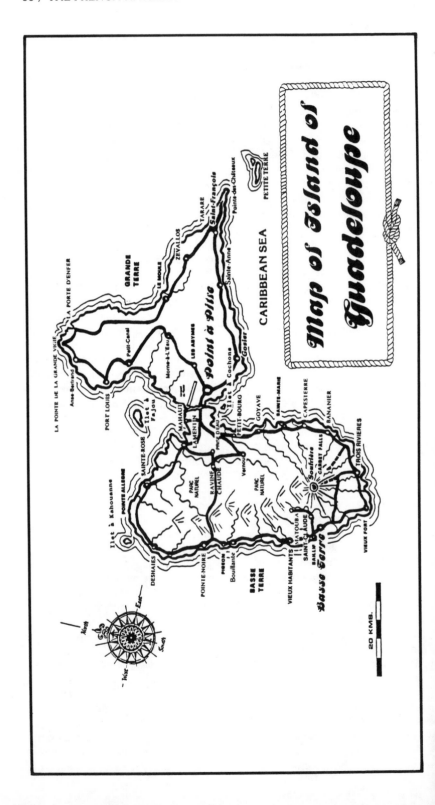

doubling every five years. The important foreign income from this source is a major competitor for the top place in Guadeloupe's convertible currency earnings.

Close-up on Basse-Terre

Basse-Terre is Guadeloupe's capital city and as such lies at the southwest corner of the island's largest sector, Basse-Terre, as opposed to Grande-Terre. With less than 20,000 population, the city is set at the base of one of the French Antilles highest active volcanoes, La Soufrière. The city has a long, straight sea frontage facing into the Caribbean, southwest, and is set between the mouths of two rivers—the Rivière de Pères and Rivière du Galion—and straddles the Rivière aux Herbes. Historically, Basse-Terre city was founded by Houël in 1640, making it one of the oldest colonial French settlements in the Caribbean. Its oldest existing building is Fort St. Charles, which was erected in 1643 and stands to the south of the city overlooking the Rivière du Galion. The fort's great battlements still stand and a museum has been built inside the massive walls where General Richepance and Admiral Gourbeyre lie buried. It was from these fortifications that Colonel Delgrès and several hundred of his followers threw themselves to their deaths rather than be captured by Napoleon's troops. From the same castellations one can see the new marina at Rivière Sens, across the main road to the south. In the valley below the fortress is a riding school.

Behind Fort St. Charles the Church of Notre Dame du Mont Carmel stands on the site of one of the earliest of French churches in the Antilles. A tiny cemetery is located in the shadow of the church. To the north the Prefecture occupies the Palace of Orleans in picturesque gardens. Just across the road from the Prefecture is the sports stadium. In front of the stadium, across a green valley, is the area known as Versailles with its church and fabulous Botanical Garden set out in 1881.

Following Rue Victor Hugues down from the Botanical Garden toward the dockside one passes the police station on the left and, just before the quay, the two grand structures of the Conseil General and Palace of Justice are on either side of the road. Two sports fields and Jardin Pinchon lie next to Parliament and Law Courts and, behind the Parliament buildings, along the harbor wall, is the Central Market. The colors of fruit, spices, herbs, vegetables and assorted wares vie for prominence with the color of Madras headscarves and gaudy traditional dresses in this fascinating marketplace. Along Boulevard General de Gaulle, leading north from the market, the Captainerie of the Harbor and the Hotel de Ville (Town Hall) stand out from office blocks and neat shopping streets. Up one of these lanes, just before one reaches the port itself and the Harbor Office, lies the city's cathedral. One of the main sights of Basse-Terre, the 1877 cathedral has a Jesuit facade with modern statues of the Virgin Mary, St. Peter and St. Paul.

Look for the square of Champs d'Arbaud where there are a number of typically old colonial houses

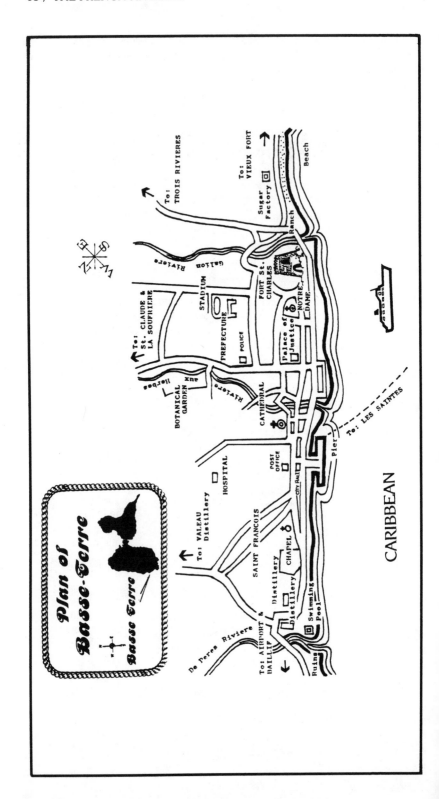

culminating in a monument to the dead of Guadeloupe in the two World Wars. Standing in the city it is difficult to imagine from the quietness of the little streets that this place has suffered so much man-made and natural turmoil. In 1590 the volcano of La Soufrière erupted; in 1635 the city was founded; in 1702 the city was attacked by the English; again, in 1759, 1763 and 1794 it was occupied by the English forces; in 1797–1798 the volcano again erupted; in 1802 the city underwent an internal riot; between 1810 and 1816 the English frequently occupied the city; in 1836 the volcano again erupted; La Soufrière blew again in 1836 and in 1890; in 1956 the mountain erupted and the city suffered earthquakes in 1976; in 1979 two hurricanes damaged the city.

As if in defiance of nature and the "sticks and stones" of mankind's inhumanity to man, the city of Basse-Terre has remained firm and un-moved. It has never undergone the devastation of Martinique's St. Pierre, entirely destroyed by volcano Pelée; it has never endured the catastrophic fire that razed its counterpart on Martinique, Fort-de-France; and never in Basse-Terre have buildings been destroyed by earthquakes such as were experienced in Point-à-Pitre in 1843. The city may be small and in the lee of a frighteningly real and active volcano but today it is at peace between the blue of the sea and the green of the mountain forests.

Touring the city can take as little as a few hours but for exploration and a proper visit to the museum, the cathedral and Botanical Garden, to visit the outskirts, such as the parks and river valleys, riding ranch and city market, one should allow at least a full day. Farther out from the capital, along the waterfront and over the River Pères toward the village of Ballif, is the city's airport.

Close-up on Pointe-à-Pitre

Although not the major administrative capital, Pointe-à-Pitre can be defined as the economic and physical center of Guadeloupe. Basse-Terre is the actual capital but its population does not exceed 20,000, whereas that of Pointe-à-Pitre stands at just under 30,000. Legend has it that the island's major township derives its name from as far back as 1654. During the governorship of Charles Houël many Dutch and Dutch Jews, persecuted in Brazil, fled to Guadeloupe and other Antillian islands. A certain Dutch fisherman, Pieter, came with this exodus and made himself popular in the region of the island where the two "wings" join—at the harbour mouth of the River Salée. At the narrow point where the Grand Cul-de-Sac of the Sea almost meets the Little Cul-de-Sac, Pieter set up his business and, from his "pitch" the French name of Pointe-à-Pitre is said to have evolved. Of course, during the numerous English occupations, the town's name was probably anglicized to Peter Point.

Of little significance except as a convenient harbor and entrance to the River Salée, the town grew quietly until occupation by British forces in 1757. During the Seven Years' War the port was improved and later fortified by the French. Continuing to expand after the Peace of Paris Treaty in 1763, the town became an important trading center after being linked by road with other parts of the island. On February 8, 1843, a great earthquake destroyed a good part of Pointe-à-Pitre and this the people reconstructed up until 1846.

From 1847 onwards a series of disasters befell the town. A fire razed the wooden houses, and in 1865 an epidemic of cholera decimated the population only to be followed in 1906 by another fire; in 1928 a violent hurricane hit the town and in 1934 another fire completed the destruction of many old colonial structures. This resulted in Pointe-à-Pitre losing most of its original buildings and being left with few historic monuments. There are, however, several old sites to be visited and these include the Basilica Saint-Pierre and Saint-Paul. Built in 1847, this cathedral is one of the oldest remaining structures to be found in the center of the town near the Place de la Victoire Square. Nicknamed the "Iron Cathedral" because of its metal, skeletal structure inside, made to withstand hurricanes and earthquakes, this is probably the best starting-off point from which to see Pointe-à-Pitre.

One of the major diversions of the town are the shopping opportunities along Schoelcher, Nozières and Faubourg Frèbault streets not far from the Basilica. Boulevard Chanzy tends to divide the town between north and south. The port (La Darse), the quays, cruise ship depot and maritime installations run around the south and west side of the town bordered by offices, banks and shops. The Musée Schoelcher, named for the emancipation leader, lies near the main or Central Market. This half-covered, colorful sight offers a riot of variegated fruits and vegetables and just in front of the Tourist Bureau on the dockside is another general marketplace. Behind here is the Place de la Victoire. It was here in 1794 that Victor Hugues fought off the English invaders. The square offers the cool shade of exotic royal palms and sablier trees. Across the way is the Place Gourbeyre, named for the admiral whose bust decorates the square, the Place of Justice and, again, the yellow and white cathedral.

In the southeastern corner of the main square is the Sous-Prefecture building fronting onto Rue Massabielle. Farther out along this street is the old nineteenth-century church of Massabielle, now in the shadow of the tower block of the same name. The hospital and Pasteur Institute lie a little farther out of town in the same direction. Just to walk back along the side of the old port and watch the schooners and sloops with their colored awnings basking in the warm swell of the Darse is a sight in itself. Just around from the Marché La Darse is Rue Rene-Boisneuf where a plaque has been erected for the Nobel prize-winning, Guadeloupe-born poet, Saint-John Perse. A visit to the St. John Perse Museum is well worthwhile, as is that to the Schoelcher Museum.

Cutting up from René-Boisneuf, along Faubourg Frèbault to the north, one passes close by another interesting nineteenth-century colonial edifice, the Chambre d'Agriculture. Farther up, the shopping colonnade meets the Boulevard Chanzy with its tree-lined freeway. Cross this and one is in the north part of town a block away from the post office. Next door to the post office is the Hotel de Ville (Town Hall) and across a beautiful parkland square is the popular Art and Cultural Center. Here one may view a variety of exhibitions in a clean, modern atmosphere and occasional cultural events may entice you to return for a fashion show, dance demonstration or craft exhibit. To the top of Faubourg Frèbault is the Centre Cultural Remi Nainsouta where similar exhibitions and events are

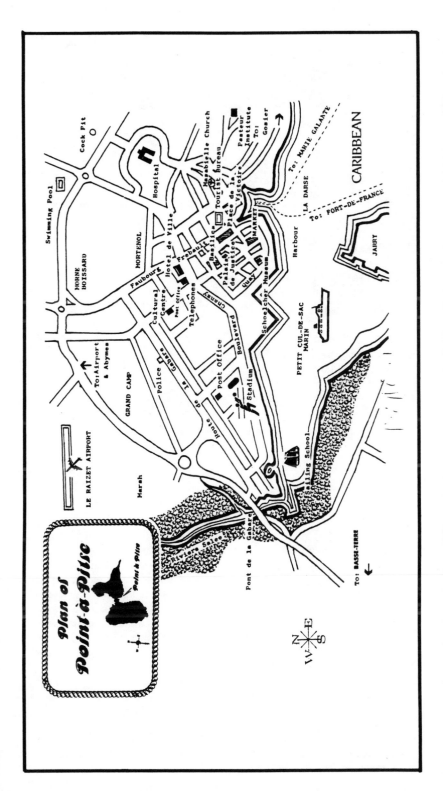

Umbrellas shield produce stands in open-air market in Pointe-à-Pitre.

held. Behind this is the fascinating Market St. Jules, just in front of the town cemetery. Behind the cemetery is the municipal stadium for sports and similar events and to the north of this, Route de la Gabare leads to the mouth of the Rivière Salée.

If one is short of time one could allow a half-day sightseeing tour of the town of Point-à-Pitre. However, if you have a taste for old French colonial architecture, wooden fretworks and ornate iron grilles, one should linger here a little longer. If you are inclined toward photography, the colorful wares, headdresses, shawls and remarkable antics of the stall-holders of the many markets should keep you enthralled for hours. If you have a penchant for discovery, walking the tiny, wood and corrugated-iron-shacked streets and alleys, the view of the island's oldest and largest rum factory, just before La Carénage old harbor, and digging out the town's history in its cathedral and museum may take you longer than you expected. Should you be a shopper or even window-shopper, the duty-free stalls and bazaars of the port area, the displays of Frèbault and Nozières streets could keep you enthralled for many hours. Just on the northern edge of the city is the island's main airport, Aéroport International du Raizet.

Discovering the Island

With one half of the island flat, with plantations and beaches, and the other mountainous, with a 74,000-acre national park, Guadeloupe is no easy island to view in one simple excursion. Initially it is divided into two quite different halves that vary in

Guadeloupe comfortably one should divide sightseeing into at least three full excursions. Again, the "neck," or central area of the island, between the two wings of Grand-Terre and Basse-Terre, should be covered by a seventh excursion.

Gendarmes enjoy traffic lull in Pointe-à-Pitre.

terrain as well as access. Grande-Terre, to the east, has a comparatively flat landscape and is crisscrossed by a network of roads that do not easily give tour access to all its attractions and, for comfort, must be divided into at least three excursions. Basse-Terre, to the west, is mountainous and a most difficult region to navigate due to the few roads crossing the steep peaks and deep gorges. One road cicumnavigates the region, running around the coastline but even so, in order to visit the most important sights of this section of

The seven suggested tours around the two halves and central part of the island of Guadeloupe, plus full-day excursions in the town of Point-à-Pitre and the city of Basse-Terre, could take a total of ten days if one includes detours to specific sites and botanical or mountaineering excursions. There are many more diversions in both the countryside and under the sea, on the beaches and in the national parklands but, for the excursionist, these tours are the best recommendations either by car or sightseeing coach. The volcano of

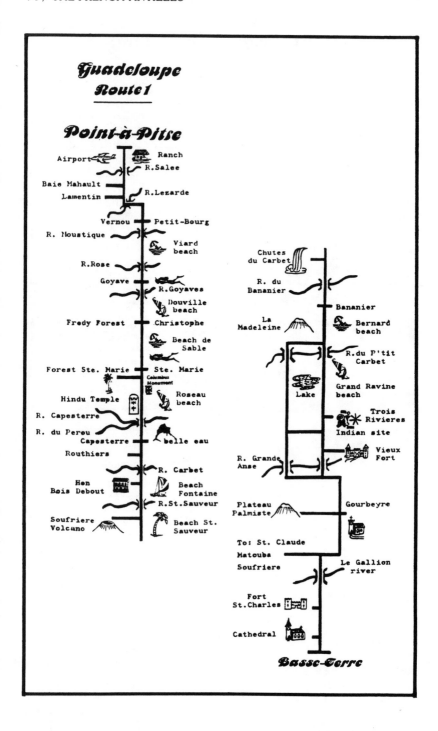

Soufrière requires a separate tour and a guide is needed to point out the paths and landmarks on the lunar-type landscape.

Excursion No. 1: Pointe-à-Pitre to Basse-Terre.

A freeway runs out from Point-à-Pitre across the Riviere Salée with views of the yachting port to your left as you travel west. Also on your left, through flat mangrove and marshy land, one passes a riding school before a network of interchanges when the route to Petit-Bourg should be selected. The road north goes to the ancient buccaneers' hideout called Baie Mahault. Before entering the seaside village the route passes over the Lèzarde River and, after the fishing settlement, over the Moustique River. Views of the azure sea across the wonderful beach resorts of Viard, Anse a Douville, the hamlet of Goyave, Anse Sable and scattered hamlets appear typically Caribbean. The next village, Sainte-Marie, also has a fine beach but look out to your left carefully and you should spot the monument to the first landing of Christopher Columbus: November 4, 1493. Here one can make a detour through Neuf-Chateau where you can visit the nursery of IFAT (Institut des Fruits et Agrumes Tropicaux). Roseau beach comes next and, after Pointe Constant, a Hindu Temple to Changy on your right. All along the way the high slopes of the foothills of La Soufriere and its sister mountains accompany your route to the right-hand side of the road. Rivers like the Capesterre and Perou are crossed, just two of the hundreds of streams and rivers cascading toward the blue-green Caribbean. Capesterre-Belle-Eau is the next small township to pass through and this has a reputation as a good fishing port. This area has also the tradition that it was here the secrets of the benefits of the plants manioc and cassava were divulged to the settlers on the island. Plantations of both root vegetables can be seen on either side of the road. Just after

the bridge over the Rivière du Grand Carbet is a turn to the right. Note the magnificent avenue of royal palms planted in the last century by the native writer Pinel Dumanoir. The avenue is known as Alle Dumanoir. The little lane leads up to the boyhood holiday home of the poet Saint-John Perse when he was a boy. The celebrated French Nobel prizewinner lived from 1887–1975. Look up to the mountains from here as there are generally good views of the volcano and the waterfalls. After crossing the River St. Sauveur there are tracks on the right that can take you on a stiff walk, eventually to the highest of the three waterfalls of the Chutes du Carbet which so impressed Columbus. The three Carbet falls are from 66 feet, 361 feet, up to the 375-foot fall. The river that feeds the fall finds its source in the Soufrière Volcano and empties into the sea at Capesterre-Belle-Eau. Anywhere along the road on this southeastern coastline of Basse-Terre there are opportunities to take walking detours up the steep side of the 4,813-foot high La Soufrière volcanic mountain, its foothills, or river gorges and smaller waterfalls. Beautiful beaches continue to present marine vistas along the left-hand side of the road, Anse à la Fontaine, Anse St. Sauveur and, after Bananier—literally an important banana-growing center—and the Barracuda Beach hotel, are Anse Bernard and Anse Grand Ravine. If Pointe Coq Souris, just before Anse Grand Ravine, refers to the laughing cock, it is no coincidence. In almost every village and hamlet on Guadeloupe there is a cock-fighting pit. Cock fighting is a national sport where two trained cocks, fitted with lethal spurs, battle to the death in a specially constructed pit. Winning cocks are well prized and fetch large sums of money as bets are placed on the winning cockerels. Trois-Rivières (Three Rivers) is no stranger to the cockfight. This attractive little township, set on the hillside with its colorful fruit and fish market and quayside where boats ferry visitors to Les Santes, has a historic background of its defense against the English in 1703. Most important about the history of the region are its pre-history sites. Set out by the Arawak Indians almost 2,000 years ago, a great number of large flat stones have been littered across a wide area of parkland. The rocks have been incised with strange and undeciphered characters and pictographs relating to life in the early Indian villages. These petroglyphs are similar to many found on other Caribbean islands like Puerto Rico and in the Dominican Republic. From this site in Guadeloupe three of the giant relics have been removed to museums in New York, Paris and Berlin. The Parc Archéologique des Roches Gravées has a fine exhibition center with displays related to the site and the entire collection is set in an attractive botanical garden. Just after the detour to the archeological park, back on the main road, the more interesting route is to divert south onto a narrow secondary road toward the hotel on Pointe de la Grande Anse. The Grande Anse beach is a gorgeous arc of volcanic sand and its promontories lead round to the village of Vieux Fort and Pointe à Launay. From here good views can be had of the Les Saintes islands just seven miles to the south. The old fort, established by Liénard de l'Olive in the first quarter of the seventeenth century, even withstood the onslaught of Hurricane David in 1979. With a little church, a handicraft center where one can buy locally-made needlework and, at the right time of the year, the site of a traditional fete, this pretty fishing village shelters under the deep-cleft ravines of the 700-foot-high Monts

Caraïbes. Following the road around from Guadeloupe's southernmost point, the four-mile beach of Anse Turlet is one of the most spectacular on this part of the island. Just after a sugar refinery on the right one crosses the Gallion River into the capital of Guadeloupe, Basse-Terre.

Excursion No. 2: Basse-Terre to Pointe-à-Pitre

Leaving the center of Basse-Terre and heading out toward the airport, one should glance up the valley made by the River des Peres to the town of St. Claude and the village of Matouba perched under the peak of La Soufrière's volcano. The largest of the volcano's craters is known as "Napoleon"! Famed for mineral water springs, the area contains a volcano museum and an ancient 1823 hospice and has a history going back to the emigrees of the eighteenth century. Passing the airport to the right, one enters the fishing village of Ballif, which has a record of historic skirmishes with British invaders in the early eighteenth century. Up in the hills just past Ballif are a number of Arawak Indian petroglyphs beside the Plessis River. Rocroy Beach is a fine tourist resort with hotel just before the small town of Vieux-Habitants where the road turns inland slightly. One of Guadeloupe's oldest settlements, Vieux-Habitants boasts the oldest church on the island. More beaches and deep river clefts before the anchorage of Marigot's small inlet, Petite Anse and Anse de la Barque, are not only shaded by palms but overlooked by the beginning of the famed foot-path across the mountains, known as the Trace des Crêtes. Fascinating scenery along this coast is matched by high forest up in the 1,000-foot high peaks and the great ridge of the Pitons de Bouillante—named for the next fishing village to be passed. Bouillante's church lies on the right as does the distillery for rum just after the village, another resort before Pigeon hamlet and another with its tiny islets of Goyaves, marking the beginning of one of Guadeloupe's only marine reserves. This under-water game reserve is a major attrac-tion for divers and researchers from across the world. After passing a fa-mous beauty spot the road winds around Point Zombi to another fine beach marking the end of the re-serve. Just after the point, at a place named Mahaut, one should double back, up alongside the valley of the River Colas in order to cross the great mountain peaks of Les Mamelles. A breathtaking climb with sharp bends leads to a breathtaking view just off the main road at Morne à Louis, almost 2,500 feet up. Between the twin breasts of Mamelle de Petit-Bourg and Mamelle de Pigeon, the road has detours where one can go by way of the Grosse Montagne For-est or stop and take the trails to Morne Léger. Further on, passing stunning views at every turn, is the public park with all necessary mod-ern amenities and the Maison de la Forêt. From this delightful stopover there are mountain tracks through tropical forest, exhibits of local natural attractions, species of vegetation, and a picnic area overlooking the valley of the Petit David River. Another picnic beauty spot looks out toward the great Morne Moustique, or Joffre, at 3,675 feet. The area of parkland here is known as Parc Tropical de Bras-David. Not the least of this mountain

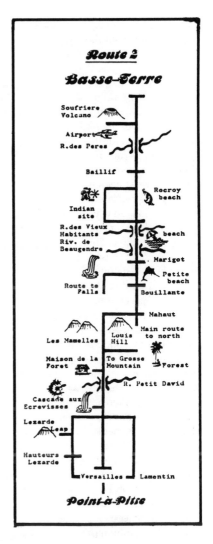

route's attractions are the fabulous waterfalls of Ecrevisses, the Saut des Ecrevisses and the Cascade. The "Crayfish Falls" can offer a refreshing dip in sparkling pools and mountain-cool rivulets and, just a short detour off the main road, is the village of Vernou with another waterfall, the

Saut de la Lezarde. Barbotteau is the hamlet where the road leads back to Vernou but also where the road leads either down to Lamentin on the north coast or past the Tabanon rum distillery, past several smaller distilleries, to the main Pointe-a-Pitre freeway. At the interchange with the road to Petit-Bourg take the left fork to the north at Versailles until the "spaghetti junction" of roads taking the exit to Pointe-a-Pitre, bypassing Baie-Mahault and crossing the Salée River before reaching the town itself.

Excursion No. 3: Basse-Terre to Lamentin

Basse-Terre lies on the southwest tip of the island section of the same name and Lametin is almost diagonally opposite on the north coast near the village of Baie-Mahault and the township of Pointe-à-Pitre. There are several ways to reach the north side of Basse-Terre but the scenic route chosen here is the coastal road that runs around the perimeter of the western islet. From Basse-Terre, the capital city of Guadeloupe, it is necessary to head north along the same route traversed in the previous excursion (2) and passing the village of Ballif, the town of Vieux-Habitants, Marigot, Bouillante and several beaches to the hamlet of Mahaut facing the beach. Then comes Anse Colas, which is followed by another long beach resort, Anse Caraibe. Behind Anse Guyonneau is the Maison du Bois with its craft center on the entrance to the lane leading to the track known as Trace des Contrebandiers (Smuggler's Footpath). In the basalt-colored town of Pointe Noir, dating back to the 1600s, there are the ruins of an ancient fortress and then the road begins to hairpin up to the site of an old cavern, then down again to the beginning of another trail, the Trace Baille Argent

Sofaia, leading across the mountains to the village of Sofaia. Lakes and ponds in the rain forest include Grand Etang, Ase de Pique (Ace of Spades) and Etang Zombi (Zombi Pond). Back on the coast, near the beach of Baille Argent, is the "Path of Discovery" on the left. Another beach lies to the left before the road cuts inland and then doubles back to Deshaies, its picnic site of the Batterie de Deshaies and the anchorage itself just over the hilltop. Just past the village is a site of antiquity behind the tiny police station. Gros Morne looks down on the village from 673 feet up to the seaward side, dwarfed by the giant mountains and river valleys to the right. Terrific beaches for diving, snorkeling, spearfishing and all water sports, Grande Anse and Anse de la Perle are passed before the naturist beach and the Hotel of Club Mediterranee Fort Royal. Plage de Clugny is another naturist beach just before Anse Vieux-Fort and Pointe Allègre—Guadeloupe's most northerly point. Just by the two beaches is an ancient site dating from 1635. The little island off Clugny is the Ilet a Kahouanne, famed for its spearfishing, deep-sea fishing and haven for boating enthusiasts. Anse du Vieux-Fort has the historic background of being the place where the first settlers landed on Guadeloupe. Plessis d'Ossonville and Liénard de l'Olive arrived here from St. Kitts to the north, in 1635, building the first fortress on the island. Just past Pointe Allègre, on the left-hand side of the road, is an ancient site of archeological interest connected with the first landing. There are a large number of cannon batteries around this coastline, many with armaments still intact. Further on, the road joins with one leading to Grande Anse across the point, nearby is another fine beach and, after the old distillery of the Comte de Loheac, is the splendid Plage la

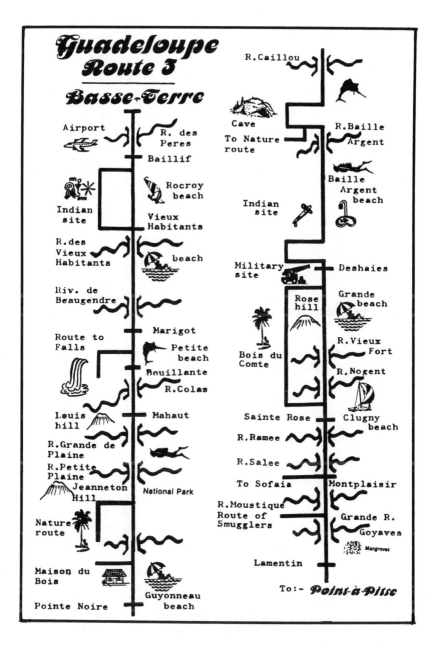

Guadeloupe Route 3
Basse-Terre

Airport
R. des Peres
Baillif
Rocroy beach
Indian site
Vieux Habitants
R.des Vieux Habitants
beach
Riv. de Beaugendre
Marigot
Route to Falls
Petite beach
Bouillante
R.Colas
Louis hill
Mahaut
R.Grande de Plaine
R.Petite Plaine
Jeanneton Hill
National Park
Nature route
Maison du Bois
Pointe Noire
Guyonneau beach

R.Caillou
Cave
To Nature route
R.Baille Argent
Baille Argent beach
Indian site
Military site
Deshaies
Rose hill
Grande beach
Bois du Comte
R.Vieux Fort
R.Nogent
Sainte Rose
Clugny beach
R.Ramee
R.Salee
To Sofaia
Montplaisir
R.Moustique
Route of Smugglers
Grande R. Goyaves
Mangroves
Lamentin
To:- Point-à-Pitse

Ramée. Another ancient site, La Ramée, is found on the roadside to the left just before one enters the town of Sainte Rose. With its myriad little islets and coral reefs, Ste. Rose is becoming a major tourist attraction. All along this northeast coastline of Basse-Terre there are cays, reefs, is-

lets and isles like Fajou, tempting the sailor and diver alike. Spearfishing is popular in these cays as is scuba diving among the astounding varieties of coral and marine growth. From the road one can see the variegated water as it shimmers over reefs and shallows on the way to the little village of Montplaisir. A lane leads to a small distillery and one then passes over the Moustique River and the Grande Riviere Goyaves at la Boucan (named for the buccaneers—or the bacon-producing pigs!). More flattish land and sights of mangrove swamps and marsh before the crossroads of Chantilly are revealed where one turns off left to the township of Lamentin. Several colonial buildings here are worth a visit. On the road south of Lamentin, near the sugar factory of Montagne, is the famed sulphur spring of Ravine Chaude, a spa on the River Goyaves—the longest and largest river in the whole of Guadeloupe.

Excursion No. 4: Central tour from Pointe-à-Pitre

A short tour that covers a little bit of everything—beach and sea views, mountains and waterfalls, architecture and culture. As in Excursion No. 1 the route should be taken out of Pointe-à-Pitre to the west, across the River Salée and into Basse-Terre. On the left-hand side, immediately after the bridge over the Salée, lies the peninsula of Jarry, a new industrial area. After mangrove and marsh the road divides at "spaghetti junction" and one should divert to Baie-Mahault, north of the main route. Baie-Mahault is named for the type of mangrove that abounds here and the settlement was once an eighteenth-century hideout for pirates. The bay itself is popular with watersport enthusiasts and the village earns its living from fishing. There is a cock pit in the village and a small church. A special festival is also held here. After visiting the portside one should return up the same street, taking the second turn on the right which leads onto the main road again. Some woods and sugar cane edge the route to the settlement of Lamentin where

one diverts from the direct road to enter the tiny town. Lamentin also has a small church, a distillery for rum, and also holds its own special festival. Although not on the coast exactly, Lamentin is attractive for its French colonial architecture. Continuing through the main street one should arrive at a crossroads with the main road again. Cross the highway at Chantilly and head toward Bagatelle and then Gross Montagne with its sugar factory and outlying rum distilleries. This is a great sugar-producing area and the little village, not surprisingly enough, entertains itself with cockfighting. From Montagne one should take a detour west, across Guadeloupe's longest river, the Goyaves, up to Ravine Chaude with its famed hot sulphur springs and spa. Beyond here, the Bras de Sable River, a tributary of the Goyaves, leads up into the forest of the Grosse Montagne. Back on the road from Montagne through Fontarabie at Prie d'Eau one comes to a junction, with the track leading to the trail of the forest de Grosse Montagne. This pathway runs along a ridge with spectacular views and mountain woodland, tropical forest and across deep ravines to the junction with the main cross-country roadway at Les Mamelles—the "Two Breasts." Back on the road at Pris d'Eau the route crosses the main highway at Barbotteau and continues to Vernou. Another famous scenic trail from here leads into the hills and to the very summit of La Soufrière volcano, if one has the time and energy! The track is known as Trace Merwart, which joins the Trace Victor Hugues and which crests the peak of Morne Moustique (Joffre). Much nearer the hamlet of Vernou are the two most visited sights of the region. Within a short walk are the falls of the Cascade aux Ecrivisses and, even nearer, the Saut de la Lézarde offers the most picturesque settings for woodland and waterfall photography. At Vernou, sadly, the road ventures no farther into the mountains and one should continue around the hairpin bend and head east toward the lower, coastal slopes. Cocoyes and Hauteurs-Lézarde are two small hamlets on the way and views on the route are quite rural. Joining the peripheral main road it is a good idea just to detour to the right slightly in order to take in the lovely port town of Petit-Bourg. On the harbor side there is a famous beauty-spot, or lookout, over the Petit Cul de Sac Marin and its numerous coral reefs. Not much farther south is the site of Columbus's first landing on the coast of Guadeloupe at Sainte Marie. There is memorial of the event erected in 1916 and designed by the sculptor Bacci on the site. On the return route to Pointe-à-Pitre you will notice acres of sugar cane fields and banana plantations with their blue plastic bags protecting the ripening fruit. Across the Lézarde River the road passes through the hamlet of Versailles to Moudong and the large interchange near Baie-Mahault. Just taking a right turn here leads you back into the main thoroughfare of Pointe-à-Pitre.

Excursion No. 5: Pointe-à-Pitre to Sainte Anne (circular)

From Pointe-à-Pitre one should head toward the University on the eastern outskirts and the sailing resort and marina Du-Bas-du-Fort. Keep to the main highway heading east and one passes the Fort Fleur d'Epée on the right-hand side of the road. This eighteenth-century fortress is well preserved and stands on a hill commanding La Grande Baie. From its battlements one has a fine view of Pointe-à-Pitre, the mountains of

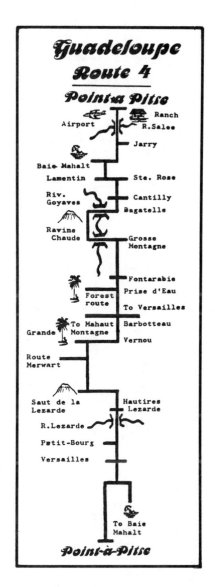

Basse-Terre, Marie Galante and Les Saintes islands. The island of Dominica is also visible from here and one should visit the dungeons, which still seem to echo to the cries of battle when the English wrested the fort from the French in 1794. A drawbridge and moat give the fort a really swashbuckling air. A drama theatre is nearby. The side road skirts south to a small lake before passing an athletic stadium on the right and then enter-

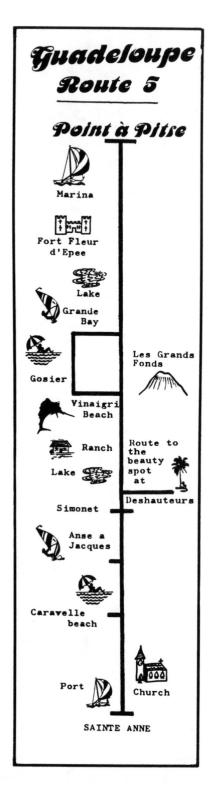

Guadeloupe Route 5

Point à Pitre

- Marina
- Fort Fleur d'Epee
- Lake
- Grande Bay
- Gosier
- Vinaigri Beach
- Ranch
- Lake
- Simonet
- Anse a Jacques
- Caravelle beach
- Port

Les Grands Fonds

Route to the beauty spot at Deshauteurs

Church

SAINTE ANNE

ing the town of Gosier. A typical French beach and watersport resort, Gosier offers all the delights of seaside activities and has the added attraction of a naturist beach and the tiny, offshore, Islet du Gosier. Rejoining the main road eastwards a riding ranch is passed on the right, between the mangroves, and a large marshy lake before the hamlet of Simonet and the picnic area by the beach of Anse Jacques. More beaches and coves string along the coast until one reaches Sainte Anne. Yachts bob in the anchorages while beaches, hotels and a variety of shops belie the original seventeenth-century atmosphere of the town when it was named for Queen Anne of Austria, wife of Louis XIII. Once an important port for the exporting of sugar, the only boats now, apart from tourist craft, are the gaily-painted fishing smacks of the locals. Once sacked by the British in 1759, Ste. Anne has now been raided by sun worshippers and can boast one of the best beaches on Grande-Terre—Caravelle Beach. Visit the little church to the north of the township and maybe snorkel over the reefs so close to the shore. See the statue of Victor Schoelcher, champion of emancipation, in the town square. The return road to Pointe-à-Pitre cuts back across the Grands Fonds and is known locally as the Switchback route. Karstic hills of limestone have created fascinating scenery which is dotted with ruined sugar mills. Keep to the road through Fouché, through the green hills to Deshauteurs where there is a lookout, or famous beauty-spot. Continuing along the winding route one should come to Bouliqui and Céligny hamlets and follow on down to the town of Abymes. The road skirts Abymes but it is possible to detour there to view this town that was built in the early 1700s. The town is renowned for its amphitheatre-shaped cemetery. On All Saints Day it is a veritable fairyland, ablaze with a thousand candles brought by a long line of devotees. From here it is but a few minutes, past the airport on the left, to the main part of Pointe-à-Pitre.

Excursion No. 6: Pointe-à-Pitre to Pointe des Châteaux

Head first for the airport, which should come up on your left as you leave town. The eighteenth-century township of Abymes (which holds special religious festivals and its own carnival) with its athletic stadium on the left is passed when one takes the right fork in the road at Quatre Chemins. Over green hills and through carpets of sugar cane, the road weaves through tiny villages like Chazeau and Rouseau. Roadside shrines and little churches, tiny cottages and school houses seem to be scattered at random along the route until one comes to a tiny pond and the village of Chateau-Gaillard. After the hillside village a series of cliffs can be seen across marshland to the left and the rum distillery of Bellevue. The next turn off to the left, allbeit only a lane, leads to the resort of Baie du Nord-Ouest, a beach and hotel. The reason for the detour is the nearby interesting site of the Sentier de Decouverte du milieu, an ancient site. Just a few minutes along the sea road to the east lies the town of Moule. Set on a magnificent horse-shoe-shaped beach on the mouth of the river which runs down the Ravine Gardel, Moule is a historic sugar port and fishing village. Not only does the town have a late seventeenth-century background but it is a region famed for archeological discoveries from Arawak and Carib Indian times. Laid siege by the British in 1794 and 1809, near the port are the remains

of an eighteenth-century fortress. Visit the famous museum "Edgar Clerc" in Moule. The quaint church in the town square dates from 1850; in 1928 Moule suffered considerable damage from a hurricane. All around the area are remnants of ancient Indian settlements and just a little way out at Morel an Arawak village has been unearthed. Even more macabre is the Beach of Skulls and Bones. Here the sea had uncovered the remains of Carib warriors and both French and British soldiers who fought for possession of the region so long ago. While thinking of the historic events which occurred in this now peaceful town, try to count the number of antique anchors that jut from the harbor's silt when the Atlantic swell falls back at low tide. Continuing out of Moule to the east, past the hotel and gorgeous bays of Anse Conchou and Salaboue'le, keeping to the coast, one comes to the Porte d'Enfer—"The Gate of Hell," some magnificent cliffs which carry the same name as their more famous counterpart, farther north along the rocky coast. Inland from here is the colonial mansion of Zevallos; there is an ancient Indian site here and also a cock pit. You will have to divert from the coast road to Zevallos to join the main road that leads on to Saint François. Before entering the town itself it is an interesting detour to continue around the north part of the Ste. Marthe district, past the Airport of St. François, along the straightest coastal road on the island, past succulents and cacti on the arid promontory, past Anse Kahouanne and Petite Kahouanne, to the easternmost point of the island. Anse de la Gourde, on the north side of the spit of land, and Plage de Tarare disguise the sudden ruggedness of the jagged Pointe des Chateaux and the stupendous view from the Pointe des Colibris (Hummingbird Point) of La

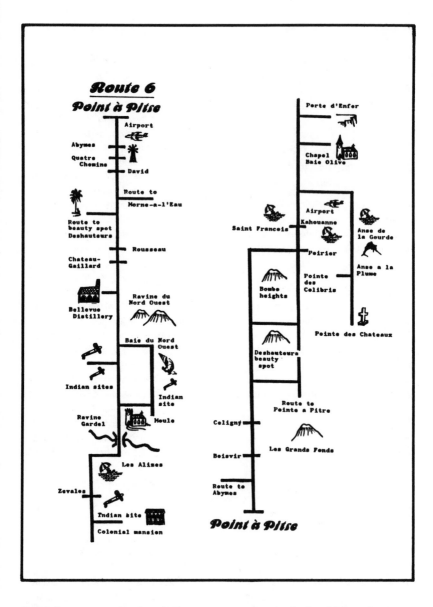

Route 6
Point à Pitre

Airport
Abymes
Quatre Chemins
David
Route to Morne-a-l'Eau
Route to beauty spot Deshauteurs
Rousseau
Chateau-Gaillard
Ravine du Nord Ouest
Bellevue Distillery
Baie du Nord Ouest
Indian sites
Indian site
Ravine Gardel
Moule
Les Alizes
Zevales
Indian site
Colonial mansion

Porte d'Enfer
Chapel Baie Olive
Airport
Saint Francois
Kahouanne
Anse de la Gourde
Peirier
Anse a la Plume
Bombe heights
Pointe des Colibris
Deshauteurs beauty spot
Pointe des Chateaux
Route to Pointe a Pitre
Celigny
Les Grands Fonds
Boisvir
Route to Abymes

Point à Pitre

Désirade, not six miles distant; the Iles de la Petite Terre and Marie Galante. Note the century-old cross on the point. Back in the developed fishing village of Saint François, don't miss its eighteenth-century church and some wooden colonial-style buildings. The historic buildings contrast sharply with the modern beach hotels, marina, golf course, tennis and shopping facilities. Similarly contrasting are the local fishing boats sometimes jostling with the varied pleasure-craft plying the waves off white, sandy beaches and lobster-filled coral reefs. Celebrated for the site of a Summit Meeting, the Hotel Méridien Guadeloupe commands one of the most evocative sites on the entire island. Taking the road out of St. François, one sees ancient steam-driven sugar mills lying deserted by modern technology like that just off the main road back to Pointe-à-Pitre. Along the road you may also spot the curious plants that grow head and shoulders above the waving sugar cane. Their stubby heads are known locally as "sucrotes" or "tour du Père Labat"—the Father of sugar and rum production in the French islands. Taking the road north, instead of through Ste. Anne, through the Bombo area, Douville is the first hamlet you will pass through, with its tiny church, then Grands-Fonds and its crossroads, Bouliqui, Boisvir—detouring the town of Abymes—and on to the town of Pointe-à-Pitre.

Excursion No. 7: Pointe-à-Pitre to Pointe de la Grande Vigie

This is the longest but most comprehensive of island tours on Grande-Terre. It is a circular excursion around the northern part of this section of Guadeloupe and takes the north road out of Pointe-à-Pitre past the airport to Abymes. One is quickly through this small township which dates from the eighteenth century and just after Abymes the road which forks to the right should be selected at Quatre Chemins. Crossing some interesting karstic country with its curious mounds and hillocks, one comes to the hamlet of Jabrun du Sud after the junction with the road out east to Moule. Said to be related to the Monaco royal family, and descended from the aristos escaping the Guillotine in Pointe-à-Pitre during the French Revolution, the unusual, fair-haired, pale-skinned people here are one of the mysteries of the fascinating French West Indies. Far to the west, on the coast near the Canal de la Belle Plaine through the coastal mangrove swamps, the outlying Ilet à Cristophe is a bird-watcher's paradise. Farther up the west side of

Grande-Terre is the little village of Vieux-Bourg, a pretty fishing settlement isolated by vast areas of mangrove. Both Ilet à Christophe and Vielle Bourg can be detoured to the village if time permits. The central town of Grande-Terre is Morne-à-L'Eau. Constructed near the end of the eighteenth century, a large canal, the Canal des Rotours, was built in 1826 to drain the low-lying Grippon Morne-à-L'Eau. The rum distillery of Berville stands just to the east of the town. Continuing north through a flank of hills facing mangrove and marsh, through Roujol, take the left turn at the "T" junction through the fishing village of Petit-Canal and around more mangrove to Port Louis. With a pretty beach, Anse de Souffleur, a cock pit and interesting churchyard, Port-Louis is a major fishing center for the region. A little farther north from the town, past the beach, is a beauty-spot known as Pointe d'Antigues. The history of the town itself includes an intense bombardment by the English naval forces in 1809. To the east of the town is the food-producing factory of Beauport and an old sugar mill. North out of Port Louis takes you past more ruined sugar mills to Anse Bertrand, another fishing town with its own beautiful beach, Anse Laborde. From here, past a sugar factory, the road hugs the coast and is not well built up. Continue northward to the very end of the track. The region you pass through was the last domain of the native Carib Indians on the island until the mid-nineteenth century. This is Guadeloupe's northernmost point, called Pointe de la Grande Vigie, well named for its fantastic views out over sheer cliffs that sweep around the rugged coastline. From a designated sightseeing point one can make out Désirade to the south, thirty miles away; Antigua, north forty-two miles; and occasionally, Monserrat's moun-

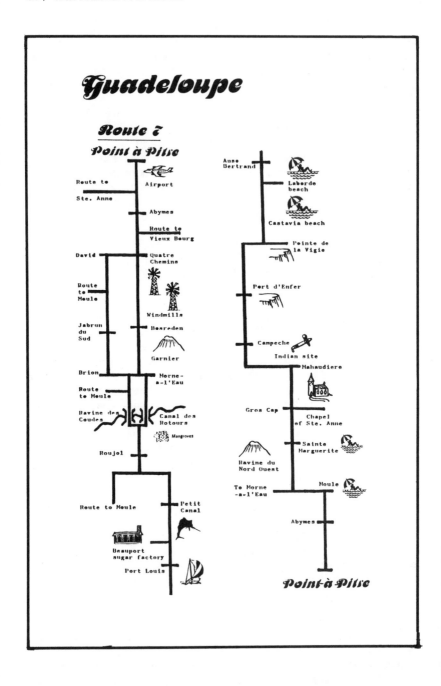

Guadeloupe

Route 7
Point à Pitre

Route to Ste. Anne

Airport

Abymes

Route to Vieux Bourg

David

Quatre Chemins

Route to Moule

Windmills

Jabrun du Sud

Besreden

Garnier

Brion

Morne-a-l'Eau

Route to Moule

Ravine des Coudes

Canal des Rotours

Mangroves

Roujol

Route to Moule

Petit Canal

Beauport sugar factory

Port Louis

Anse Bertrand

Laberde beach

Castavia beach

Pointe de la Vigie

Port d'Enfer

Campeche

Indian site

Mahaudiere

Gros Cap

Chapel of Ste. Anne

Sainte Marguerite

Ravine du Nord Ouest

To Morne-a-l'Eau

Moule

Abymes

Point-à-Pitre

tains almost fifty miles north. Retreating from the magnetic seascapes one can either follow a clifftop path or take a track detour to the most celebrated beauty-spot on the north coast. The footpath skirts coves and pretty beaches like Anse de la Pointe Nord or Pistolet Beach and leads to the stunning viewpoints of the Porte d'Enfer, "Hell's Gate." The sea has carved great chasms, caves and funnels out of the craggy rocks and cliffs.

Waves boom sonorously in unseen caverns. During the earthquake of 1843 a great natural arc of rock collapsed here leaving curious rock formations and grottos. One cave is named Madame Coco and there are two major lookouts with one splendid beach. The legend of Madame Coco relates that she appeared one day to be walking across the waves carrying a parasol then suddenly she disappeared. It was thought that many Caribs jumped to their deaths from the cliffs in this area in the past to escape capture by settlers. One can continue south on a cart track, passing on the left a small pond at Marie Thérèse, turning left at Campêche, with houses lining the roadside, and right to the ancient site Mahaudière. After searching for the historic site, head south through more sparse countryside, arid grassland and scrub to Gros Cap. It is wise to make a short detour here to the Chapel of St. Anne, perched on the cliffside with spectacular views out across the beach of Anse de la Savane Brûlée.

Take the small track back to the main road after these breathtaking sights and continue down toward the south through attractive coastal scenery until you pass the site of a pre-Columbian village on your right and the beach resort of Baie du Nord-Ouest on the left. After this, you are in Moule and the route to take is the same as that in Excursion No. 6, only reading from Moule to Pointe-à-Pitre. This route is through Chateau Gaillard, Quatre Chemins and Abymes.

These seven tours around the beautiful island of Guadeloupe cover the most important sites, both modern and ancient, scenic and historic. They are intended to encourage individual exploration of the island by hire car or similar means. The attributes of the major tourist beaches, hotels and resorts are not covered in depth as they are well known and easily appreciated by selective visits. (Note: Information on La Soufrière is best obtained from the officials and guides.)

Wildlife

It is probably because the island of Guadeloupe has such a lengthy and varied coastline, more than 150 miles with many cays and islets, that the most prolific wildlife is marine. Famed for lobsters, crabs and shrimps, Guadeloupe's shores and reefs are also a treasure-trove for shell collectors. Murex, conch, triton and abalone delight the enthusiast as much as the oysters, mussels and sea urchins whet the appetite of the gourmet. From colorful parrotfish, French angelfish, queen triggerfish, cardinals and peacockfish in the maze of brain, fan and staghorn coral, to the deepwater fish like marlin, wahoo, tuna and barracuda, the

seas are alive with nature's aquarium of colors and sizes. No scuba, snorkler, glass-bottom boat tripper or gamefisherman, shore-fisher, spearfisher or pure conservationist need travel farther than this marine wonderland for variety and excitement.

On the land the island's spectacular flora range from high, tropical rain forest to cactus and scrub, from a myriad selection of palms to some of the most spectacular flower displays anywhere in the world—just visit the flower market! Fruit, spices and herbs, vegetables and nuts provide color in pineapples and bananas, brilliance in delicacies like mango and pawpaw, variety in melons and roots or tubers and surprise in avocado, breadfruit or cashew (notice how the nut grows outside the bloom, something very rare in the vegetable kingdom). Coconuts may be familiar to us all but in Guadeloupe listen to how many uses the coco palm has in everyday native life. For the visitor it is a novelty to place a hisbiscus blossom behind a loved-one's ear—in Guadeloupe it is de rigeur! From bamboo to oleander the staggering selection of wild undergrowth and cultivated garden plants is bewildering. Sugar cane seems to grow everywhere, out of roadside banks and between the cracks in walls—surely this is the sugar island of the Indies. Up in the high mountain jungle and forests one can find some of the rarest of plants and flowers, the bromeliads and finest orchids, attached to the trunks and branches of the host trees. To experience the wonder of Guadeloupe's spectacular variety of flora, the botanical gardens are a must. There are more than 186 miles of marked country footpaths and trails through Guadeloupe's forests.

Creatures on land are few and far between. Nothing of any danger lives on Guadeloupe—the only thing to watch out for is the sap from the manchineel tree which can be corrosive if you shelter under its branches during one of the country's short storms. Small lizards, an insect called the "scieur de long," frogs, singing crickets (cicadas), a few bats and brilliant butterflies constitute the main populace of animal life on Guadeloupe. Mammals include the raccoon, "raton laveur" in French. The raccoon is the symbol and mascot of Guadeloupe's national parks. A large rodent known as the agouti is also quite common on the island. However, bringing the creatures of the air into focus, one must not forget the wealth of birdlife to be found in and around the island. Frigate birds and pelicans wheel over the coastal waters, hummingbirds and warblers hover around bush and shrub, thrushes, clown-like tody and cici, flutter around breakfast tables and doves and the gli-gli bird frolic around the beachside resorts. Cattle egrets follow their selected grazer for the insects they disturb and the occasional buzzard circles over some morsel of carrion. Color and variety of size of the birdlife on Guadeloupe comfortably challenges that of most other Caribbean isles.

An ibis is often seen in the mangrove regions of Guadeloupe.

Shopping

There are a number of specially-designated craft shops on the island and paintings of local scenes, basketwork and a number of handmade ornaments, like those made from dried fruit, seeds and pods (the calabash is a good example) are the usual wares. Decorative shells and turtle/tortoise shell carved items are on sale but one should be aware that certain items are prohibited entry into some countries. Pieces of coral and coral jewelry make good buys. The stalls also stock a variety of stuffed or preserved fauna and fish. Porcupine/puffer fish makes a spiky souvenir, difficult to transport; a stuffed baby alligator makes an unusual talking piece, but beware restricted imports. Stuffed iguanas come into a similar category. Best buys for economy and novel usage are the straw *salako* coolie hats, or the *bakouas,* a wide-brimmed version. Other straw and woven items make useful gifts as do the good variety of postcards on display everywhere. Brightly colored Creole "dou dou" dolls are another good idea for gifts as are the printed fabrics, Madras dresses and scarves.

For the duty-free liquor or perfume buyers, there are a range of exciting shops on several of Pointe-à-Pitre's main thoroughfares. Best buys are the local rums, from the dark (aged up to twelve years old) to the white or silver label rums. Havana cigars can be purchased at attractive prices and Guadeloupe coffee is among the best in the Caribbean. Discounts are available from some stores and even genuine French clothing and cosmetics can be less expensive than elsewhere. In some shops traditional musical instruments share shelf space with records and cassettes of local melodies, another interesting souvenir. Don't forget the fantastic variety of fresh flowers in the markets.

Banking

As throughout the French Antilles, the currency is in French francs but the U.S. dollar is accepted almost everywhere. Banks in the capital Basse-Terre include:

> Banque de Antilles Francaises, 24 cours Nolivos. Tel: 81.25.54.
> Banque Populaire, Rue du Dr. Cabre. Tel: 81.31.35.
> Caisse D'Epargne, 6 rue Baudot. Tel: 81.14.47.
> Banque National de Paris, 13 rue Maurice-Marie-Claire. Tel: 81.21.12.

In the main commercial town of Pointe-à-Pitre there are similar banks including:

> Banque des Antilles Francaises, Place de la Victoire. Tel: 82.25.93.
> Banque Populaire, Rue A. R. Boisneuf. Tel: 83.45.03.
> Caisse D'Epargne, Rue Commandant-Mortenol. Tel: 82.87.52.
> Banque National de Paris, Place de la Rénovation. Tel: 82.96.96.

There are also banks in Le Moule, Raizet, Gosier and Jarry. Other banks include Banque Francaise Commercial, Chase Manhattan Bank and Credit Agricole.

Churches

Being predominantly a Roman Catholic country, Guadeloupe has many churches of this faith. Also on the island there are worshiping facilities for Protestants, Evangelicals, Adventists and Methodists. Pertaining to the Catholic faith, one sees numerous roadside shrines when traveling around the island.

Hotels on Guadeloupe

Of the more than fifty hotels on Guadeloupe the number of beds actually available throughout the islands which make up Guadeloupe, including guesthouses and private house accommodation, totals almost 5,000. Practically all accommodations are either on beaches or not far from the sea's edge. Some are attached to marinas and some are chalets, apartments or condominiums. Eight hotels have facilities for meetings and the Centre des Arts et de la Culture (The Cultural Center) has six meeting rooms and a theatre capacity for up to eighteen hundred delegates.

Arawak Hotel
Pointe de la Verdure, Village Soleil
97190 Gosier. Tel: 84.24.24

160 double rooms and 8 suites. Two restaurants, Three bars. Tennis, pool.

Auberge de la Distillerie
Vernou, Petit-Bourg.
Tel: 94.25.91/94.01.56

7 double rooms and 1 suite. Restaurant, two bars in quaint country hotel.

Auberge du Grand Large
St. Anne, Route de la Plage.
Tel: 88.20.06

10 double rooms in small beach inn.

Auberge De La Vielle Tour
PLM Azur, Gosier. Tel: 84.23.23

80 rooms. Beach, pool, restaurant, nightclub.

Auberge J.J.
Gosier. Tel: 84.14.85

10 rooms in this small, conveniently located inn.

Bungalow Village
Gosier. Tel: 84.04.47

16 rooms in small resort.

Callinago Beach Hotel
Gosier. Tel: 84.25.25

40 rooms in this PLM Azur hotel. Callinago Village nearby with 115 rooms.

Canabis
Gosier. Tel: 84.11.33

13 room hotel/inn.

Cap Sud Caraibe
Petit-Havre. Tel: 88.96.02

10 rooms.

Caribe Relax
Ste. Anne. Tel: 88.05.69

14 rooms. Gardens, restaurant, bar, disco.

Carmelita's Village Caraibe
St. Felix. Tel: 84.28.28

10 rooms in this secluded inn.

Club Med Caravelle
Sainte-Anne 97180. Tel: 84.21.00

Beach resort. 300 twin rooms. Restaurant, bar, pool, tennis.

Coucou Des Bois
Petit-Bourg. Tel: 95.42.25

11 rooms.

Creole Beach Hotel
Gosier. Tel: 84.26.26

156 rooms in park setting. Restaurant and bar, discotheque, sports.

Ecotel-Guadeloupe
Gosier 97190. Tel: 84.15.66

44 rooms near beach. Pool, tennis, golf. Two restaurants, two bars.

Le Flamboyants
Gosier. Tel: 84.14.11

14 rooms.

Fleur D'Epee Novotel
Bas du Fort 97190, Gosier.
Tel: 90.81.49

186 double rooms. Beachfront, pool, tennis, watersports.

Frantel Marissol
Bas du Fort 97190, Gosier.
Tel: 90.84.44

Beach hotel. 200 rooms. Two restaurants, two bars. Tennis, watersports.

Golf Marine Club Hotel
La Marina, St. Francois BP26.
Tel: 88.41.87

74 rooms. Near golf course, marina, beach, sailing. Restaurant and bar.

Grande Soufriere
Saint-Claude 97120. Tel: 81.41.27

20 rooms. Country inn with views of volcano or sea.

Hamak Hotel
St. Francois 97118. Tel: 88.59.99

56 bungalows. Restaurant and two bars. Golf, watersports.

Honore's Hotel
St. Francois. Tel: 88.40.61

10 rooms in secluded location.

Hotel De Basse-Terre
Basse-Terre. Tel: 81.19.78

14 rooms in this small hotel.

Hotel Meridien
St. Francois 97118. Tel: 88.51.00

271 rooms on beachfront. Tennis, pool, golf, watersports. Three restaurants, two bars, disco.

Hotel de la Rade
Le Moule. Tel: 23.50.92

8 rooms in this small inn.

Hotel De Recroy
Vieux Habitants 97119.
Tel: 98.42.25

12 rooms. Near volcano and rain forest. Open-air restaurant.

Hotel Relaxe
Basse-Terre. Tel: 81.18.84

12 rooms in the capital region.

Relais Bleu Antilles
Raizet, 97139   St. Claude, 97120
Tel: 590 90 03 03   Tel: 590 80 01 27
Gosier, 97190
Tel: 590 90 81 46

Hotel Salako
Gosier, Box 8, 97190. Tel: 84.22.22

120 rooms. Restaurant, bar, beach-front, pool, tennis, watersports.

Hotel Les Trois Mats
St. Francois 97118. Tel: 88.59.99

36 rooms. Near golf course, tennis, watersports.

Hotel Toubana
St. Anne, Box 63, 97180.
Tel: 88.25.78/88.25.57

50 rooms. Beach, pool, tennis, fishing.

Jacaranda
Ste. Anne. Tel: 88.05.69

18 studios, 3 rooms for 4 persons. Near beach.

Le Bougainville
Pointe-à-Pitre, 9 rue Frebault 97110.
Tel: 82.07.56

36 rooms. Restaurant and bar.

Le Coucou des Bois
Petit-Bourg, Montebello.
Tel: 95.42.25

11 rooms. Restaurant and bar.

Le Madrepore
Gosier. Tel: 90.81.46

30 bungalows. Pool.

Le Totabas
Durivage Sainte-Anne, Box 30.
97180. Tel: 88.25.60

44 beachside rooms. Two restaurants, two bars.

Les Alizes
Le Moule. Tel: 23.33.72

34 rooms.

Les Flamboyants
Gosier. Tel: 84.14.11

14 rooms.

Les Gites de Blonval
Section Blonval/Roche, St. Francois.
Tel: 82.30.95

4 bungalows for two or four persons.

Les Marines de Saint Francois
St. Francois. Tel: 88.54.55

200 apartments. Tropical park, watersports, pool.

Marina Village
St. Francois. Tel: 88.05.69

14 studios. Nautical sports.

Marissol
Gosier. Tel: 90.84.44

PLM Azur with 200 rooms. Pool,
discos, sports, nautical activities.

Mini Beach Hotel
Ste. Anne. Tel: 88.21.13

7 rooms.

Motel De Sainte Anne
Ste. Anne. Tel: 88.22.40

11 rooms in motel style.

PLM Village Soleil
Marina-Bas-Du-Fort 97190, Gosier.
Tel: 90.85.76

105 studios. Restaurant, bar, pool.

Relais du Moulin
Chateaubrun, 97180, Sainte-Anne.
Tel: 88.23.96/88.13.78

20 bungalows around ancient mill.
Pool, restaurant.

Serge's Guest House
Gosier. Tel: 84.10.25

5 apartments, 6 studios. Pool.

Residence Karukera
St. Francois. Tel: 88.60.90

127 bungalows and studios. Pool,
tennis.

Sernida's Hotel
Dampierre, Gosier.
Tel: 84.32.47/84.04.08

7 rooms.

Sprim Hotel
Gosier, Bas du Fort.
Tel: 90.82.90/82.31.54

20 studios and 2 apartments. Sports.

V.V.F. Guadeloupe
St. Francis. Tel: 88.59.47

68 studios and 6 larger rooms. Restaurant, bar.

Village Viva
Gosier. Tel: 90.87.00/90.87.66

30 rooms.

Restaurants and Nightlife on Guadeloupe

If there is one outstanding memory of Guadeloupe hospitality it must be the bonhomie and care with which the locals present their delicious native dishes. It has become increasingly popular in many hotels and restau-rants to provide traditional native cui-sine in one way or another. Not that there is a shortage of eating places where one can enjoy Créole dishes but that the visiting gourmets are de-manding the exotic, fiery dishes for which the island has become famous. There are more than 200 restaurants on Guadeloupe.

The Guadeloupean reverence for the precise preparation of Creole dishes is reflected in the ritual of the "Ti Punch" (cane syrup, white rum and zest of lemon) as a pre-meal appetizer and the traditional, old or aged dark rum after the meal, which demonstrates the respect that both native people and those who want to follow suit have for the carefully prepared local delicacies. Some special island fare can take days to evolve, marinating in mysterious concoctions of herbs, spices—not to say rum—with ingredients collected from secret places at precise times of the year or month, cooked and arranged for the gourmet much as an artist would create a masterpiece, whether it be a tropical soup or stew, or a favorite seafood dish, vegetable salad or fruit surprise.

Just the very names of the dishes bring the taste buds to the height of anticipation with native specialities such a *poulet farci aux lambis*, capon with delicious conch; *crêpe aux fruits de mer*; *coquilles St. Jacques* with avocado; langoustine steak or turtle steak, swordfish steak or steak of shark; palm or chrisophone salads; real fruit ices made with exotic produce such as mango, pawpaw, sweet or soursop, or pineapple; and the most inexhaustive list of cocktails anywhere on earth! It is often thought that Columbus first found the pineapple on Guadeloupe and, as a keen botanist, introduced the fruit throughout the West Indies. The gamut of food and drink on the island is as varied as that found anywhere. Much needs translation: Boudin Créole—a spicy, black pudding served hot; Calalou—a soup made with crabs, tomatoes and gumbo (like a spinach); Crabes Farcis—stuffed land crabs; Oursin, or chadrons—sea urchins; Blaff—fish poached Créole-style; Colombo—a curry used in mutton and chicken dishes; Chatroux—a small octopus cooked in red bean stew; Lambis—the giant conch with beautiful shells; Belengere—eggplant; Giraumon—pumpkin; Anguille—delicious eel; Vivaneau—red snapper fish; Tazar—tunafish; Colas—yellowtail fish; Coulirou—like a sprat; Homard—lobster; Langouste—crawfish; Tortue—turtle; Harangs—herrings; Burgots—sea snails; Accras—cod fritters; Matoutou—a special shrimp; Ouassous—fresh-water crayfish.

Most restaurants on the island now serve at least a few of the delightful Créole recipes and one can guarantee that just about every ingredient is hand-picked fresh almost from the doorstep! A special variety of fruit called "citronella" grows only near the volcano of Soufrière. The number of eating places is almost as bewildering as the selection of dishes one could choose from. In Pointe-à-Pitre try the Côte Jardin at Marina du Bas-du-Fort; Le Gargantua, La Route du Rhum, La Frêgate, or Danielli, in the same district. Still in Pointe-à-Pitre, La Canne à Sucre at 17 Rue Henri IV or La Plantation on Centre Cial de la Marina. In Gosier, on the beach, is Le Mérou d'Or and, nearby, Le Pescatore, or Chez Violetta at Périnette-Gosier. Other restaurants in Gosier include Le Récif at Montauban, L'Albatros at Bas-du-Fort, Chez Rosette and Le Bistrot. Out at Anse à la Gourde, Pointe-des-Chateaux, is La Langouste Chez Honoré; in Ste. Anne, Le Mini Beach and Le Bistrot; at Anse-des-Rochers, St. Francois, Les Oiseaux, Ranch, La Ciboulette and Madame Jerco; and at Anse-Bertrand, Chez Prudence. Other recommendations on Basse-Terre include Relais d'Orleans, the Tropic, Chez Paul at Matouba, Le Karacoli at Deshaies, Gîte des

Mamelles in Petit-Bourg and the luxurious Auberge de la Distillerie at Vernou.

Nightclubs can be found in most of the large hotels like the PLM Azur establishments, Meridien, Club Med and others. In total there are about fifteen nightclubs like La Cascade, Le Caraibe, Mandingo, New Land and Rum Keg Bar in Gosier; La Chaîne in Saint-Felix; Acapulco and Bet-à-Feu in St. François; and others across the island like the Club 007, Le Neptune and Le Cercle. Look for the local group "Kassav"—champions of the popular music style called the "Zouk." Casino de Gosier-les-Bains in Gosier and Casino de Saint-François in St. François offer gambling facilities including blackjack, roulette and Chemin de fer. There are five cinemas on the island.

Communications and Information

The telephone code for Guadeloupe island is 19 followed by 590. In Pointe-à-Pitre there are two post offices, one on Boulevard Chanzy and the other out in the Bergevin district. In Basse-Terre the post office is located just behind the Town Hall or Hotel de Ville.

Telex: 919. Telegrams: telephone 89.11.11. The postal code is 971.

With 23 clinics and 5 main hospitals, Guadeloupe is one of the best medically served islands in the Caribbean. The Central Hospital in Pointe-à-Pitre is in Abymes, to the east of town, Tel: 82.98.80/82.88.88. In Basse-Terre, Tel: 81.00.30. The hospital is at Cité Jacinthe to the north of the city. Seaside medical aid can be summoned from Tel: 82.91.08.

Police in Basse-Terre can be contacted at Tel: 81.11.55 located on Rue V. Hugues. In Pointe-à-Pitre the police are to the north of town at Route de la Gabare, Tel: 82.00.17.

The Tourist Bureau is at 5 Square de la Banque, B.P. 1099, F-97159 Pointe-à-Pitre, Tel: 82.09.30. Information Bureau at the airport, Tel: 82.11.81.

Taxis are available at most centers, hotels and at the airport; bus travel is most economical and car rental is available as follows: Avis, Tel: 82.33.47, Hertz, Tel: 82.00.14, Budget, Tel: 82.95.58, Jumbo Car, Tel: 83.60.74, Sol Tour, Tel: 83.39.15; and several more local hire companies operate on the island. For group tours there are many sightseeing buses and coaches and, for small groups, a sight seeing taxi can be quite economical. Sea excursion details may be obtained at most hotels and vary in schedules, destinations and prices. Anything from a small dinghy to a 60-foot sloop may also be hired. For the golfer there is the excellent Robert Trent Jones course of 18 holes at St. Francois. Tennis is available at most hotels as are a variety of watersports.

To and From the Island

Air France, Air Canada, American Airlines, Pan American and Minerve are the international airlines that serve Guadeloupe. Links with Europe are by British Airways or Air France via Paris. The island's own airline is Air Guadeloupe, which covers much of the Caribbean region in connection with Air Saint Barth. LIAT, Caraibes Air Tourisme and Safari Tours also fly within the Caribbean to Guadeloupe. Internationally, cruise liners visit the island from France; Miami, U.S.A.; and from Cayenne in South America. Many local Antillian shipping lines have vessels that also dock at Pointe-à-Pitre.

The telephone numbers for Pointe-à-Pitre International Airport, Raizet, are 82.99.48 and 82.11.81. The airport is just under two miles from the town.

CHAPTER VI

Marie-Galante
"Sombrero Island"

Size and Location

The largest of Guadeloupe's satellite islands, which include Les Saintes and La Desirade, lies just over 25 miles south of Grande Terre. The 59 square miles of Marie Galante are located halfway between La Desirade and the British Commonwealth island of Dominica. The capital is Grand Bourg on the southwest side and its two other main towns are also positioned on the coastline, St. Louis to the east and Capesterre to the west.

Physical

Circular in shape and rising in the center to a crown, the limestone terrain of Marie Galante quickly acquired the nickname "Sombrero Isle" from its unusual similarity to the Mexican headgear. The roundish perimeter has a circumference of 52 miles and the middle of the island is divided by two faults, which split three plateaus. From Anse du Vieux Fort to Anse Piton, "La Barre" is a 492-foot high cliff rising from "Les Bas" in the northeast to "Les Hautes" in the remaining two-thirds. The river of Vieux Fort runs along the base of most of "La Barre." The upward tilt of the Capesterre region of the island forms the source of the island's other main river, the St Louis; others include the Bambara, the Coulée Oubliée and the Jeannot River. A tiny lake in the north is known as the Grande Bassin. Morne-Constant is Galante's highest peak at about 670 feet and the Trois Islet region to the east is swamp and marshes. A reef runs to south and east of the Capesterre coast and the major tourist beaches lie along Marie Galante's western side.

Climate

Marie Galante has a pleasant climate, considering its tropical location, because it is exposed to cooling sea breezes. Some of these can become blustery and up to hurricane force between June and the end of November. Hurricane warnings are not uncommon in this part of the tropics but are predicted and usually pass over. The temperature on the island can vary from 76 degrees F (24 degrees C) end December to March, and rise to 81 degrees F (27 degrees C) July and August. Sea temperatures are never below about 73 degrees F (23 degrees C).

Population

The island has three separate communities which total in number around 19,000 people. They are known as Saint-Louis, Capesterre and the largest, Grand-Bourg, with over 10,000 inhabitants. The French-Norman ancestry can still be identified in the people when one notes the European blue eyes, fair hair and light skin often seen.

Language

French and the local Creole dialects are all understood. The dialects vary with the occupations and the fisherfolk, which Marie Galante is renowned for, have a special patois. English is understood in part in some more popular tourist areas.

Holidays and Festivals

As with its language, Marie Galante's celebrations follow the pattern of those on the main island—Guadeloupe. Apart from New Year's Day, Labor Day (May 1), Assumption (August 15), Armistice Day (November 11), Christmas Day and Easter Monday, Ascension and Whit Monday, the French Isles include Bastille Day (July 14), Schoelcher Day (July 21), All Saints' and All Souls' (November 1 and 2). All Saints' is a special, moving festival—all candlelight and Sunday best, with children's processions and graveyard vigils. Carnival contrasts on Ash Wednesday and Shrove Tuesday with its flamboyant celebration of Mardi Gras and more—colorful, cacophonous and characteristically Caribbean. Local events, *fêtes communales,* occur in Grand-Bourg (December 8), St. Louis (August 25) and Capesterre (July 26).

History

Known to be inhabited by ferocious Carib Indians for several centuries before it was discovered by European explorers, Marie Galante probably has a history going back to Arawak times.

On his second, 1493, voyage to the Antilles of the Caribbean, Christopher Columbus sighted land here on Sunday, November 3. It was the second island to be discovered on that expedition, after Dominica, and was named after the admiral's flagship, the Marigalante, or Maria Graciosa. The shape of the island immediately stimulated the Spanish sailors to dub the land "Sombrero" but because of the lure of larger Guadeloupe in the distance, Columbus decided not to put in to the circular islet.

Not until 1648, on the orders of Governor Charles Houël, was Marie Galante finally settled by Europeans, 150 years after its discovery. Houël intended to raise sugar cane on the island and with a small band of colonists proceeded to exterminate the resident Caribs. It is said that many Indians resorted to suicide from the craggy cliffs of the northeast coast. The men were encamped at Vieux Fort and when Houël returned to the island in 1653 with one hundred men he proceeded to erect a fortress at Grand Bourg.

In 1676 the island was attacked and overrun by the Dutch. In 1691 the English took possession of Marie Galante, as they did again in 1703. Five years before they managed a takeover of the main island of Guadeloupe, the English in 1754 again occupied the circular island. The poor African slaves working on the sugar, tobacco, indigo, coffee,

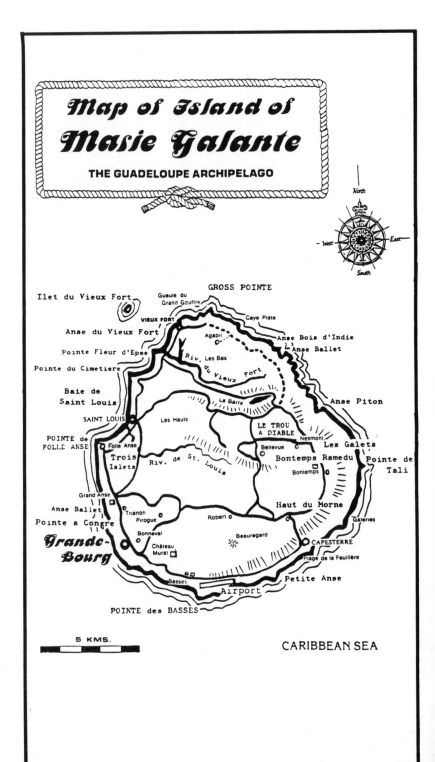

cotton and cacao plantations must have been unsure as to which language they should be learning at any one time! Marie Galante had changed hands, from Carib to French, to Dutch, etc., etc., about ten times in just over a century.

There was no doubt that the island had great agricultural potential. During the early days of French occupation, under one Jacques de Boisseret, Lord of Temericourt, Marie Galante flourished and its settlers prospered. Known during that time as "The Paradise of the French West Indies" or "The Garden of Guadeloupe," this was certainly a prize worth fighting for as both the Dutch and the English had discovered. After five years of sorties against Guadeloupe the English took Guadeloupe in 1759 and twice more, during the Napoleonic era, in 1808 and 1815, Marie Galante fell to their hands. The French were not inactive themselves in the sixteenth and seventeenth centuries and their navy was often defending French claims in other parts of the Caribbean.

Once the island finally returned to French hands in 1816, Marie Galante became a hive of agricultural activity and plantation owners grew rich. Grand mansions, like that of Dominique Murat, were erected and hundreds of sugar cane windmills dotted the island. The typical "pile" houses, now few and far between, were commonplace and every available patch of land was being turned to either sugar or bush and tree crops. Rum distillieries sprang up to assuage the thirst of the planters and this industry quickly established Marie Galante as a prime Caribbean producer of rum. A short decline in the trade occurred just after emancipation in 1848. Few major events occurred on the island except for the dedication of the sugar industry until 1901, a year before Mt. Pelée on nearby Martinique erupted, a great fire leveled a large part of the main township, Grand-Bourg.

Today, Marie Galante is part of the Region of Guadeloupe and therefore is administered by Guadeloupe which, in turn, is part of the European Economic Community and a region of France.

Trade, Industry and Economy

Ever since the establishment of settled communities on Marie Galante during the mid-seventeenth century, the island was given to raising sugar cane. Initially, this crop vied with tobacco, cacao, coffee, indigo and cotton as the island's major crop but, due to the selective nature of the other plants, sugar quickly spread a waving sea of green across the circular terrain. By the middle of the eighteenth century there were seventy-two sugar mills across the almost sixty square miles of island. Each of these mills was owned by a separate plantation family. By the end of the 1800s the ancient mills, most of them wind-driven, were replaced by four main sugar factories, due to the speed and efficiency of the machinery of the Industrial Revolution. The four factories, named Pirogue, Grand Anse, Le Robert and Dorot, were located across the island and served by a chain of distilleries which produced the island's famous rum. By this time most of the plantations cultivating other cash crops had all but disappeared.

Fishing was traditionally a rewarding occupation of the islanders and the fisherfolk became known across the Caribbean for their skills and mastery of boatcraft. The waters around Marie Galante are rich fishing grounds and the island still exports tuna, lobster, conch and turtle meat. Fine pasture land across the flatter parts of the island and on the rolling limestone hills, supports goat and cattle as in the past, but new strains of livestock have been introduced as the demand for meat increases.

Today, although most of the old sugar mills and three of the factories no longer operate, five distilleries continue to produce the much-sought-after island rum. Dorot, once an ancient mill, now supplies the growing export trade with rum as do the Poisson, Bellevue, Bielle and Le Salut distilleries. Just the one sugar factory at Grand Anse remains to process the island's dwindling sugar crop. The most famous of Marie Galante's rums is that named Père Labat after the celebrated French Dominican missionary who resided during the early eighteenth century on Guadeloupe. In rural areas fields of yam, cassava, beans and fruits may be seen.

Tourism is now becoming an important part of the island's economy and Marie Galante's export trade majors in its fine, strong rum, or *rhum* in French.

Close-up on Grand-Bourg

Although this picturesque town was devastated by an extensive fire in 1901 that demolished many of the more ancient structures, the tiny capital retains much of its old French charm. A little more than 10,000 people actually live in Grand-Bourg and the township supports two hotels, several small restaurants, a post office, chapel and police station. Les Basses Airport is just two miles to the east and from a little jetty a regular ferry service runs to Guadeloupe. The best day of the week to see Grand-Bourg is Sunday when the populace dresses its best and the traditional *foulard et madras* costume is often seen. The colorful dress and scarf-like headgear date back to early slave days—ask about the significance of the tying of the Madras.

The main street of the town, leading in from either St. Louis or the airport and Capesterre, links with Rues Presbytére, Cimetière and Eglise and, near the Place de l'Eglise, runs down to the waterfront. There are few sights in the town but one should visit the Eco-Museum of Marie Galante in the Murat sector of Grand-Bourg. On display are artworks and exhibits of local customs and traditional items, a few antiques and examples of early living on the island.

It is only from Grand-Bourg that one can hire a car to tour the island. Fishing trips can be organized from the jetty or from the main hotel, Auberge Soledad. Bicycles and mopeds may also be rented at Soledad and excursions to places of interest, like Château Murat, are often organized from there. Don't forget to ask to see one of Grand-Bourg's cockfights!

Discovering the Island

Grand-Bourg, with St. Louis and Capesterre, make up the three cantons of Marie Galante and each has popular beaches, resort areas and notable

sites. Capesterre has the most significant chapel, Saint Anne's, and as each of the towns hug the coast, all offer excellent fishing facilities. Although most visitors start their tours around the island from Les Basses Airport or the Grand-Bourg ferry, a regular boat service links Guadeloupe with St. Louis.

Being circular in shape, Marie Galante has a road that follows the coastline, almost encircling the whole island. The main road links Capesterre with St. Louis, through Grand-Bourg and another crosses the island from Capesterre to link with the main route just north of the capital. Other roads follow river courses and gullies joining outlying cottages, old sugar mills and hamlets. All along the roadside, as in mother France, one can see little crosses and shrines that testify to the staunchly Catholic faith of the islanders. A complete leisurely tour of the island takes more than four hours but the visitor usually prefers to take several short excursions to points of interest from the town of arrival as most visits are less than a full day.

However, touring the island from Grand-Bourg, follow the coast road to the north out past the cemetery on the left, skirting Le Petit Trou à Diable, with its subterranean river, on the right. The windmill ruins you will see on the way include Bonneval, Roussel and the Trianon. The famous white sands of Anse Ballet come on the left after Pointe à Congre. The beach of Ballet Bay is a popular sunbathing resort and is overlooked at one point by the raw sugar factory of Grande Anse. At the next promentory, Folle Anse, from where several mangrove-marsh mills can be seen, the resort of Rivière St. Louis commences. This beach, leading to the bay and township of St. Louis itself, runs for about three miles, with the port in the center. St. Louis has a harbor, lighthouse and the nearby rum distillery of Poisson. From here some tours may take the cross-country route to Capesterre.

Continuing along the beach, out of the tiny, smart port, one reaches Pointe du Cimetière, famed for its fine scuba fishing and the beaches of Anse Mays, or Canot and Vieux Fort.

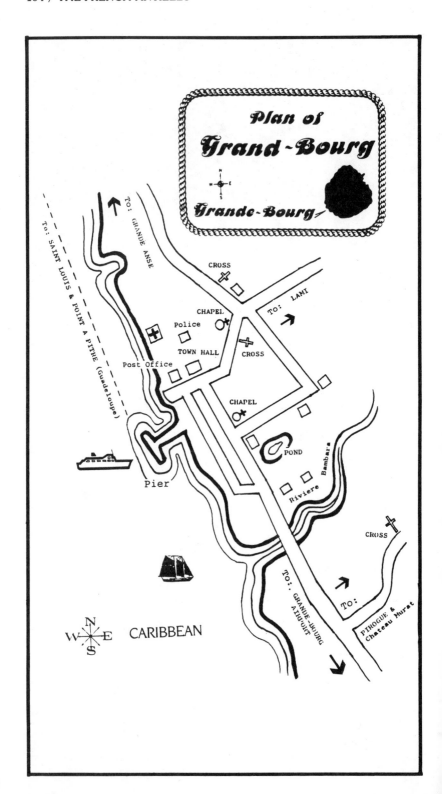

On this road there are spectacular views of the blue Caribbean and the town of Saint-Louis behind you. Vieux Fort was the site of the first settlement of French colonizers and has a graphic history. Not so romantic, however, are the charcoal-burning and fishing activities of today! The site of the fortress is on the seaward side of the road. The deep, wide Rivière du Vieux Fort meets the coast road just before the school of Vieux Fort on the right. A notable Englishman, John Waller, who visited Marie Galante during the British occupation of the islands, waxed lyrical in 1807 about the lagoon. "A more beautiful stretch of water was never seen than this, winding around the base of the hills," he wrote, "as beheld from their summits. . . ." Nearby Merlet mill offers excellent views of the lake. Looking out to sea from the village one may make out the low islet of Vieux Fort. The odd, thin-slatted and thatched roofs of the village cabins are most picturesque and nicknamed *gaulette* in the local dialect. The thatching is typical of all houses of fishing or plantation workers up until the eighteenth century.

One of Marie Galante's most spectacular sights may be seen next on the northernmost point of the island. Huge waves crash against the cliff sides of the Gueule Grand Gouffre, "The Mouth of the Giant." The coastline here has natural sea arches carved in the cliffs by the emerald tides and the best viewing point is from Caye Plate. Along the road to the clifftop beauty spot are two of the most endearing of all ancient ruins on the island, the windmills of Cambrai and Agapy. Agapy has an unusual mill shaft. Many steep cliffs, high points and bays indent the west coast for the next few miles as the road detours inland through quite hilly countryside until at Grande Barre one meets the cross-island route that follows the Barre, or fault, from St.

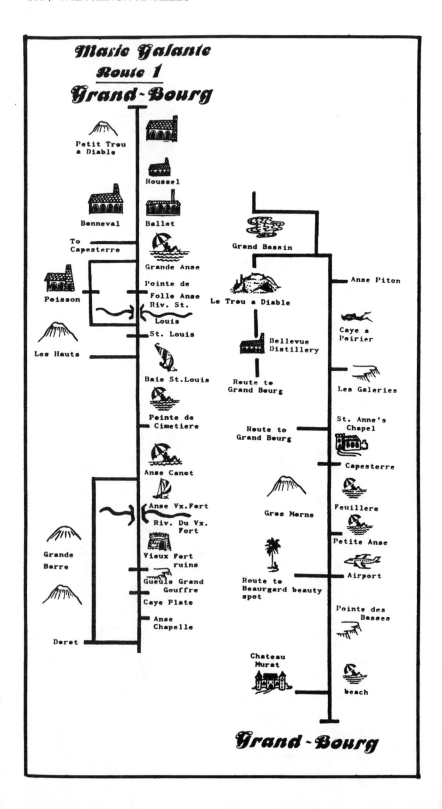

Louis in the east to Capesterre in the west. The distillery of Dorot is near Grand Bassin village and its lake-like stretch of water.

It is from this junction that one visits the Trou à Diable, or "Devil's Hole." This unusual rock formation in the limestone is an underground grotto about 328 feet in length. Stalactites and stalagmites create an ethereal atmosphere around the cave's subterranean lake and a guide is needed to point out the best sights. The tour of Devil's Hole can take about one hour. There are two alternative routes south to Capesterre from the natural spectacle. One runs through Les Balisiers region past the Bellevue distillery, joining the main road after the long cliff-fault that conceals the St. Louis River. The main route crosses to a more built-up road nearer the coast and bordering on les Galets Mabouya region. There is an ancient site of interest on the cliff side overlooking the reef. More old mills dot the roadside on the six-mile trip from Devil's Hole to Capesterre. With a coral reef running parallel to its shoreline, Capesterre boasts the two important resort beaches of la Feuillere and, further south, Petite Anse. To the north of Capesterre port is the spectacular sight-seeing vantage point of Les Galeries. Giant waves crash into caverns and sea caves at the foot of breathtaking cliffs where even the raucous Caribbean sea-bird screeches cannot be heard above the thunderous boom of foam on rock. Just a half-mile south of the town, on the airport road, is an old site of historic interest.

From Capesterre and its chapel of St. Anne, quaint streets and neat houses, one can take either the coast road past the airport to Grand-Bourg or, for those with a thirst for most spectacles and more history, the "black route." This road runs about nine miles across a less spectacular terrain of plantations and fields but passes two of the island's important sites. The chalky road might often be used by the traditional ox-cart of the island, loaded with sugar cane or thatching fronds for windbreaks or outhouse roofing. Not three miles out of Capesterre, on the right of the road, down a small track and near the ancient mill of Beauregard, across the depression of a river valley from Le Salut distillery, is a famous lookout. From this point one has a fantastic view so typical of this part of the island.

Back to the main road, one passes on the right the entrance to the Bielle distillery. Follow it down to the junction with another route leading to Grand Anse on the west coast. Take the left fork and almost immediately to your right, is the Pirogue sugar factory. The fascinating history of the nearby pool tells that upon the announcement of the abolition of slavery on the island, the workers occupied the distillery and emptied the entire rum stock into the pond. All night long, or so the tale goes, the slaves drank from this dubious cocktail—hence its name, the *Mare au Punch* or "The Punchbowl." Just a few miles farther on from Pirogue the road comes down to meet the coastal route and the outskirts of Grand Bourg once again.

If, instead of turning right into the town itself, one turns left along the coast toward the airport of Basses, there is an opportunity to view the old coffee plantation house of Murat. Just under *Morne Rouge*—Red Mountain—is the Château Murat. Sadly the name has no connection with the noted Murat, husband of Caroline Bonaparte; the name is of a Dominique Murat, a one-time lawyer who lived in Capesterre in the late eighteenth century. Mademoiselle Murat, a student at the Fine Art School in Paris and an accomplished architect, constructed the mansion in about 1832. Restored after many years of dereliction, the typical manor house has often been considered ideal for conversion into a hotel but now remains an interesting historical site. In the earthquake of 1843 the colonial mansion and mill suffered substantial damage. Don't miss the plantation's windmill to the north of the Château, Moulin Ducos. Along the shore near here are some beautiful beaches between the Pointe des Basses and Grand-Bourg. A fine coral reef runs the length of this two-mile resort.

Wildlife

Marie Galante is not noted for its wildlife—most of which comprises of goats running wild on the hillsides of "Sombrero Island"! Cattle and oxen are a familiar sight, but these are domesticated and no really wild animals inhabit the tiny island.

However, along the coasts the prolific birdlife and fascinating marine animals like the large sea turtles quite make up for the lack of wild elephants on Marie Galante! Here, the ornithologist is in his element, as are the scuba diver, snorkel enthusiast and fisherman. Seabirds wheel and dive off spectacular cliffs on the is-land's north and east coast and on the ten miles of reefs the tropical fish population never ceases to amaze.

Watch the fishermen on the beaches or take a boat out on a fishing excursion from any of the three ports to experience the wonderful variety of colorful fishes that abound in the tempting waters. Here, the fishermen land enormous lobster or crayfish and the conch shellfish with its pearly cream and pink shell provides the ingredients for local soups. Tuna, bonito, often marlin and wahoo are just some of the game fish caught here.

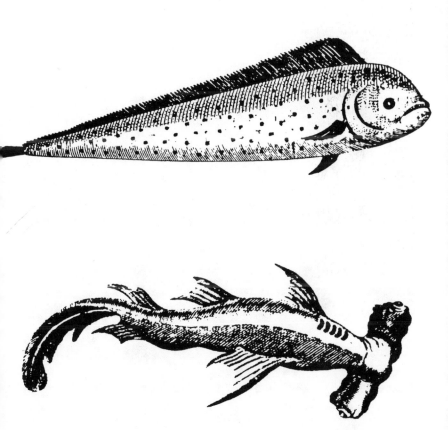

Shopping

What does one purchase as a reminder of a paradise island? Little can bring back memories of peace and tranquility, of thundering sea-pounded chasms, of the gentle clop of ox hooves on dusty chalk tracks, or palms rustling on secluded beaches. However, why not try buying a few bottles of the island's famous rum, or *rhum?* The magic of Père Labat's excellent spirits will lull you back to those soft breezes and lazy time on sandy shores. Père Labat Rhum is stronger than both those of Guadeloupe and Martinique—perhaps the reason for the islander's laid back hospitality?

Banking

Banque Antillaise, on Place de l'Eglise, Tel: 87.20.46; Banque Nationale de Paris, between de l'Eglise and Beaurenom, Tel: 87.20.10; and Credit Agricole, on Rue du Cimetière, Tel: 87.20.40, are the island's only banks—all in Grand-Bourg.

Churches

On this strictly catholic island there are many tiny churches and also the large chapel of Saint Anne in Capesterre.

Hotels on Marie Galante

At the last count there were just six hotels on the island, all except one in Grand-Bourg.

Auberge Soledad
Grand-Bourg.
Tel: 97.92.24/97.93.18

20 rooms, 8 of which are air-conditioned. Local-food restaurant.

Hotel Le Belvedere
Grand-Bourg, east of the airport.
Tel: 87.22.32

7 rooms. Restaurant and nightclub.

Hotel Latin Quartier
Grand-Bourg. Tel: 87.20.39

5 rooms.

Chez Hajor
Grand-Bourg

9 rooms.

El Rancho
Grand-Bourg

3 double rooms.

Hotel Le Salut
Saint-Louis. Tel: 87.21.67

15 rooms. Restaurant.

Restaurants and Bars on Marie Galante

Fish and seafood dishes, particularly the giant crayfish, are specialities of the Marie Galante cuisine. The spicy, hot, Créole sauce is a local way of adding zest to the meal—as if the Père Labat *rhum* is not enough!

The "giraumont" pumpkin is a favorite ingredient in soups and stews, and eggplant, or "belengere," is a popular vegetable.

Try fish dishes fresh from the waters at Le Bêkêke, Tel: 87.22.24; on the beach at Feuillère, near Capesterre, or one of the tables of the El Rancho, where a terrace grill supplements the restaurant, snack bar and adjoins its discotheque. Bébélé is a Creole favorite of breadfruit, peas, bananas and crab. Aux Crabes and Au Coquillage, on the St. Louis road,

are just what they purport to be and offer excellent local concoctions of fresh seafood. One of the two La Maille, "Fish Net," restaurants, either No. 1 on Rue Presbytère, in Grand-Bourg, and No. 2 in Rue Desmarais, St. Louis, may be a refreshing change from beach barbeque and both are moderately priced. Try the Bouton d'Or in Etang-Long, Saint-Louis, which has a varied menu, or the Bambou Club in Capesterre, Tel: 97.96.98. Both the Soledad and the Belvédère hotels in or near Grand-Bourg have distinctive restaurants and the Salut hotel in St. Louis also has its own restaurant. Arc en Ciel, also in St. Louis, is becoming popular.

Communications and Information

The telephone code for Marie Galante is the prefix 97 and there are post offices in Grand-Bourg and in Saint-Louis.

There is a hospital in Grand-Bourg, a pharmacy and dispensary. Tel: 97.81.42.

The police station on the island is at Grand-Bourg. Tel: 97.90.03, near

the hospital, on the west side of town.

There is no Tourist Bureau on the island as tours are organized from that in nearby Guadeloupe.

Cars and taxis may be hired at the airport and some forms of transport can be rented from the Soledad Hotel.

To and From the Island

About a one-and-a-half-hour trip by boat from Pointe-à-Pitre on the General Dugommier (Tel: 82.54.86), or the Marie Galante, by Regina (Tel: 99.80.65), Madras (Tel: 83.12.45), or the Delgres (Tel: 82.03.50) takes the visitor to Grand-Bourg or St. Louis. The number of Les Basses Airport on

Marie Galante is 87.20.09. By air there are daily flights from Raizet Airport in Guadeloupe to Basses Airport and the flight takes about thirty minutes. Both Air Guadeloupe (Tel: 82.28.35) and Air Antilles (Tel. 82.12.25) fly to the island.

CHAPTER VII

La Désirade "The Longed-For Land"

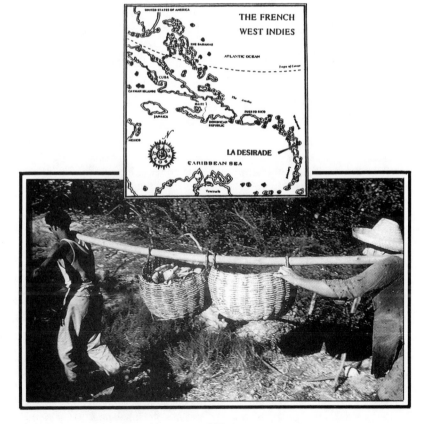

Size and Location

Just about seven miles in length and little more than a mile in width from one to the other end of the almost rectangular island, La Désirade lies on its own off Grand-Terre, Guadeloupe. This tiny island has Grande Anse as its capital township, located on its southwest corner. Only five miles from Guadeloupe's westernmost point, the island has only one road, running the entire length of the southern coast. In area, La Désirade is about eight-and-a-half miles total.

Physical

Long and thin, this island is rather like a table with a ridge down the eastern side. Grande Montagne, at just under 900 feet, is La Désirade's highest point. Several other peaks, like Souffleur and Morne Cybèle, break the desert-like limestone terrain and a fine coral reef shelters a good part of the island's south beaches. A few subterranean streams cross the upland ridge and some lead down to the indented and craggy north coastline. A large bay, the Porte d'Enfer, breaks into this north shore and opposite, on each side of Grande-Anse town, are two small lagoons. Anse d'en Haut, Baie Mahault near Le Souffleur village, and that near Anse d'Echelle in the southwest—are the three resort beaches.

Climate

The aridity of the climate on this exposed island has never contributed to its popularity although its beaches are ideal for sunbathers. At some times of the year, June to November, winds, often quite strong, can cool the island but temperatures can rise to well over 85 degrees F (29 degrees C) and can drop to about 75 degrees F (23 degrees C) from the end of December to March. Nights can be very cool but the sea temperatures, particularly on the beach (south) coast, do not usually drop below 73 degrees F (23 degrees C).

Population

About 1,800 people live on La Désirade and many are descended from colonists including Bretons, fisherfolk and settlers who tried to eke a living from the poor soil in the early part of the twentieth century. During the Revolution, when the wealthy aristocrats were being persecuted, a few sought sanctuary on La Désirade and when emancipation came to Guadeloupe in 1848 freed slaves joined the swelling numbers of isolated exiles.

Practically abandoned by the mainland people and left to their own devices, the inhabitants of the island grew quarrelsome and the land was avoided by passing ships. However, by the early part of the twentieth century, Bretons, Petit Blancs (outcast mulattoes from Guadeloupe) and pioneers established a base at Grande-Anse and attempted to raise sheep, cotton and vegetables and to live from creating a fishing industry. The barren soil defeated them and drove many to search elsewhere for a more hospitable clime.

By the time the middle 1950s had arrived, the leper colony, established during the early half of the eighteenth century, had also been abandoned by the nuns and life on La Désirade was probably at its lowest ebb. Tourism is now giving the islanders some hope for the future—certainly more than its first inhabitants—and some tourism income supplements the meager living drawn from the sea.

Language

As with all satellite islands of Guadeloupe, the local people have adopted their own form of dialect, which differs slightly from the correct French. The Créole patois of the residents of La Désirade is more often in use than French, particularly with the fisherfolk.

Holidays and Festivals

La Désirade has no special fêtes or celebrations. Apart from New Year's Day, Labor Day (May 1), Assumption (August 15), Armistice Day (November 11), Christmas Day and Easter Monday, Ascension and Whit Monday, the French Isles include Bastille Day (July 14), Schoelcher Day (July 21), All Saints' and All Souls' (November 1 and 2), only Assumption is the main festival.

History

There is little evidence to point to early habitation on the island before the early eighteenth century. Few mariners, whether traders, colonists or pirates, bothered to mention the island deserted since the days of Columbus.

It was Christopher Columbus who gave the inhospitable land its curious name. Meaning the "sought after land," La Désirade was thought to be thus dubbed as the great admiral searched for the elusive Indies. "La Désirade"? was his possible exclamation on sighting the rocky coast on the night of November 2, 1493. The second voyage of the Spanish fleet across the Atlantic Ocean had dangerously depleted the ship's water supply and Columbus was anxious to find fresh supplies. However, not finding a suitable mooring on this first-sighted island in the darkness, the expedition sailed on to replenish supplies on Guadeloupe. In the earliest maps the island was named "y de Sorana."

During the early eighteenth century the island was a haunt for the infamous pirate Captain Bar-

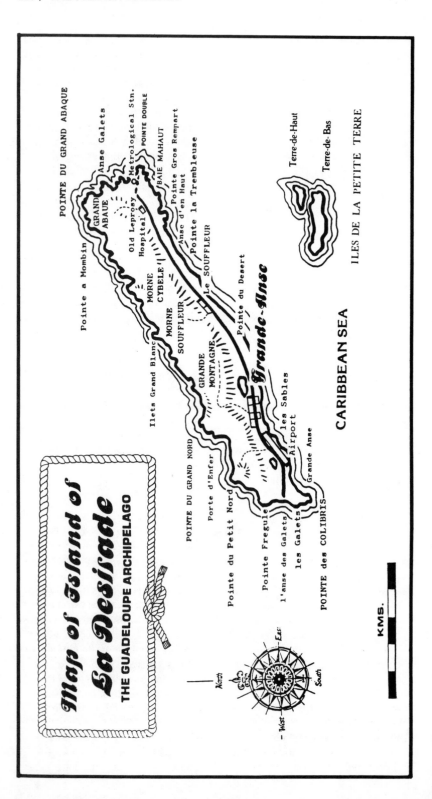

Map of Island of
La Desirade
THE GUADELOUPE ARCHIPELAGO

KMS.

tholomew Roberts. Corsair, Captain George Lowther, captured a brigantine off here and the pirate John Evans captured the 200-ton "Lucretia and Catherine" off Désirade on January 11, 1723.

In 1725 an outbreak of leprosy on Guadeloupe prompted the authorities to secure a refuge for the sufferers. La Désirade, undesirable and deserted, a short distance offshore, and easily isolated, was the perfect solution and so a colony of lepers was established at Baie-Mahault. The Governor of Guadeloupe, Moyencourt, banished all sufferers to the colony which was run until 1954 by the Sisters of Charity.

The idea of using the island as a place of internment soon gained popularity and when on July 15, 1765, the king ordered all rogues, undesirables, the bastards of nobles (often those of mixed black and white races), gamblers, debauchers and vagabonds exiled from Guadeloupe, resulted in the 'unwanted island' gaining its first consignment of healthy (or semi-healthy) residents. Later, during the French Revolution when the wealthy aristocrats were being persecuted, a few sought sanctuary on La Désirade and when emancipation came to Guadeloupe in 1848 freed slaves joined the swelling numbers of isolated exiles.

Trade, Industry and Economy

A frugal, hand-to-mouth existence is eked from fishing and from cultivating sparse crops, raising goats and domestic animals on the island. Some of the fish caught is destined for export to mainland Guadeloupe and tourism has recently improved prospects for craftware sale and guided tours of the island.

Close-Up on Grande-Anse

This tiny village, the largest settlement on the island, was established early this century and has just one main road. Between twin lagoons, the four or five houses, two post offices, church and a few tiny cottages line the island's only road. Grande-Anse lies almost at the end of the island's highway and boasts an airport that accepts light airplanes. The highlights of the township are the pretty little church and the one hotel, La Guitoune, with its five rooms, tiny restaurant and cocopalms. The undisturbed beach fronting the hotel offers ideal barbeque locations and on the Fêtes Communale (Assumption) the celebrations of the village extend along to the Guitoune.

Farther along the beach is the Quatier desert Salines, where the Oasis offers economic accommodations. Les Sables beach is also an attraction of Grande-Anse as are the fishing boats so often drawn up on its shoreline. If you want to see a cockfight on the island, however, you will have to drive to Baie Mahault, farther to the east.

Diving and fishing have now brought visitors and tourists to Grande-Anse and its ferry service brings the curious and the adventurous to the village ten times a week.

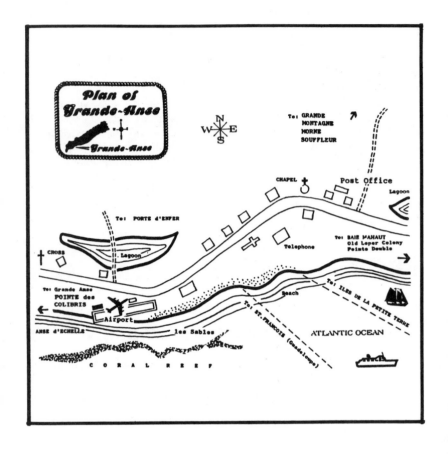

Discovering the Island

Although there are few real discoveries to make on La Desirade, there are many to make in and under the seas that surround this isolated isle. With just one road, the detours and opportunities for grand excursions are limited. Only seven miles in length, the narrow road runs from just west of the airport, through Grande-Anse, terminating at the ancient leper colony buildings near Pointe Gros Rempart.

About halfway along the short road is the hamlet of Le Souffleur with its tiny houses and lighthouse. Boats are built on the strand near this little village and its beach is a favorite for those who venture from the area of Grande-Anse. At Baie Mahault there is another beach on the right and from the end of the track, near the lepers' cemetery, a walkway leads up to the spectacular lookout at Pointe Double. Here the visitor will see the weather-monitoring station, and walks lead out along the stunning cliffs of the eastern coast. Anse Galets is an especially popular spot to stop and admire the views.

Walking is the best way to view the island and see the remarkable variations in scenery from one side of the narrow island to the other. From sweeping, sandy beaches in the south, just over the ridge of low mountains, gentle slopes of sparse scrub and cactus lead across to a much-indented coast stretching from Pointe Grand Abaque, in the farthest northeast, to Pointe du Grand Nord and Pointe du Petit Nord, embracing the Porte d'Enfer—the Gate of Hell bay near the southernmost tip of La Desirade. The nearest point of the island to Guadeloupe is the Pointe des Colibris—"Hummingbird Point." Opposite, on Guadeloupe, the matching spit of rock has the same name. Alternative walks take the visitor up to the summit of the Grande Montagne (896 feet) and the path up to the top of Morne Souffleur (679 feet). Morne Cybèle may also be scaled, particularly en route to the craggy, northern coast with its caves, sea tunnels and blowholes.

It really is under the water that one can appreciate the tropical aqua-scenery of coral ledges, jungles of sponges and great forests of sea ferns. These seas, although nominally the Caribbean, are actually in the Atlantic Ocean and the island is one of the farthest east of the Antilles, if not the easternmost of all the Leeward Islands. Multicolored fish in crystal-clear waters attract many diving enthusiasts and sub-aqua spear fishermen. Game fishing is also a

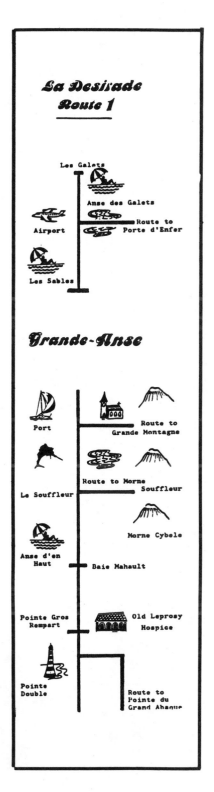

sport enjoyed off this coast and one could even take trips from La Désir- ade out to the nearby great deeps of the Atlantic for huge sports fish.

Wildlife

As explained, the variety of tropical and large game fish is bewildering and La Désirade certainly has an unusual selection of species. It is on the island's excellent coral reef, in the south west, that the best spots for diving are found.

Curious animals also have made this island their home. The ferocious-looking but harmless iguana, said to be a tasty ingredient in local dishes, is often seen darting in and out of the limestone karsts of the desert terrain. The "Englishman's Head" cactus plants provide shelter and perches for several varieties of birdlife and the cavernous, sheer cliffs to the north, provide home and hunting-ground to a remarkable number of interesting seabirds.

Back to the land, and the casual visitor might remark on seeing some of the guinea-pig-like animals darting into holes and crannies in the rocks. These are the agoutis, also a delicacy among the islanders who seem to have inherited their forebears' taste for anything edible! Other wildlife that dash around the arid landscape include pheasants; another delicacy imported by early La Désiradiennes?

A gouti.

Shopping

Without real shops, this subject is somewhat academic but enterprising islanders are beginning to create an interesting number of souvenirs that are displayed in the open air for tourists arriving by boat or plane. Handicrafts and conch shells are, as yet, the sum of tourist trophies available here.

Banking

There is no bank on La Désirade.

Churches

Only one small church exists on the island. It is located north of the main road in the center of Grande-Anse, facing the beach. This is a Roman Catholic Church.

Hotels on La Désirade

La Guitoune
Grande-Anse. Tel: 20.01.22

5 rooms with a little beach.

L'Oasis
Quartier Desert Salines.
Tel: 20.02.12

This little hotel has a small restaurant and lies on the beach.

Camping can be catered for on the island at Baie-Mahault and Grande-Anse.

Restaurants and Bars on La Désirade

L'Oasis, also a hotel, has facilities for serving a limited number of diners and specializes in local and some international dishes. The only other restaurant on the island is that at Le Galete—Les Salles. It is called the Aerodesire and, as the name indicates, is near the airport. This restaurant also serves local cuisine and is a little more expensive than the Oasis. Try the ultra-fresh sea food.

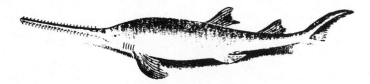

Communications and Information

There are two post office facilities in Grande-Anse on La Désirade, one each side of the main street. Area code is 20 prefix.

There are no medical facilities on the island but First Aid is locally at hand. Dispensary Tel: 20.01.00.

The police may be contacted at Tel: 20.01.62.

There is no Tourist Board facility on La Désirade; the nearest is on Guadeloupe.

Due to the small size of the island, no taxi or rental car service is available.

To and From the Island

About three-quarters-of-an-hour trip by ferry from the Saint-François Marina on Guadeloupe brings the visitor to Grande Anse daily. On some days there are two return journeys. With ten trips a week, the ferry is supporting the transport of visitors from Raizet Airport on Guadeloupe.

Flights are twice a day and are only on Saturday and Sunday. The flight takes about a quarter-of-an-hour on a light aircraft. For reservations on Guadeloupe Tel: 83.06.61; or, at the airport, 82.28.35. On La Désirade Tel: 20.01.82.

Les Îsles de la Petite-Terre

Two tiny, white sand beach-girded, desert islands lie just a dozen miles southeast of Guadeloupe near La Désirade. The uninhabited islands are covered by cactus and brushwood and can only be reached by boat, a ten-mile trip from Grande-Anse. Mysterious birds, giant crabs and iguanas live on the islands named Terre de Haut and Terre de Bas.

CHAPTER VIII

Isles Les Saintes "Eight Apostles"

Size and Location

In total, these islands cover just 5½ square miles and lie directly south of the town of Trois Rivières on Basse Terre, Guadeloupe. Of the eight islets, the second largest, Terre-de-Haut, is no more than three miles in length and less than a mile and one-half in width, narrowing to under one-half mile in places. The largest isle is Terre-de-Bas, a roundish island just over three miles in diameter. Grand Ilet, Ilet à Cabrit, La Coche, La Redonde, Les Augustins and Le Pate are all miniature islets with no habitation. Being just six miles south of Guadeloupe, these idyllic, peaceful isles make perfect weekend resorts.

Physical

Just the tips of a volcanic mountain range appearing like green droplets on the blue Caribbean, Les Saintes vary in size and shape with beautiful beaches, desert isles, rain-forest terrain and the occasional peak that rises to a maximum of just over 1,000 feet. Morne de Cameau, at 1,014 feet, is the highest peak and the tiny islets like Le Pate can only rise to under 100 feet. Hills, valleys, bays, inlets, cliffs, chasms, gentle beaches and tiny lagoons make up the general topography, which is never dull. The cluster of islands offers a change of pretty and spectacular views around every point. On a peninsula to the west of Terre-de-Haut island is a bay of basalt, "organpipes", and the famous miniature "sugar loaf" mountain.

Climate

Although the islands are not far from the mountains of Guadeloupe that attract heavy rainfall, Les Saintes are comparatively drier and more arid, tempered by the trade winds which bring a welcome freshness to the air that reduces the humidity. In parts the islands are quite arid and temperatures can rise to 82 degrees F (28 degrees C) during July and August, dropping to 76 degrees F (24 degrees C) during December to April. January to April is the height of the season because of the cool breezes and number of dry, sunshine hours. Sea temperatures rarely drop below 72 degrees F (22 degrees C).

Population

The people here are mainly descended from the Bretons, Normans and Poitevine races that settled here as "poor white" colonists centuries ago. Mingling with the many black slaves who were required to tend the few acres of sugar cane that the white population could not cope with, the islanders' skin colors range now from white to dark and hair can be flaxen-gold, red-ginger or long black tresses. Noted as some of the best fishermen in the Caribbean, Les Saintois are charming and hospitable. They can often be seen, especially on festival days, wearing the traditional garb of the sailors—red shirts, yellow scarves, blue pants and the famed "salako," a flat parasol-shaped, Indo-Chinese-style hat called in common parlance "chapeaux annamites." With the green and blue of the natural background and the colors of the costume, the photographer or painter has an artist's palette of primary shades to work from! About 3,500 Saintois live on the two inhabited islands, most on Terre-de-Haut.

Language

French is the official language of Les Saintes but, as in all the islands of the French Antilles, the patois comes through in everyday speech, particularly in market-places and down by the fishing communities. Few Saintois speak any English but the growing influx of English-speaking tourists is changing this.

Holidays and Festivals

On Terre-de-Haut the main celebration falls on August 15th and is the Fête Communale of the island, celebrating Assumption. St. Nicolas Day is the Terre-de-Bas festival, occurring on the 6th December. Apart from New Year's Day, Labour Day (May 1), Assumption (August 15), Armistice Day (November 11), Christmas Day and Easter Monday, Ascension and Whit Monday, the French isles include Bastille Day (July 14), Schoelcher Day (July 21), All Saints' and All Souls' (November 1 and 2).

History

No evidence of pre-history occupation has been found on any of the Saintes islands and this is not surprising since there is no natural source of fresh water. Today the islanders desalinate sea water, having previously resorted to catching rainwater in giant cisterns. Caribs and Arawaks may have visited the islands briefly for food and fishing but nothing is known of the group until the date November 4, 1493.

Having already discovered La Desirade and Marie Galante on his second expedition of discovery in the Indies, Christopher Columbus sighted this cluster of islands which he named Los Santos, or Les Saintes. Possibly, in sailing past, Columbus may have miscounted twelve islands instead of eight; however, with typical religious zeal, the admiral was inspired to give them a pious name, after all, it was All Saints' Day. Could he have noted the organ-pipe-like basalt stacks on Terre-de-Haut? Drawn on by the overshadowing size of Guadeloupe, the fleet of Colum-

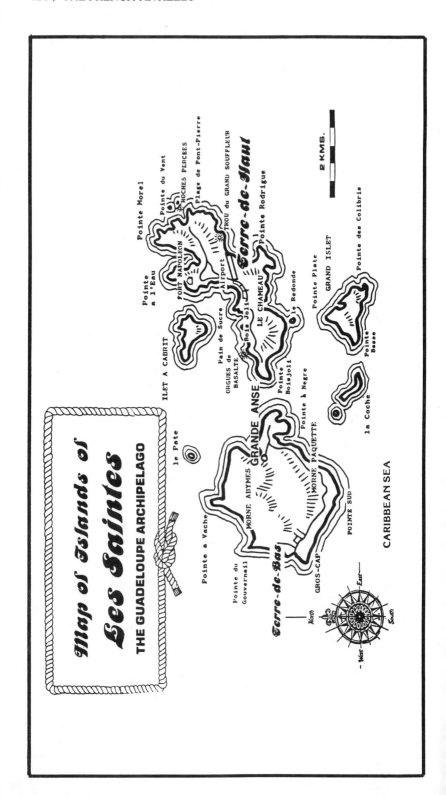

bus decided to bypass the Saintes although they were noted on Captain de Cosa's chart of the period as "Todos Santos," "All Saints."

It wasn't until 1648 that any European community attempted to settle on Les Saintes. Even then, the establishment of a fortified outpost was only a strategic move and designed to protect the flank of nearby Guadeloupe. The move to erect an armed emplacement on the islands gave them the name of the Gibralter of Guadeloupe. From that date on, the islands became the scenario for many struggles between French and English colonizing forces in the Caribbean.

On August 4, 1666, an English battalion sailed in to attack the heavily fortified island of Terre-de-Haut. They stood off in the "roads" and during the night a violent storm ravaged the fleet. Together with 200 Carib supporters, the French were able to defeat the English force to the indignation of Captain Henry Morgan, who more or less controlled the English activities in the West Indies. This victory by the French over the English is celebrated in the annual festival of August 15, the day on which the English surrendered. In 1780 the French erected a new fort, now Fort Josephine, on Ilet à Cabrit.

One of the most decisive sea battles in the course of the colonial history of the Caribbean was fought off Les Saintes on April 12, 1782. Admiral Rodney, the Earl of Albemarle, had by then become the scourge of the West Indies and, leading the British forces, had captured the Spanish capital, Havana, Cuba, twenty years earlier. During the 1780s he was based on the island of Dominica, just south of Guadeloupe. On that April day within sight of land the English fleet of fifty ships under Rodney's command caught the fleeing French flotilla and proceeded to decimate

their thirty-four warships. The French, under Admiral Comte de Grasse, were escorting one-hundred-and-fifty merchant vessels loaded with goods to the Hispaniola port of Santo Domingo. Superior in firepower to the French—3,012 guns to the French's 2,246—Rodney scored an overwhelming victory and a great prize; not only had he captured the commercial fleet, the English flag was to fly over the Isles des Saintes for the next thirty-three years. Admiral Rodney escorted the captured Comte de Grasse back to London, England, and subsequently the Treaty of Paris was signed which finally ceded the Saintes to the French in 1815. The important encounter was named the "Battle of The Saintes" or the "Trafalgar of the Antilles."

In 1809 the English occupational force leveled Fort Louis, which was reconstructed as Fort Napoleon in 1867. Lord Nelson's victory in the Battle of Trafalgar all but cut off the French West Indies from any kind of support from mainland France and those outlying islands suffered most. Les Saintes was almost abandoned and it was only the determination of the Békés, or poor whites, which kept the islands' heads above water. These tips of volcanic masses could not support the large sugar cane crops like those of neighboring Marie Galante and the islanders were really on their own when emancipation freed the black slaves in 1848. For agricultural reasons, the islanders had almost become divided themselves as to race and color. In Terre-de-Haut the population was mainly white and in Terre-de-Bas most people were black. The islanders resorted to fishing, tending the few sheep that the arid land and sparse grazing could support and, above all, taking to the boats. Les Saintois became renowned sailors the world over and their expertise more or less saved the archipelago from ruin. Smuggling and fishing were the islanders fortes and they excelled in both occupations. Today, fishing is the mainstay of the islands, officially, although tourism has grown to astounding proportions over the past few years. Almost ten times the population in numbers of tourists now visit Les Saintes and facilities for visitors are becoming quite sophisticated.

Trade, Industry and Economy

There is little to say about the Isles des Saintes, languishing in the shadow of the great sugar-producing islands of Guadeloupe and Martinique. Sugar growing dwindled to a trickle in this archipelago, which has little rainfall and no other source of fresh water except that for domestic use from desalination plants.

All that is grown on the islands is for local consumption and the fishing industry supplies a little of its harvest for export to Guadeloupe. There is not much else in the way of commerce or industry and there is not even a distillery in the island group. Together with La Désirade and St. Barthélémy, Les Saintes is one of the three French Antilles with no legal rum industry. The island does, however, make its own special conconction of Bay Rum; not the drinking rum but a medicinal potion which is purported to cure rheumatism. This ancient recipe, together with conch shells, "salako" hats, the skins of iguana and some local craft work comprise the islander's income from sales to tourists.

Tourism industry is benefiting the Saintois also in revenue from the island's hotels and restaurants, escorting groups of visitors and guiding tourists over points of interest or taking them on boat trips. Beach resorts also hire out watersport equipment and rent facilities for diving and sailing enthusiasts.

Close-up on Bourg

Just one main road comprises the little town of Bourg on the north coast of Terre-de-Haut. The street follows the curve of the bay and its tiny harbor. Red-roofed houses, often painted in patriotic colors of the Tricolour—red, white and blue—string along the seafront and up the lower slopes of Le Chameau's sister peak. Narrow streets wind up into the gentle hill behind the bay with rust-colored corrugated iron roofs and neat porches.

Near the white-painted jetty that is served by a regular ferry, the model church stands on a hillock overlooking the sleepy, bungalow-style homes on the beach side. The chapel, with its square tower, denotes the dividing line between the fishing community in the south of town and the more well-to-do families of the Mouillage sector. The paved main street, with the odd colonial fretwork carving or wrought-ironwork balcony, leads to the north half of the town that sports a pizza cafe. The south part, called Fonds du Cure, has three or four local food restaurants and a hotel.

Along from the jetty, toward the southeast, a small spit of land juts out into the bay creating two semicircular sandy bays. The broadcasting station is farther on and behind the town a

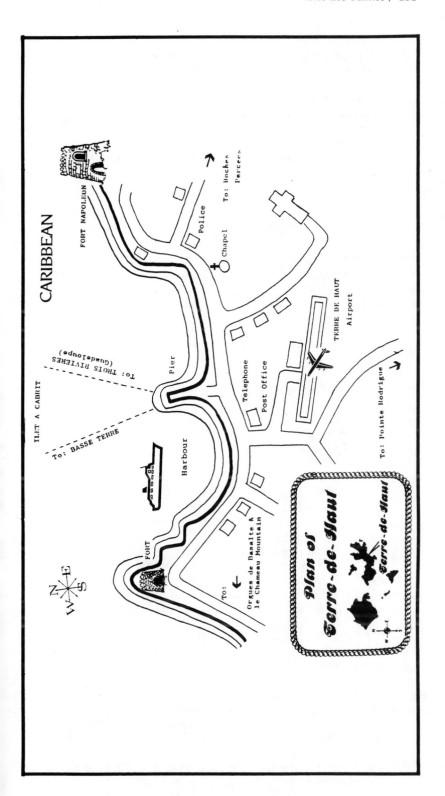

little airstrip accommodates twin otter aircraft and light airplanes. Cruise ships frequent the harbor as do many local schooners and yachts. A total of fifteen restaurant and seven hotels on the island ensures facilities for visitors to the town of Bourg.

In the north part of town the road encloses a residential area at the foot of the hill on which Fort Napoleon stands. Coco palms and tropical trees gird the beaches, which are often dotted with colorful fishing boats and nets hung to dry in the sun. Low mountain peaks and rolling hills, some covered with woods and scrub, ring the town, which nestles in quiet seclusion facing out towards the small Isle à Cabrit and Fort Josephine.

Discovering the Islands

Without leaving the island of Terre-de-Haut one can experience the typical life of the islanders—watching the fishing fleet come in, photographing the men in their salakos and traditional costume, visiting historic sites, enjoying the beaches and watersport activities or tasting the distinctive food of the islands. On the main island there are several walks that one should try to make which broadens the horizons of the town itself. Not far from the outskirts of Bourg a path leads past the naval dockyard of L'Anse Mire (Quatier Maison Blanche) and up the hill to Fort Napoleon. Originally Fort Louis, destroyed in 1809 by the British, this square structure inside a curiously shaped battlemented wall was constructed in 1867. Fine views from the summit and the fort's great vantage point belie the fact that, however strategic, the fort never fired a shot in anger. Green wooded slopes reach down to crescent bays and steep cliffs from the fort, which now serves as a museum. The surrounding gardens are now of great botanical significance.

Across the Baie du Marigot is Pointe Morel and, beyond that, the resort bay of St. Pierre with its famous "Pierced Rocks" standing out of the sea. Sea arches are a specialty of the French islands and these Roches Percées on Les Saintes are good examples. The bay is also a popular fishing spot. It is here that pirates had their hideouts and later the bay was well used by smugglers. A picnic area on the next point overlooks the beauty spot known as the Trou du Grand Souffleur—a cave used by pirates and a spectacular cleft in the cliffs into which the sea surges. At the other end of the island is another beauty spot known as the *Orgues de Basalte,* literally the Organs of Bassalt. These are in geological terms stacks made of volcanic bassalt that resemble organ pipes. Here, also, is the famed Sugar Loaf, Pain du Sucre peak, a miniature of that in Rio de Janiero and which gives the whole region the title of Mini-Rio. Hotel Bois Joli looks out across the bay to this spectacular natural phenomenon. Above the hotel is the highest point of the island, Le Chameau—The Camel. This peak rises to 1,014 feet and offers stunning panoramic views around the entire island archipelago. Try to spot Dominica far to the south. Across a small point from the hotel is one of the French Antilles' few naturist beaches.

Ilet à Cabrit is a rocky islet within a half mile from the town of Bourg. On each side is a stretch of water—to its north the Passe de la Baliene (Whale

Passage) through which the ferry to Guadeloupe sails and, to the south, the route of the ferry to Terre-de-Bas, through the Passe du Pain de Sucre (Sugar Loaf Sound). On Cabrit's 279-foot-high peak sits Fort Josephine. Originally Fort La Reine, this oldest of Les Saintes' fortresses was first constructed in 1780. The existing structure dates only from the early nineteenth century. There is an important anchorage on the west side of the island on a vast sweeping bay. The six abandoned bungalows on the nearby summit are the remnants of a resort complex.

Terre-de-Bas (the low island) is not so low; its high point, Morne Abymes, rises to 961 feet. The Passe du Sud, between Bas and Haut, is just under a mile wide although the island's main settlement, Gros Cap, lies on the other, western side of Terre-de-Bas. The town is square in layout and has a ferry landing at the end of its main street. The ferry, which links the island with both Basse Terre on Guadeloupe and Terre-de-Haut, on the voyage from Bourg, passes the tiny islet speck called La Pate. The town has the usual church, police station and post office and a short distance away is the airfield.

A track winds through the valley between Morne Abymes and the 685-foot peak of Morne Paquette to the famous beach resort of Grande Anse although the road to the airfield continues on around to the beach by a more circuitous route. This beach is the best on any of the Saintes islands and it offers all the advantages and facilities of any vacation resort. Just one hotel and one restaurant make this getaway isle an intimate one and it justly deserves the accolade of "wild and free island." One of the most interesting historic sites of the island is the little seventeenth-century church not far from the beach at Grande Anse. The other church, on

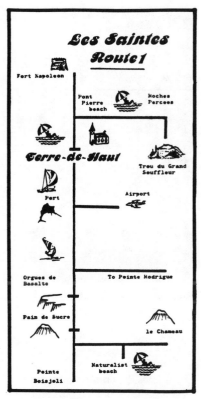

the edge of Gros-Cap town, has a cemetery that contains some ancient sailors' tombs surrounded with sea-shells.

From the largest island of Terre-de-Bas, at the jetty of Gros-Cap, one can take an excursion by sea, south of the island, past the smallest of the Les Saintes, Les Augustine, to the isle of Grand Ilet. This flat island is uninhabited and has no particular interest except that some deserted beaches attract the complete Robinson Crusoe or Man Friday and it has a pretty lagoon. Just across the sound between Grand Ilet and Terre-de-Bas, one can see the little mound of La Redonde—nothing to do with the island of Redonda near Antigua. Across the Passe des Dames, on the return journey to Terre-de-Bas, is the remaining of the eight islands of the archipelago, La Coche, also uninhabited—also long, thin and low.

Some work in sugar mill of 1850 was mechanized.

Wildlife

Les Saintes do not have many spectacular forms of wildlife but can claim to have one of the Caribbean's most fearful-looking beasts, the iguana. The coat of arms of Terre-de-Haut, surmounted by five sailing galleys forming a crown, sports a bright green iguana on a stylized wavy sea above a castle. Two mythical fish support the crest, resting their tails on an anchor. Both green and yellow varieties of this hideous throwback to prehistoric reptilian times thrive in the arid, desert-like terrain. Iguanas are completely harmless and are fascinating to watch, like their smaller cousins, the many types of little lizards that dart around the sunburned rocks. Strangely enough, although the islands are dry and waterless, the lush vegetation in some regions is reminiscent of more damp climates and flowers bloom around every garden and along the roadsides. In the drier inland areas, scrub and varieties of cactus present a totally dif-

ferent face to the blazing days and starlit nights. Sea birds are common in the more isolated areas and in the coves and inaccessible cliffs along some shorelines.

As throughout the French islands, the tropical fish are too diverse to mention by name; it remains only to say that the seas around the Saintes are prolific in all forms of sea creatures, mollusks, turtles, tuna and dolphin. Blenny nibble at your toes

while paddling in the shallows and giant grouper inquisitively nudge the diver off coral reefs. Out to sea the deepsea angler can hook barracuda and yellowfin and the spearfisherman can take snapper and jackfish. The islands are a paradise for anyone with the slightest interest in the sea, its creatures, or the pleasures it and they can provide. Don't forget, Terre-de-Haut is the island that the famous underwater expert Jacques Cousteau selected from a world of islands as his favorite diving location and shore.

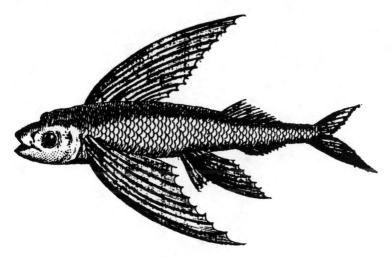

Shopping

There is little shopping to be done on these islands that tend just to bask in the shade of the great shopping boulevards and arcades of nearby Guadeloupe. Bay Rhum (for back ailments), a few items of craft work, the salako or "chapeau annamites," some basket weaving, shells, iguana skins, stuffed fish and the delicious, local delicacy—the coco-tart—are about the sum total of items for sale to visitors. The best souvenir is the remembrance of the happy people, the gorgeous beaches, interesting walks and, of course, the lasting suntan—free!

Banking

There is but one bank on the Les Saintes islands. It is located in Bourg—Credit Agricole.

Churches

Including the largest, red-roofed church in Bourg, the oldest, seventeenth-century church in Terre-de-Bas, there are just three Roman Catholic churches on the two inhabited isles.

Hotels on Isles Les Saintes

Los Santos Plhiazur
Marigot Beach. Tel: 99.50.40

54 air-conditioned rooms. Restaurant, nautical sports. Beachside under the shadow of Fort Napoleon.

Hotel Bois Joli
Terre-de-Haut.
Tel: 99.50.35/99.52.53

24 rooms, most air-conditioned. Two beaches (one naturist), fantastic views, sports, restaurant, bar.

Hotel Jeanne D'Arc
Fonds-de-Curee, Bourg.
Tel: 99.50.41

10 rooms, some air-conditioned. Watersports

Hotel Kanoa
Pointe Coquelet, Terre-de-Haut.
Tel: 99.51.36

14 rooms. Restaurant, bar, watersports.

La Saintoise Hotel
Terre-de-Haut. Tel: 99.50.52

10 rooms. Restaurant, bar, watersports.

Les Anarcardiers Auberge
Terre-de-Haut. Tel: 99.50.99

10 rooms.

Le Poisson-Volant Hotel
Terre-de-Bas. Tel: 99.80.47

9 rooms. Restaurant, nightlife.

Restaurants and Bars on Les Saintes

For the size of a group of islands, only two of which are inhabited, and with visitor accommodations for just 250 or so persons, the number of restaurants on the Saintes Islands is encouraging. A number of seafood specialities abound and the range of fish dishes seems unlimited. *Courts bouillons* are a favorite with every kind of *fruits de mer* included. Conch is a popular addition to many dishes or can be enjoyed on its own as at the Mon Paradis or the Le Casse-Croûte in the south (fishermen) sector of Bourg. In Le Mouillage, past the spired church, the elegant Le Genois, as a change, serves pizza; and La Paillotte, on Place de Marigot, serves lambi, or conch, as a soup. On Route de Pomière the Jonathan Restaurant serves a blaff with fresher-than-fresh fish as does the La Caraibe or the La Concorde on the Pompiere-Marigot beach.

Deliciously tasty local food can be enjoyed as well as more western-style foods at the hotel restaurants like the Bois-Joli or Les Amandiers, at the Jeanne d'Arc, La Santoise, Kanoa, or Azur Los Santos at Marigot. Flying fish or prawn dishes are as popular as swordfish steaks or turtle fillets at restaurants like Coconut's or the Coq d'Or or La Redonde. At Chez Line, in the Mouillage district of Bourg, or the Le Relais des Iles on the Pompiere road, try the classic dessert dish of the islands—"Tourment d'Amour" (the "Torment of Love"), a pastry made with deliciously fresh coconut, oozing with succulent, sweet cocomilk.

Communications and Information

The telephone code for Les Isles des Saintes is 99. There are post offices in Bourg, on Terre-de-Haut, and in Gros Cap on Terre-de-Bas.

There is no hospital on the islands but there is a dispensary at Tel: 99.50.39 and a Pharmacy at Tel: 99.52.48.

The two police stations, one near the church in Bourg and the other opposite the church in Gros-Cap, can be called by dialing 99.53.77.

There is no Tourist Board Office on Les Saintes.

Few cars run on the tiny islands but several minibuses are said to run between the airport on Terre-de-Haute and the main hotels where car hire or taxi arrangements might be arranged.

To and From the Islands

A twin Otter airplane with twenty seats flies a regular service from Pointe-à-Pitre on Guadeloupe to Terre-de-Haute and Terre-de-Bas island airfields. Flights are expensive and boat crossing is recommended for those who do not mind a choppy one-hour trip from Trois-Rivieres on Guadeloupe or a two-hour voyage from Basse Terre. Regular sailings are available and details can be had— Tels: 83.40.93, 99.50.68 or 81.24.83.

CHAPTER IX

Saint Martin "The Friendly Island"

Size and Location

Lying just above the 18 degrees North Latitude, similar to that of Puerto Rico, the entire island of St. Martin/Maarten covers an area of 37 square miles. The island itself is divided politically into two parts—the Dutch part, to the south, has an area of 16 square miles and the French, northern territory is 21 square miles in total area. About equidistant from Puerto Rico (144 miles west) and Guadeloupe (140 miles southeast), the island is the farthest north of all seven of the French Antillian territories. The capital of French Saint Martin is Marigot, on the eastern bay of the same name.

Physical

The island can be compared in shape to a Henry Moore or Joan Miro sculpture but with jagged edges and irregular holes. Almost lopsided and triangular, the main landmass is pierced by lagoons and salt ponds and one "wing" is almost completely occupied by a vast lake—one of the largest natural lakes in the Antilles. With arid limestone, indented with karstic action and by numerous bays, coves and inlets around its perimeter, Saint Martin/Maarten is more hilly in the northern French half. The island's highest point is also in the French Quatier, Pic du Paradis, at 1,391 feet in height. The great lagoon, in the west, is divided laterally to the Dutch and French sides and the French part is attended by two low islands, Ilet Pinel (Penal Island) and Caye Verte. Several other tiny islets dot the bays of the east coast but one important island further out, also belonging to the French is Ile Tintamarre.

Climate

Sunny and warm throughout the year, St. Martin has a constant temperature average of 80 degrees F (27 degrees C) cooled by fresh Trade Winds. The inhabitants call it Sunshine Island, although short sharp showers occur during late summer and early fall.

Population

About 11,000 people live on the French side of the island, nearly 8,000 less than in the Dutch half. As well as those islanders who are descended from early French settlers, there are traces of migrations from surrounding islands. Some evidence of the black influence from early slavery time can still be seen throughout the island.

Language

As the island is divided, both Dutch and French are spoken on St. Martin/Maarten. On the French side the language is almost exclusively French with a dash of patois and English is widely understood because of the island's exposure to English-speaking tourists.

Holidays and Festivals

The French side celebrates several exclusive events such as Mardi Gras, Ash Wednesday and Fête Nationale on Bastille Day. St. Martin's Day, November 11, is celebrated on both sides of the graphic line known as the border. Apart from New Year's Day, Labor Day (May 1), Assumption (August 15), Armistice Day (November 11), Christmas Day and Easter Monday, Ascension and Whit Monday, the French isle includes Bastille Day (July 14), Schoelcher Day (July 21), All Saints' and All Souls' (November 1 and 2).

History

Before its discovery by Europeans, this island was inhabited by ferocious Carib Indians. Pre-Columbian remains have been found at several sites on the island. Mainly Tainos (Arawak) cultural objects have been unearthed, which shows that both Amerindian tribes had spent time there until the explorers arrived. Caribs knew the island as "Sualovegia"—island of salt.

On the celebration of St. Martin (San Martino) of Tours, November 11, Christopher Columbus sighted the island, sailed into the large bay on its west coast, and was subsequently driven off by the Indians. With him was Father Raymond Pane, a missionary of the Order of St. Jerome, who returned to study the Ameri-Indian way of life a few years later. The year of discovery was 1493 and it was Columbus's second voyage through the Caribbean.

The Indians were left to their own devices for almost another 150 years, apart from Father Pane's efforts to decipher the cults of early Tainos; Europeans avoided the island because of the cannabalistic tendencies of the Caribs. It was not until the latter half of the 1630s that the first French filibusters, a smattering of pirates seeking lairs and a few shipwrecked sailors, began to spend any length of time on the island. Being so far north and in close proximity to the Spanish treasure routes, freebooters, corsairs and buccaneers used the island's indented coastline to

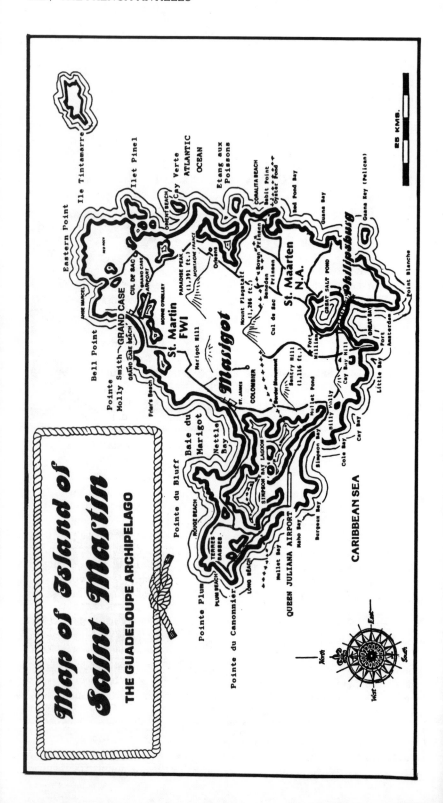

evade detection after raids on shipping. The French had built a fort as early as 1629 which Spanish settlers reerected high above Pointe Blanche in 1633. The French governor of the region, Longvilliers de Poincy, in 1637 then decreed that the island of St. Martin be claimed for the French Crown.

No sooner was this done than the Dutch drove out the French claimants and by 1640 the Spanish had sent 53 shiploads of troops to oust the Dutch settlers. The Spanish took occupation of the Dutch fort built on the island and remained in control for eight years. Seeing no further gain than making salt and keeping itinerants at bay, the Spaniards began to abandon the island in 1643. Almost directly, in 1644 the Dutch, under the governor of Curaçao, Peter Stuyvesant, attacked the Spanish at their settlement (Fort Amsterdam as it was to become) and in the skirmish while trying to hoist the Dutch flag, had his right leg injured. Stuyvesant's leg was subsequently amputated and reputedly thrown into the sea from one of his fleet of eleven ships.

A French-Dutch peace treaty was signed in 1648 after the Spanish had completely left St. Martin. Romantic stories of how the two powers divided up the land still persist. It is said that a walking contest around the perimeter of the island would decide on the area to fall to both French and Dutch. The respective forces each chose their champion, both of whom walked in opposite directions in order to circumnavigate as large a section of the island as possible for their country. Mount Concordia was selected for the starting point and the saying goes that the Dutchman's stride was impeded either by Jenever gin or by the wiles of a cooperative French maiden! Whatever the true story, the Dutch ended up with 16 square miles, and the French with the lion's share, 21 square miles. The French accepted the northern part of St. Martin and the Dutch the south— Sint Maarten.

However amicable this agreement might have seemed, it did not prevent the English and other forces raiding the settlements constantly over the following 168 years. English ma-

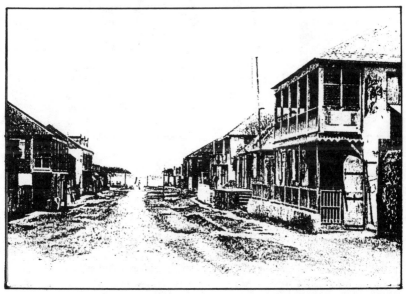

Main street of Marigot around 1900

rauders pillaged plantations on the French side between 1740 and 1742. Between 1763 and 1785, the governor of St. Martin, Auguste Descoudrelles, requested new settlers to help maintain the economy—all he got was English volunteers! In 1793 a Dutch force of twelve men occupied Fort St. Louis in Marigot, the capital of the French side! English forces took the island in 1794 but it was recovered two years later by Victor Hugues for the Dutch. The English established control in 1799 and again in 1808. Within 200 years the island had changed hands sixteen times and it was not until 1816 that the French and Dutch were installed for the last time. On September 21, 1819, a terrific hurricane followed by a tremendous earthquake devastated St.

Martin. In 1839 the Treaty of Mount Concordia was revised and the dividing line established.

Since 1963 the French part of Saint Martin has been, with Saint Barthélémy, an arrondissement of the island of Guadeloupe and with status as a region of France lying within the EEC. St. Martin administers the island of St. Barts by means of a mayor. Today tourism has brought riches to the island as a whole and both French and Dutch sides benefit from an increasing tourist trade. The red, white and blue flag, whether in vertical (French) or horizontal (Dutch) stripes, flies over the island announcing one of the only outposts in the world where two major powers live together in shared harmony.

Trade, Industry and Economy

From the earliest times of occupation the island has been a noted source of salt, obtained by evaporation of sea water in great salt ponds. Early settlers also produced tobacco, indigo and, much later, sugar and agricultural products. Never particularly important in the trade of the West Indies, both French and Dutch strived for several regularly interrupted centuries to carve a living from the island. Simpson Bay was the original site of the Dutch capital and Orleans, in the east-central part of the island, was the first French capital. By reason of convenience both centers were shifted to their present sites, Philipsburg and Marigot, in 1733 and 1760 respectively.

Constant harassment of trade and changes in allegiance made it difficult for the islanders to establish a solid identity in the Antilles but the Dutch did have the advantage of the

Netherland's West India Company in the seventeenth century and the French benefited from their own equivalent. When indigo and tobacco trades began to wane, "King Sugar" took over and slaves were imported to tend, harvest and process the crops. Emancipation in 1848 freed many of the sugar plantation workers and from that time the industry went into a slow decline. During the 1870s a little cotton was grown to support the waning sugar and livestock industries.

Practically ignored during both World Wars, St. Martin managed an almost self-sufficient economy, scraping a living from the salt industry at Grand Case and from a few agricultural exports to North America. The salt manufacturing business kept going on Saint Martin right through until 1967—about the time that the tourist industry started to take off.

Tourism now is the mainstay of both the Dutch and the French sectors and it is improving the islanders' lot in leaps and bounds. The Dutch-side tourist industry is far in advance of the French efforts to bring sophisticated tourist facilities to their part of the island, as was witnessed in the unfinished folly of La Belle Créole appart-development. However, the part-island's 36 beautiful beaches are a secret that will take the international tourist set no time at all to unlock. Marigot is also home to a distillery that produces a very special brand of French Rhum.

Slaves processed, as well as tended and harvested, the sugar crop.

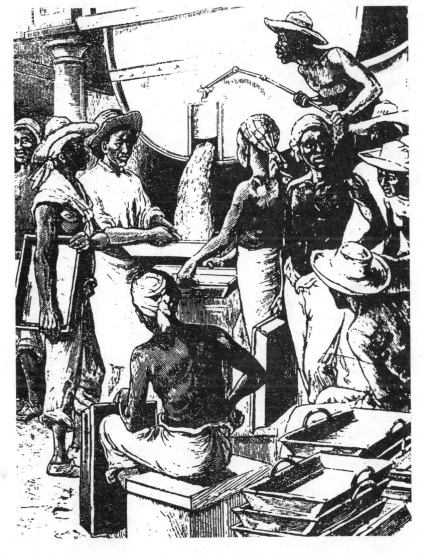

Modern methods of sugar harvesting are mechanized.

Close-Up on Marigot

The name, however pretty, comes from a marshy area of ground behind the present capital. Marigot's location is unique; it lies on a vast bay really divided into three sweeps—Baie Nettle, Baie de la Potence and, in the middle, Marigot Bay itself. The great, horseshoe-shaped arc, which is a popular anchorage, is more than a mile and a half across and is situated above the huge lagoon of Simpson Bay on the west coast of the island.

Established late in the eighteenth century because the original capital of Orleans was found unsuitable, Marigot has little signs of antiquity except the moldering Fort Louis (Fort du Marigot) on the hill overlooking the township. The fort's cannon are rust-ing and, as there is no museum in the town, little is being done to preserve the eighteenth-century bastion. In the town itself with its two main streets, Rue de la Republique and Rue de la Liberté, there are several quaint, colonial-style houses with trims of gingerbread fretwork, red roofs and white-painted verandas. Grand'Rue du Bourg, leading down to the long, wedge-shaped quayside, has a number of older buildings.

A little path leads from the Saturday marketplace along the harbor up to the site of the old fort. It is from this path that the extent of the small port can be viewed best. Tropical vegetation blossoms between red and white tiling or corrugated-iron house-

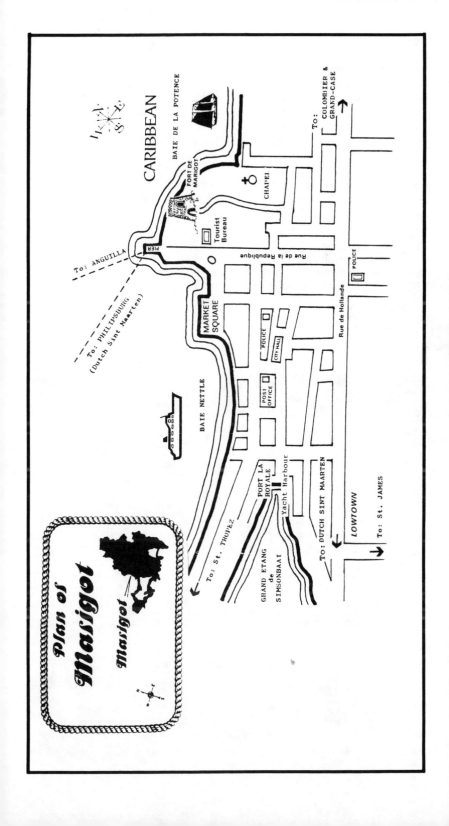

tops and in the background gentle hills slope away from the azure waters of the bay. Yachts and motor craft bob in the languid swell and the quiet of the town is broken only by tinkling halyards against metal masts and the bustle of fishing boats and the local scow emptying its cargo. Rue du General de Gaulle and Sandy Ground can be picked out from the heights that command spectacular views over to the newer hotel and marina developments and even to parts of the Grand Etang de Simsonbaai.

In the center of the town, at the junction with Republique and Rue de Holland, is the wooden Gendarmarie building and at the end of Rue d'Anguille is the harbor arm of Port La Royale. Back along Charles de Gaulle, the City Hall is on the left before the junction with Waterloo Alley that leads to the Market Square on the main quayside. This tiny town has few roads and a window-shopping walk from one end to the other would take less than a half-hour—depending on your duty-free purchases. The Tourist Bureau is located just under the hill fort, near the pier. Ask about car hire here, about renting boats, getting a guide for an island tour or even news of the latest cockfight in town!

Discovering the Island

Turn right out of Marigot and you are heading toward the Dutch part of the island—Sint Maarten, via St. James and the little Mount Fortune on the right, just before the Concordia Monument on the border. If this small obelisk was not in place and the "Welcome" signs not red and blue (Dutch and French), few would realise they had stepped into the territory of a different country and another language. The monument itself is un-possessing, a miniature "Cleopatra's Needle" on a plinth of stone steps on a flat scrub and pasture field on the left side of the road as you leave St. Martin. The dates 1648 and 1948 are inscribed in bronze on the monument and one looks over to the dinghies and yachts in the waters of Simpson-baai.

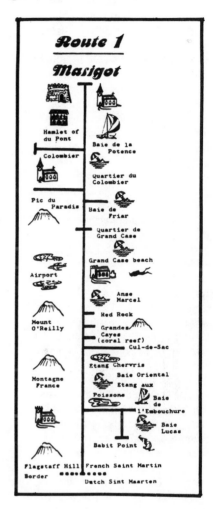

If you take the right fork out of Marigot you head toward Sandy Ground and the long, thin spit of land that leads to Terres Basses and which divides the Caribbean Sea from the calm waters of Simpson Bay. The resort peninsula of Pointe du Bluff is on the right and there is an important site of antiquity on the point. Terres Basses is an islet in itself as it is really reached by the narrow causeway. Low mountains back beautiful beaches and resort areas on the great lagoon. Rouge Beach, Plum Beach and Long Beach are the larger bays with little Cupecoy inlet coming before the invisible line defining the Dutch-French boundary. Simpson Bay Lagoon itself is split in two by the border and it is the south side of this large stretch of water that has been developed for tourism by the Dutch.

St. Martin, to the south of Marigot, the Lagoon and Terres Basses are purely for the recreational element as sailing and sunbathing are the main preoccupations. North from Marigot one comes to the real St. Martin—a large triangle of land with hills and mountains, sheep grazing and hillside chalets overlooking pretty, sandy bays and rocky coves all around the island's perimeter. It is inland where the people are still in their Rip Van Winkle mode, where the inhabitants of lonely crofts and farmhouses still use the language of Shakespeare and still raise cattle in walled pastures and sheep on the green foothills.

Taking the road north out of Marigot, the hamlet of du Pont lies on the right under the lee of Pic du Paradis, the island's highest peak at 1,391 feet. Just a little farther along the road is the pretty village of Quatier du Colombier and it is from here that a narrow road leads to the summit of this small mountain. The views from this centrally located peak are stunning and this is an ideal vantage point for photographers. By taking the right fork, away from Paradis Peak, the little homestead of Colombier nestles under another small mountain, Flagstaff. Note the beautiful white home of the Gumbs family. At 1,286 feet this fourth highest summit on St. Martin offers views down into the Orlean quarter and toward Philipsburg, the capital of the Dutch sector of Sint Maarten. The border between the two halves of the island runs across the top of Mt. Flagstaff. The road does not lead to Flagstaff's summit but it is a short walk that should be made for the spectacular views. Can you make out Saint Barthelemy to the southeast? Or Saba far in the distance to the southwest? On the eastern flank of this mountain a number of pre-Colombian artifacts have been discovered, possibly of Taino Indian origin.

Back on the main coastal route, after Quatier du Columbier, the road bends left to the north and one enters the town of Grand Case. It is really only in St. Martin that one would call Grand Case a town as really it is a glorified shopping precinct, resort hotel strip and beach-oriented commerce center. Pretty enough, this is a real Creole village on a picturesque beach and lies along the promenade between Point Molly Smith and Bell Point (It is not difficult to note that the English certainly left their names, if not their mark, on St. Martin after successive sorties and five periods of occupation). Does one detect a touch of the Irish in the name of the 1,150 foot high Mount

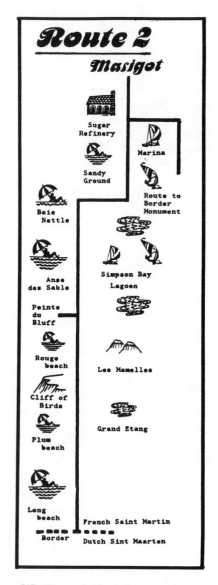

O'Reilly overlooking Grand Case, the salt pans and the magnificent curving bay? From the higher ground one can see Anguilla to the north and boat trips regularly visit the island. In Grand Case one can take some colorful photographs of Creole markets, shop in a number of duty-free boutiques or even watch a cockfight with the locals. Grand Case is important to the visitor because this is the site of the French island's airport, slightly smaller than Juliana airport in the Dutch quarter; most arrivals from Guadeloupe or neighboring islands will disembark here. Grand Case was once six times larger than Marigot according to records but in 1819 a violent hurricane and an earthquake devastated the town reducing its 250 houses to just eight. Note the Lawrence Wattle house with its typical fretwork veranda, built in 1897, and another antiquity—hurricane-struck ruins of Grand Case bridge made from lime blocks.

Follow on round the bay to where the road cuts off to the right; at this point you will find a path leading to the idyllic Anse Marcel, Red Rock Peak, Eastern Point and the coral-reef-girt bay of Grandes Cayes. Further on along the N.7 main road a narrow route leads down to the famous village of Cul de Sac, its popular anchorage and harbor and offshore retreat of Ilet Pinel or Penal Island (what a glorious place for a prison colony!). Cul de Sac used to be known throughout the Caribbean for its agricultural produce. Far out from Cul de Sac port is the magical island resort of Ile Tintamarre, an essential boat excursion. Ask the boatman about trips to Sandy or Dog Island, to Saba, Saint Barthelemy or Anguilla.

Back on the road and skirting the Etang Cevrise, or Chevrise Lagoon, beautiful curving Baie Orientale with its attendant desert island of Caye Verte and naturist beach, the direction suddenly heads due southwest to the delightful Quarter of Orleans. Sheltered by the sweep of Mount France, or Vernon Mountain, this comparatively large township is constructed part on the Lagoon of Fishes and part in the valley below Mount Flagstaff. Beyond the lagoon is the great arc of the Bay Orientale on the Baie de L'Embouchure, a popular resort for sun-seekers and water-sports enthusiasts. In the center of Orleans a narrow track leads out to the last two of St. Martin's twenty-two recognized beaches. Baie Lucas and its Coralita Beach is the most easterly of the island's resorts and if you follow the path up to Babit Pointe you can look down to one of Sint Maarten's most famous resorts, Oyster Pond. Having come this far around the island it is just another two minutes' drive to the border and another few minutes of pleasant (Dutch) countryside before skirting the great Salt Pond and entering "Little Tropical Holland," in the shape of Philipsburg, the Dutch Sint Maarten capital. Why not make a complete island tour and take in all the sights of the Dutch sector as well as the French?

Visiting Philipsburg and Sint Maarten

Philipsburg is an attraction included on most tours of the Caribbean, on cruise-liner itineraries and on island-hopping excursions. Sint Maarten's own international airport can claim to be one of the busiest in the West Indies and an extra influx of visitors come from just across the "border"— French Saint Martin.

It is not just the Aladdin's Cave of duty-free shopping (said to offer the best buys in the Americas), the bustling markets or the casinos and shows that draw the crowds of holidaymakers and tourists. Philipsburg offers a good cross-section of interests, like the 300-year-old Fort Amsterdam, the typical, Dutch-style buildings with their gables and "Hollandaise" decorations, the old courthouse and the neat churches, gardens, verandas and balconies painted in pastel shades.

In addition, the Dutch side of the island provides facilities for almost any form of water sports, golf, tennis and rambling tours. In the hills behind Philipsburg and the Great Salt Pond (now being reclaimed) are rolling hills with grazing sheep and cattle, tiny farmhouses and ancient homesteads like the 1730s and a typically Dutch colonial mansion at Cul de Sac. The summits of Sint Maarten's low mountains offer excellent views of the Dutch part of the island and even ocean vistas out as far as Saint Barthelemy and Saba.

On the miles of gorgeous beaches, coral sand strands and cliff-ringed bays and coves a varied assortment of seaside activities await like snorkeling over coastal reefs, water skiing and wind surfing, scuba diving, deep-sea fishing excursions and sailing.

Back in the capital, Philipsburg, the main road, Front Street, and its parallel, Back Street, offer all the gastronomic delights one would expect of this "Little Holland in the Tropics." Sample the wonderful cheeses, Dutch Jenever gin, Holland-style steaks and the famous Dutch beers. Take a cruise out to Prickly Pear Island for a barbeque lobster meal or lash out on the Indonesian Rijsttafel (rice table)—a thousand delights in one spicy dish! Don't forget to change some cash into Dutch Antillian currency—the Guilder or Florin; many visitors hang on to the "square nickel" as a souvenir of their visit to another country—on the same island!

Wildlife

For the really exciting wildlife on St. Martin one should just look under the surface of its clear, blue seas. A veritable wonderland of anemones, sponges, gorgonias and corals, swarming with myriad varieties of fishes from cardinals to angelfish, parrot fish and butterfly fish, sergeant majors and doctors. The reefs around St. Martin's coast are gardens full of marine life, especially those off the Grandes Cayes in the northeast of the island, Ilet Pinel, Flat Island (or Ile Tintamarre), and the barrier reef of Green Key.

Deeper waters, whether the Atlantic Ocean on the east or the Caribbean Sea to the west, teem with

sportsfish like marlin, wahoo or king-fish, amber and yellow jack, grouper and tuna. Marine turtles can sometimes be seen as can the feared barracuda and shark. A particularly spectacular phenomenon is the magical luminescence occasionally seen at night along the shoreline or in the wake of a boat. This is caused by millions of tiny plankton that drift in the warm waters and reveal their phosphorescent lights, like a luminous stardust, when waves break against the shore or a boat cleaves the waters where zooplankton abound. Some species of whale feed only on these microscopic animals but the chances of seeing a whale on just one or two boat trips are slim.

Above the seas of Saint Martin a great variety of seabirds congregate; gulls, pelicans and cormorants dive for fish and the magnificent frigate bird, or man o' war bird, wheels in solitary majesty above cresting waves searching for crop-filled terns to pirate for a meal. Inland, several species of hummingbird, doves, pigeons and the ubiquitous bananaquits flit around brilliant-colored flowers, dust-bathe in sandy gullies or pester breakfasters on outdoor terraces. Don't forget to go to the falconry display of eagles, hawks and vultures on the hilltop overlooking Simpson Bay lagoon.

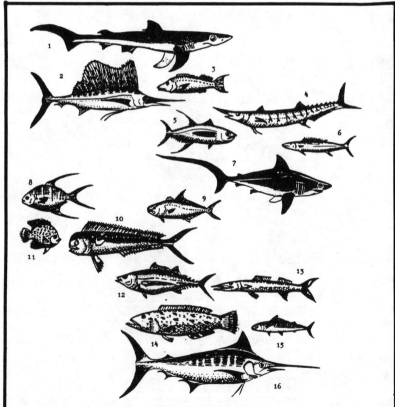

Game Fish of the Antilles: 1. Mako Shark 2. Sailfish 3. Gray Snapper 4. Wahoo 5. Yellowfin 6. Bonefish 7. Tiger Shark 8. Palometa 9. Almaco Jack 10. Dolphin 11. Chub 12. Blackfin Tuna 13. Barracuda 14. Rockfish 15. Rainbow Runner 16. Blue Marlin

Shopping

Saint Martin is a duty-free paradise for shoppers searching for anything from the most exclusive French perfumes and fashions, exotic jewelry, watches, cameras or electrical equipment. Most goods can be purchased both in Marigot or in Philipsburg for about half the price one would pay back home. As for souvenirs, in French St. Martin the islanders create batiks, silk paintings and water colors. Shells, like the queen conch, conch pearls and woven handicrafts are popular. T-shirts, postcards and the colorful postage stamps of Dutch Sint Maarten are a less expensive choice whereas an original idea is to cajole your local chef for a few really traditional Creole recipes to take home. Don't forget the island's rum (rhum, in French)—if you visit Sint Maarten you might be captivated by the unique taste of their 200-year-old guavaberry liqueur.

Banking

There are two banks in Marigot: Bank of the French Antilles on Rue de la Republique, Tel: 87.52.31; and Banque Francaise Commerciale also on the same street in the center of town, Tel: 87.53.80.

Churches

There is one church in Marigot, two in Grand Case, two in Orleans and one in Colombier. The national religion is Roman Catholic but Anglican, Methodist, Baptist and other Protestant services are held on a regular basis.

Hotels on Saint Martin

There are 20 hotels on the island and one naturist hotel. Nine of the hotels are in the capital, Marigot. Le Pirate, on the edge of town, is a residential hotel. Four hotels offer meeting room facilities and theatre hire.

La Samana
Baie-Longue, Tel: 87.51.22
85 rooms and apartments. Pool, restaurant, bar.

Le Royale Louisiana
Avenue General de Gaulle, Marigot, Tel: 87.86.51
14 duplex, 4 triples and 29 rooms in delightful, Creole-style block. Restaurant and lounge.

Coralita Beach Hotel
Oyster Pond, Lucas Bay,
Box 175, Tel: 87.31.81
76 air-conditioned studios. Restaurant and bar, beach bar, tennis.

L'Habitation de Lonvilliers
Anse Marcel, Tel: 87.33.33
253 rooms and suites, 52 apartments. Two restaurants, three bars, beach, all water and land sports.

Saint-Tropez Beach Hotel PLM Azur
Marigot, P.O. Box 120, Tel: 87.54.72
118 air-conditioned rooms. On the beach with watersport activities.

Happy Bay
Grand-Case, Tel: 87.55.20
40 suites and 20 rooms on La Savanne. Pool, watersports, restaurant and bar, entertainment, tennis.

La Belle Creole
Pointe du Bluff, Tel: 87.58.66
159 rooms, 17 suites. Two restaurants, three bars, at Pointe des Pierres a Chaux, low rise, tennis.

Palm Plaza Hotel
Rue de la Republique, Marigot,
Tel: 87.51.96
18 air-conditioned rooms, three suites.

Petite Plage
Grand Case, Tel: 87.50.65
Motel, 12 apartments with air-conditioning.

Le Grand St. Martin Hotel and Beach Resort
Galisbay, Marigot, P.O. Box 99,
Tel: 87.57.91
46 studio and two-level suites. Two restaurants and a bar.

Le Galion Hotel
Baie de L'Embourchure, P.O. Box 1,
Marigot, Tel: 87.51.77
62 rooms, suites and bungalows. Situated on Orleans beach, diving, tennis, watersports.

Hostellerie L'Hermitage
Rue de la Liberte, Marigot,
Tel: 87.50.33
10 air-conditioned rooms. Restaurant and bar.

Chez Martine
Grand-Case, Tel: 87.51.59
8 rooms. Beachfront, open-air restaurant.

Beausejour Hotel
Marigot, P.O. Box 67, Tel: 87.52.18
10-room guesthouse with air-conditioning.

Hevea or Ho-Mai Hotel
Grand Case, Tel: 87.56.85
Eight rooms, restaurant.

La Marina Royale
Marigot, Tel: 87.57.28
58 rooms with 14 suites, watersports, sailing.

Captain Oliver PLM Azur
Oyster Pond, Tel: 87.30.00
24 bungalows, terrace restaurant, bar, marina, boutique.

Grand Case Beach Club
Baie-Orientale, Tel: 87.51.87
76 rooms, theatre, meeting room.

Club Orient (Naturist Hotel)
Baie-Orientale, Tel: 87.33.85
Designated a nudist hotel with its own secluded beach, 90 rooms.

Royal Beach Hotel PLM Azur
Baie de Nettle, 97150
80 rooms, restaurant, bar, beach.

Esmeralda Mansions Resort
Baie Orientale, BP 630
Tel: 590 87 91 49
60 beach villas with private pools.

Hotel Belvedere, Cul de Sac
Tel: 590 87 37 89
Sports center and connections to Pinel Island.

Sol Hotel Ambiance
Oyster Pond   Tel 590 87 31 10

Orient Bay Hotel
Mount Vernon   Tel: 590 87 37 66

Hotel Anse Margot
Baie Nettle, 97150
Tel: 590 87 92 01
95 rooms with 35 suites on the beachfront.

Hotel du Golf
Residence St. Jean, Bellvue, B.P. 974
Marigot
Tel: 590 87 92 08
Near town centre, pool with jacuzzi.

Hotel Roselys
Concordia, Marigot 97150
Tel: 590 87 70 17
40 studios and 8 duplex, restaurant and pool.

Bertines Restaurant and Guest House
Savana Grand-Case, 97150
Tel: 590 87 58 39
Good value accommodation and meals.

Restaurants and Bars on Saint Martin

There are more than 60 restaurants on St. Martin-French side. No traveling gourmet can claim to have sampled the finest of international cuisine without first making a stopover in St. Martin. However, any connoisseur of food could never make just a short visit to this island that has secured a top position in the worldwide good eating guide for many years. What this island does not lack is the most excellent of restaurants. St. Martin can probably boast some of the best eating places in the entire Caribbean.

Enough praise, and down to the essential facts. Most notably, it is fact that this is a French island and therefore offers the best selection of French wines, champagnes and brandies (cognacs). Fact, again, that this is a tropical island and, for that reason, it has the most delicious fruits and vegetables and access to a plentiful supply of fish and shellfish from the Caribbean or Atlantic Ocean waters.

Whether it be genuine French country cuisine from L'Auberge Gourmande in Grand Case, frog's legs in aspic at La Privilege Gourmet Grill on Marcel Cove or a bouillabaisse at La Vie Parisienne in Le Grand-St.-Martin, the touch of classic French cooking to the traditional standards is in the air. In the air, also, is the savory waft of specialities like "hot rock" tenderloin from Bertines on the hills of La Savane, paella or couscous from Le Ponton restaurant near the floating bridge on Sandy Ground, or bear steaks and ostrich breasts being roasted just across the border in the Dutch section of Simpson Bay!

Nouvelle French dishes are in vogue at places like Le Tastevin in Grand Case and Cornish game hen with tarragon at Le Boucanier in Rue d'Anguille, Marigot, can seduce the taste buds for your entire evening. The restaurant has a large terrace, as does Chez Martine in Grand Case, where they serve a delicious conch salad. One of Marigot's oldest houses is now La Maison sur Le Port where, on the waterfront, one can sample lobster with caviar. Famed for its desserts is La Vie en Rose on Boulevard de France in the capital and a little farther along the same street is La Calanque which specializes in veal scaloppini in morel sauce.

Sauces are a hallmark of French cooking and the island has no shortage of imagination when one can try champagne butter sauce with lobster at Le Poisson d'Or in Marigot, Madeira and cream sauce with veal at Chez Rene, near Marigot Bridge, or a brandy or wine sauce with duckling at David's, on Rue de la Liberté. Bisques and soups are given the French touch with specialities such as crème de pireaux (leek bisque) at La Nacelle in old Gendarmerie in Grand Case, terrine of fish and vegetables at L'Escapade, also in Grand Case, and scallop chowder at the Rainbow restaurant just along the waterfront. The Parisienne will feel right at home with the boeuf Wellington served in Le Santal in Marigot's west side, or the Roman, with osso buco primavera at Sebastino in Grand Case, or the spagetteria of Gianni's not a few minutes away.

This, however, is St. Martin, a tropical island with its very own tastes and specialities that mix the exotic with the conventional, the spices with the finest herbs, and the rum with the claret. This is the country of Creole cooking and the island has many native cuisineries or West Indian restaurants, mainly in the less expensive price range. There are more than ten

Creole restaurants in and around Marigot, such as Chez Max on Rue Fleix Eboue, where fish and fungi is one speciality, or crab backs at Cas d'Annie, Rue d'Anguille, turtle steak-stuffed shellfish at La Samanna, Baie Longue, or goat water in the pretty surroundings of Le Palmier on Sandy Ground. French Caribbean cooking is celebrated with chicken and baked papaya at La Rhumerie, the Colombos to be savored at Chez Lolotte in the capital, or boudins at Egnold's, on the harbor. Other delights include curried goat with christophenes to be enjoyed at La Maison des Pecheurs, crabes farcis at Chez Ninon, or poisson coffre, the local speciality at Au Petit Coin Guyannais also in Marigot. Creole preparations can be quite hot and often need a cooling dessert, such as peach souffle or the popular guava sorbet. Not alone in the international rating of fiery foods, the Creole dishes like stuffed eggplant and christophene at Le Bistrot can compare favorably with the Guadeloupian/Vietnamese "nems" at Hoa Mai, in Grand Case, or the Indonesian, sixteen-dish, rijsttafel at the Java, also in Grand Case.

Back to the moderate European dishes, there are several restaurants serving for the American or international tastes such as Waves, Le Ritz or Le Pirate. Wherever you go, however, in French St. Martin, the Gallic essence breaks through. At Jardin Bresilien a Samba evening rounds up delights such as Coquilles St. Jacques; Bistrot Marseillais offers provençale bourride; and La Nacelle serves good, plain French cookery. In an old Creole house in Grand Case, Le Toucan offers "Surf and Turf"— don't ask, try it! And another old mansion, La Mangouste, Colombier, specializes in traditional French food with the tang of the tropics, as does Clair's Country Corner, in French Cul de Sac.

Don't forget that in late May the island celebrates its "St. Martin Food Festival."

For after-dinner entertainment the choice is bewildering and if your hotel is not arranging a feature, try the Pinao Bar at Hotel Le Grand St. Martin, the Mini Club in Marigot, Night Fever in Colombier, Jardin Bresilien, or run the gamut of casinos, nightclubs and shows just across the border in Sint Maarten. Musically, apart from the time-honored "beguine", the new sound on the island is the "Zouk."

Communications and Information

The telephone code number for St. Martin is 87. Dialing the Dutch side from the French side, use the prefix 3; there are post offices in Marigot and Grand Case.

There is one of the best hospitals in the Caribbean at Philipsburg in Dutch Sint Maarten but Saint Martin has its own hospital in Marigot, Tel: 87.50.07.

The French island has a police station at Tel: 87.50.10.

The Tourist Bureau is to be found on the Rue de la Republique in Marigot, near Fort de Marigot, Tel: 87.50.04.

Cars and taxis may be hired at the airport, Babi Richardson, Tel: 87.51.11; Hunt's Sunrise, Tel: 87.51.91; Romeo Fleming, Tel: 87.50.81; A.F. Cars, Tel: 87.59.79; Saint Martin Auto, Tel: 87.50.86; Esperance Cars, Tel: 87.51.09—all in Marigot. Buses run on the island until midnight and most hotels or restaurants can assist with transport advice.

To and From the Island

L'Esperance Airport is located on the northwest side of the island about three miles from the capital, Marigot. The airport handles only the small 19-seater aircraft like those used locally by Air Guadeloupe, ALM, Liat, etc. The international airport for the island, located in the Dutch sector, and just eight miles from Marigot, is Princess Juliana Airport taking long-haul air traffic. There are several shipping routes from the island to St. Kitts, Anguilla (English), Saba and Sint Eustatius (Dutch) and Saint Barthelemy (French). Cruise liners, as yet, do not use Marigot's facilities but are regular visitors to Philipsburg on the Dutch side.

CHAPTER X

Saint Barthélémy "Land of the Hummingbirds"

Size and Location

Just 8½ square miles in area, this island is shaped like a dragon with its tail upturned. The second farthermost outpost of the French Antilles, St. Barthélémy lies 125 miles northwest of Guadeloupe and 15 miles southeast of Sint Maarten/Saint Martin, its nearest neighbor. The tiny capital is called Gustavia and is located just under the "tail" on the western side of the island.

Physical

Covered in smooth, undulating hills, karstic limestone formations and several mountain peaks, St. Barthélémy is surrounded by beautiful coral-sanded coves, sweeping bays, more than twenty noted beaches and several rocky coves. The island is quite arid but there is no lack of greenery and also some pastureland. At 922 feet, Montagne de Vitet is the island's highest point. Six large lagoons are scattered across the hilly landscape. More than twenty tiny islets and islet groups lie in St. Barthélémy's waters; Ile Fourchue and Ile Chevreau or Ile Bonhomme are the largest of these islands, which also include the Ile Frégate twin islets, Ile Toc Vers, La Tortue, Les Grenadiers, Ile Coco, Fourmis, Roches Rouge, Les Balines, La Baline (the whales and the whale), Les Saintes, Pain de Sucre (Sugar Loaf Island), Ile de la Pointe Petit Jean, Roche le Boeuf, Ile Pelé, Ile le Boulanger (Baker's Island), La Poule et Les Poussins (The Hen and Chickens)—such amusing names that they deserved inclusion!

Climate

The climate on St. Barthélémy is dry and arid with a pleasant average temperature of 72 degrees F (22 degrees C) to 86 degrees F (30 degrees C). If rain falls, it is generally at night and short and sharp in duration. December to April is the "high" season for visiting. Sea temperatures are never cold.

Population

Incongruously, in the middle of the tropics, here is an island race with fair skin, blond hair and blue eyes—surely some mistake. First French, then Swedish, then French again, the lineage of the islanders goes back to early Breton, Norman, Poitevin and Viking settlers with a smattering of pirate and buccaneer blood for good measure. The entire Saint Barthélémy (or St. Barts, as everyone shortens it) is about 3,100 permanent residents. St. Barts is the only island in the Caribbean with Swedish descendency in its makeup. Some of the older generation still wear the traditional costume and go about barefoot.

Language

Naturally, with a mixed background, the people of St. Barts share mixed tongues—some maintain their Norman dialect, others speak English, but all speak at least some French because it is the island's official language.

Holidays and Festivals

Around August 24 the Festival of Saint Barthélémy, the island's patron saint, is celebrated in a continuous fair atmosphere that lasts for a few days. A small carnival is held near the beginning of Lent. The Corossol fête occurs on August 25. Apart from New Year's Day, Labor Day (May 1), Assumption (August 15), Armistice Day (November 11), Christmas Day and Easter Monday, Ascension and Whit Monday, the French Isle includes Bastille Day (July 14), Schoelcher Day (July 21), All Saints' and All Souls' (November 1 and 2), only Assumption is the main festival. Don't forget the "St. Bart's Music Festival" held every February; the trans-atlantic sailing ship race—"La Route du Rosé," in early December, and the wine festival of "Salon du Rosé".

History

The Carib Indians living on the island had already christened it "Ouanalao" before Christopher Columbus sailed by on his second voyage of discovery in 1493. Meaning the "Land of the Hummingbirds" in pre-Columbian language, Amerindian tribes were still living on the island when it was named by the Europeans. Although it is doubtful whether Columbus or his crew ever set eyes on Saint Barthélémy the island received the name of the admiral's brother, Barthelemeo—Bartholomew. The island has been known by the same name since the earliest of charts were drawn.

Certainly discovered first by the Spanish, St. Barts was ignored for 135 years, until in 1629, the French, based on nearby St. Christopher (St. Kitts), made a halfhearted attempt at occupation. Driven off by the warlike Caribs, it was not for another nineteen years that they returned, landed and set up a stockade. The year was 1648 and again the Amerindians drove the French from the island. Bent on taking the island for strategic purposes, the governor of St. Kitts, Longvilliers de Poincy, sent sixty men to establish a stronghold under the command of Jacques Le Gendre. After about eight years of defending the fort, a raid by the Caribs set the French retiring to St. Kitts once more. In 1659 a contingent of fifty men and their wives, led by Guillaume d'Avranches from Beauvais, set up a colony on the island.

However, these peasants from Normandy and Brittany were unable to hold onto their new-found home for very long. More serious and more political was the action taken in 1665 by Colbert, who was responsible for the Royal Colonies of France. The island was sold back to de Poincy,

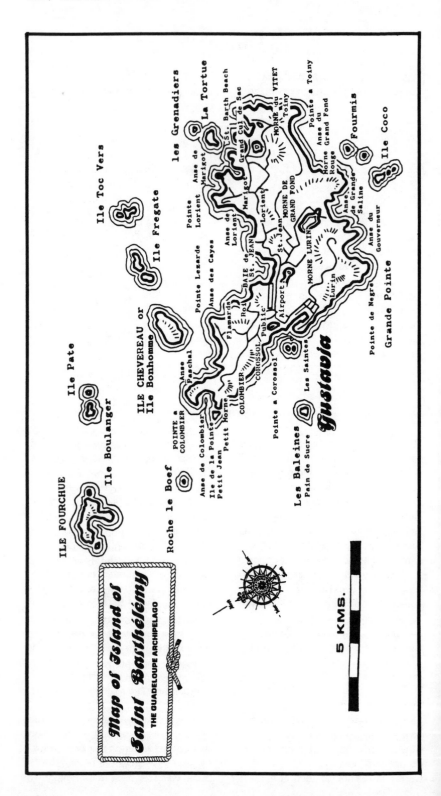

Map of Island of
Saint Barthélémy
THE GUADELOUPE ARCHIPELAGO

5 KMS.

chevalier of the Order of the Knights of Malta. Another attempt was made to settle the island in 1674, again by French Huguenots. Tobacco, cotton and vegetable produce were grown and some sheep and goats were raised on the rolling pastureland. These crops attracted the "Brethren of the Coast," pirates, maurauding buccaneers and privateers who assisted the settlers in establishing a port they named Carenage after the careening of ships (hull clearance and barnacle scraping) which was practiced there. The families, Aubins, Grêaux, Berniers and others supplied the corsairs with provisions in return for defense and by 1681 there were nearly 400 inhabitants living permanently on St. Barts.

In 1686 indigo works were established to supply the French cloth manufacturers and more family names joined the pioneers; those of Brin, Ledee, Magras, Maye and Quinquis can still be traced as can the families of Berry, Laplace and Questel. Pioneers gave succour to corsairs and buccaneers and the notorious pirate Bartholomew Roberts regularly was entertained here during the 1720s. The fearsome privateer Montbars the Exterminator, used a bay on St. Barthélémy as a refuge. The settlement, however, grew and thrived until in the year 1744 when the English, incensed by the harboring of pirates on the island who jeopardized their shipping, exiled the French to St. Kitts and St. Martin. By 1764 the exiles were permitted to return on the faith that the French authorities in control of the island desist from aiding and abetting privateers.

Having suffered enough at the hands of Caribs and being blackmailed by pirates, being dispossessed by the English and having to build their homes up from scratch again, the settlers were dumbfounded when on March 7, 1785, they learned that France had betrayed them. One of Louis XVI's ministers, the Count of Vergennes, had swapped the island and its 750 inhabitants for warehousing and free-port rights in Gothenburg, Sweden. This access to the Baltic seemed to be important for the French and as a result of the exchange the Huguenot islanders found themselves sharing their island with the descendants of Vikings who even changed the name of their one town, Le Carenage, to Gustavia, after their king, Gustaf III of Sweden.

By 1810 the population had grown to more than 6,500 and the status of Caribbean free-port had drawn considerable prosperity to the island. Livestock was being raised, cotton thrived and the island exported quantities of fruit. The few brushes with the fringe skirmishes of the Napoleonic Wars did little to disturb the island's tranquility. However, five epidemics of plague and four hurricanes decimated the population and destroyed crops and houses. Things did change. Sweden abolished slavery in 1847 and by that time there were very few slaves left to free. Those that were, soon left to find work elsewhere but this was the time when the worst disaster hit St. Barts. A great fire devastated the port and town of Gustavia in 1852, compounding all the previous ills that had beset the island.

In 1878 France purchased her former colony back from the Swedish for 320,000 francs in gold. This left the Swedish street names, paved streets and typically Scandanavian walls dividing properties. Nor did the French change the name of the island's capital. The island came under the jurisdiction of the administrative area of Guadeloupe and it is now administered by a mayor residing on nearby Saint Martin.

During the Second World War the

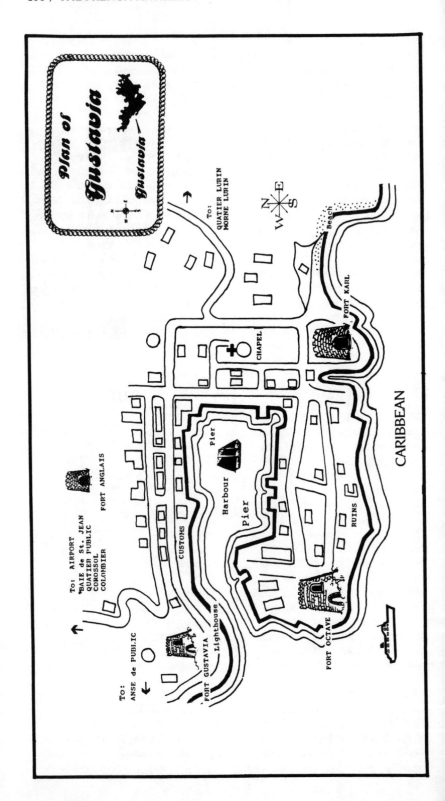

island was more or less forgotten by the outside world and suffered many shortages. It is only recently that Saint Barthélémy has been rediscovered as one of the most attractive islands in the entire galaxy of the Caribbean Antilles. The tourist trade has brought unprecedented prosperity to this tiny French enclave.

Trade, Industry and Economy

Apart from the period covering the latter years of the eighteenth century and the early part of the nineteenth century when cotton, livestock, vegetables and fruit production boomed, St. Barts economy has been negligible. During the first decade of the nineteenth century the island was exporting many thousands of pineapples and other exotic fruits to the provisioners of Europe and Scandinavia but, when disease and adverse weather conditions laid waste the plantations and crippled the workforce, the decline was one from which the island would never recover.

Today the story is changing, the balance is swinging in favor of the diligent and deserving islanders. When the first tourist hotel was constructed on the island in 1953 there was a glimmer of hope. Sadly, the hotel closed its doors in 1957 only to re-open in 1960. The airstrip, which was opened in the 1960s (although the first aircraft landed on the island in 1945), really got the tourist business off the ground and now tourism constitutes the major part of the island's income. The status of free-port still remains and the more than thirty hotels on St. Barts are often booked one year in advance.

Close-Up on Gustavia

This must be one of the prettiest, doll-house-like port towns in the Caribbean. Originally called Le Carenage by the first French settlers, Gustavia is named after the Swedish King Gustaf III, a throwback to the times of Swedish occupation. A model harbor, oblong, and with a mouth extending out to a wide, deep bay, makes Gustavia one of the best ports for shipping in the West Indies. Local cruise ships and many yachts make a beeline for this duty-free harbor, which can accommodate forty boats.

In the early days of pirates and French-English antagonism the harbor was protected by four fortresses. The ruins of these can still be made out—Fort Gustav and Fort Karl are open to the public. Fort Oscar, in the west, is not open to the public and of the fourth fort there is little trace. Not much of old Gustavia remains because of the terrible fire in 1852. Of the earlier buildings, just the belfry and clocktower of an old Swedish church, standing stone and wood-clad and corrugated-iron-roofed just outside the town, an old Swedish cemetery and a few Swedish street-signs indicate any real historic background.

The main road in Gustavia runs around the three sides of the port and can be covered in an hour's walk if one does not linger too long in the few dozen boutiques, the roadside cafes, or taking photographs of the one antique monument in Gustavia—the English Admiralty-type anchor, dredged from the bay in 1981. Two churches show dual religious allegiance. Unless you're interested to shop or laze by the dockside, mingle with the yachtsmen and tourists from St. Martin off the regular catamaran service, climb up to one of the many magnificent vantage points to view the neat little town from mountain slopes. A guide or map from the Town Hall may help in identifying some landmarks.

Discovering the Island

Apart from climbing up Morne Lurin at 630 feet to view the stunning panorama of Gustavia and its environs, Pain de Sucre Isle out in the bay, farther out the pirate lair of Ile Fourchue, scattered rocks and outcrops and the vast mass of St. Martin on the horizon, it is recommended to take the road around to Corossol. Before taking to the road one can visit Petit Anse de Galet (Shell Beach) for a dip or, on the south side of Lurin, Gouvernuer's Bay, from where Saba, Statia and St. Kitts can sometimes be sighted.

Corossol is a tiny fishing village that retains its Norman links. It may just be that you will spot here the traditional dress of the island women. This consists of ankle-long seventeenth-century-style dresses with long sleeves and high starched collar, bare feet and the distinctive Breton Calèche (kiss-me-not) bonnet. This starched, pleated white headdress—a similar style to that worn in nearl y Colombier—is known by the French "quichenottes" and is now rarely seen. In Corossol one also can still buy the famed handicrafts of the fisherfolk whose wives, while they toil on the seas, weave wicker baskets, fans and hats from the leaf fibers of the lantania palm (fan palm) trees introduced in the late nineteenth century. The people of St. Barts are almost exclusively white and so, to see them going about their everyday business in their tiny hamlets like Corossol or Colombier, just across the pass, is quite strange in this Antillian location where most populations are predominantly black or brown. From Corossol, at the northernmost point of the island, one can look out to St. Martin from Le Petit Morne, 528 feet. Near here is the triangular design of the house built for the U.S. banker, David Rockefeller, to the designs of Nelson Aldrich. The semicircular bay is a famous anchorage and sports an excellent beach. Just around the headland is an even more popular beach resort, Anse des Flamanda. Roads or paths link most of the beaches and above the pretty Anse á Galets a little school and a church on the left of the roadside indicate that one is on the right route down to the island's airport and the spectacular Baie de St. Jean.

Airplanes arriving at the tiny airstrip swoop either over the beach or across the scarped plateau to plump down just yards from the bright blue water's edge. The airport is known locally as Aerodrome la Tourmente—well dubbed for the heart-in-mouth approach. To be deposited so near such a breath-taking sweep of silver sand and beckoning sea is quite as much a jolt as the landing itself and one is compelled to cross the road and make for the azure waters. Low green hills surround the airport with red roofs peeking from behind palms, frangipani or flame trees. Hotels, stores and cafes have provided facilities for the many visitors to Saint-Jean, which boasts one of the island's few sites of antiquity and also a fine yacht mooring basin.

Continuing around the bay one comes to Lorient and another of the few bits of evidence from early St. Barts. Lorient has an ancient cemetery and church, petrol station and post office. This hamlet overlooks another of St. Barts twenty-two listed beaches, Anse de Lorient. This is one of the larger settlements on the island! From here one can return to Gustavia, a few miles back across the

mountain ridge, or continue in a number of directions following roads or paths to the east side of the island. In the center of the eastern part of the island is the Montagne du Vitet, which the main road circumvents passing by beaches such as Anse de Marigot, Anse de Grand Cul de Sac—named after the little hamlet on the hill—St. Barth (the French way of spelling) Beach, Petit Cul de Sac Beach, Pointe à Toiny Beach and the great sweep of Anse du Grand Fond. Each of the names around the island seems to be twinned with its own Quatier, or district, even though the island is so tiny. Above all these last named beaches and bays towers the 922 foot-high mountain peak, a must for views that seem to stretch the length and breadth of the Caribbean itself!

A large peninsula divides the Anse du Grand Fond from the next magnificent bay, the resort of Anse de Grande Saline. It was here that the salt pans behind the beach were used to evaporate sea water to reclaim the valuable salt. Disused now, the pans form a lagoon over which the Les Castelets hotel gazes. From this flank of the Lurin mountain one can join either the road back to Saint-Jean and the airport or follow around by the Anse du Gouverneur, yet another beauty spot and celebrated beach. Legend has it that Montibars the Exterminator, a ferocious French pirate, buried his loot near this beach.

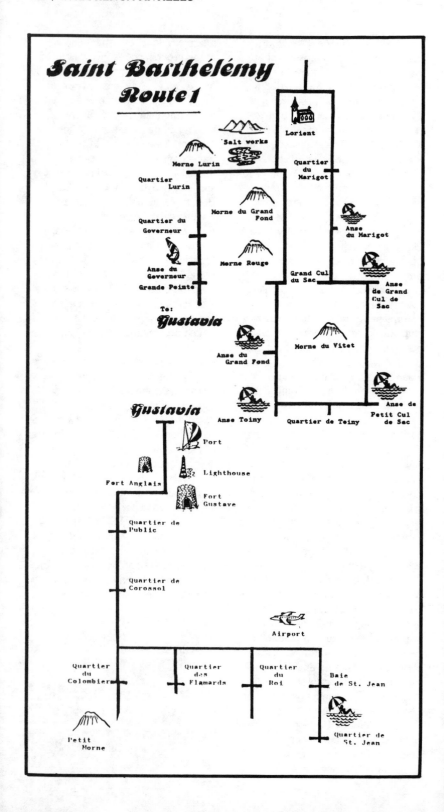

Wildlife

Does such an idyllic isle need any other diversions than its tranquil bays, golden beaches and green rolling hills? What could enhance the imitation of paradise? Few could answer these questions, but St. Barts itself has provided the answer. The hibiscus, flamboyant flowers, anthuriums and oleander blossom attract the jewels that bedeck the crown. Hummingbirds in shades of iridescent greens, shimmering gold, reds, purple, long tails dipping and diving, curved beaks probing, throng around the brilliant blooms and dart through the hedgerows. What more fitting and dazzling compliment to the island's charm. The seas, as is the case almost everywhere in the West Indies, are alive with fish and it is no surprise to see the water surface showered with silver as shoals of flying fish skim out of reach of larger predators. Turtles—one of St. Bart's islands is named Tortue after the animals—are often seen by divers or snorkel enthusiasts, lazily drifting over reef banks and coral outcrops. Angel fish in striped clouds and cardinals in brilliant crimson are just two of the myriad inhabitants of coral pools and gorgonian-clad submarine ledges. About fifteen different snorkeling locations have been identified and La Marine Service provides all the requirements for scuba diving. Yacht Charter Service and La Marine charter boats for deep sea fishing off Corossol, Flamands and Lorient. La Caleche also charter boats. Lou Lou's Marine is the only chandlery on the island.

The shrill cry of peacocks startles visitors in St. Bart's hotels.

Offshore Life of the Antilles: 1. Blue Tang 2. Flying Fish 3. Soldier Fish 4. Butterfly Fish 5. Doctor Fish 6. Queen Angel Fish 7. Sea Horse 8. Rock Beauty 9. Angel Fish 10. Yellowfin Grouper 11. Spotted Drum 12. Queen Triggerfish 13. Palometa 14. Goatfish 15. Clown Wrasse 16. Four-eyed Butterfly Fish 17. Needle Fish 18. Glasseye Snapper 19. Squirrel Fish 20. Sergeant Major Fish 21. French Angel Fish 22. Scorpion Fish 23. Gray Trigger Fish 24. Green Turtle 25. Damsel Fish 26. Lobster 27. Blue-striped Grunt 28. Spotted Moray Eel 29. Hermit Crab 30. Murex 31. Cowrie, Starfish, Lion's Paw, Coneshell 32. Sea Cucumber 33. Triton

Shopping

Many day trippers and excursion members from Marigot, Saint Martin, who arrive on the ferry and catamaran visits, browse through the thirty or so boutiques, duty-free shops and kiosks on Gustavia's wharf front. However, there is little in the way of original souvenirs of the island except for straw-work woven from the lantana palm, sandals, bags, hats, shell jewelry and hand-printed fabrics.

Luxury goods, French cosmetics and bikinis, perfumes and watches are de rigueur, it seems, for most of Saint Barts' shops whether in the capital or Saint-Jean. Locally made goods include hand-turned pottery, woven baskets and delicate, palm-straw bird shapes, T-shirts and hand-print wraps, or lithographs produced by the island's artisans.

Banking

Banque Francaise Commerciale, Rue du General de Gaulle, Gustavia, Tel: 27.62.62. Banque National de Paris,

Rue du Bord de Mer, Gustavia, Tel: 27.63.70.

Churches

The French islands of the West Indies are Catholic but here on St. Barts there is both a Roman Catholic Church and a Protestant Church in Gustavia with two other chapels on

the island. Crosses, like the large white cross on the road from Gustavia to the airport, and other shrines may be seen along the roadsides.

Hotels on Saint Barthélémy

There are about 26-1 bedroom villas; about 5-1 bedroom apartments for lease; 50-2 bedroom villas for rent; 34-3 bedroom villas and about 5-4 bedroom villas available on St. Barts. 22 hotels are listed officially and there are 12 "Petite Hotelleries."

Le Manapany Cottages
Anse des Cayes. Tel: 27.66.55

40 apartments, all air-conditioned. Private beach, bars, restaurants, grill, sport facilities.

El Ypado
Gustavia. Tel: 27.60.18

8 air-conditioned rooms.

Hotel Emeraude Plage
Baie de St. Jean. Tel: 27.64.78

30 rooms, bungalow style, 3 suites, one villa. Bar.

Hotel Jean Bart PLM Azur
Baie de St. Jean. Tel: 27.63.37

50 double, air-conditioned rooms. Restaurant, bar, pool.

Les Mouettes (Petite Hotel)
Lorient. Tel: 27.60.74

6 rooms.

Le P'tit Morne (Petite Hotel)
Colombier. Tel: 27.62.64

12 studios. Air-conditioning.

Chez Joe Motel
Corossol. Tel: 27.62.53

3 studios.

La Presqu'Ile
Place de Parade, Gustavia.
Tel: 27.64.60

12 rooms. Bar, restaurant.

Les Castelets
Lurin. Tel: 27.61.73

6 rooms, 2 villas, 2 chalets. Pool,
restaurant, bar.

Auberge de la Petite Anse
Petite Anse, Flamards. Tel: 27.64.60

16 rooms.

Hotel de la Plage
Grand Cul de Sac. Tel: 27.60.70

16 bungalows.

Autour du Rocher
Lorient. Tel: 27.64.60

5 rooms. Restaurant, bar.

L'Hibiscus
Rue Tiers, Gustavia. Tel: 27.64.82

11 rooms, air-conditioned. Restaurant, pool.

Hotel Tom Beach (Petite Hotel)
St. Jean. Tel: 27.60.43

12 rooms in cottages.

Hotel Baie des Anges (Petite Hotel)
Baie des Anges. Tel: 27.63.61

9 rooms.

Chez Cocotte
Gustavia. Tel: 27.62.39

6 rooms.

Kerjean (Petite Hotel)
Gustavia. Tel: 27.62.38

8 rooms.

Les Bougainvilliees
Gustavia

3 rooms.

Taiwana
Flamards. Tel: 27.65.01

9 rooms. Restaurant, sports, pool.

Hostellerie des Trois-Forces
Vittet. Tel: 27.61.25

12 rooms.

Guanahany Hotel
Anse de Cul de Sac. Tel: 27.66.60

80 rooms and suites. Two restaurants,
pool, sports.

St. Barths Beach Hotel/L'Hotel de la
Plage
Grand Cul de Sac. Tel: 27.62.73

36 air-conditioned rooms and 16
bungalows plus eight bungolettes.
Bar, restaurant.

Hotel Filao Beach
Baie de St. Jean. Tel: 27.64.84

30 double rooms. Air-conditioning,
pool, snacks, sports.

Hotel Baie des Flamands
Baie de Flamands. Tel: 27.64.76

24 air-conditioned rooms. Pool, bar,
restaurant, fishing.

Les Jardins de St. Jean
St. Jean. Tel: 27.70.27

Apartments and studios. Exotic gardens and pool.

Les Islets Fleuris (Petite Hotel)
Hauts de Lorient. Tel: 27.64.22
One-room studios. Pool, watersports.

Marigot Bay Club (Petite Hotel)
Marigot.
6 apartments. Restaurant, three
beaches, watersports.

Marigot Sea Club
Marigot.
11 apartments. Pool, three beaches,
watersports.

Tropical Hotel
St. Jean. Tel: 27.64.87
20 rooms. Air-conditioned, reception
bungalow, bar, pool.

Sereno Beach Hotel
Grand Cul de Sac. Tel: 27.64.80
20 rooms. Air-conditioned, garden,
pool, restaurant.

La Normandie
Lorient. Tel: 27.61.66
8 rooms. Garden pool, terrace restaurant.

Port St. Barth
Gustavia. Tel: 27.62.36
19 rooms.

Village St. Jean
St. Jean. Tel: 21.61.39
6 rooms, 20 studios and villas. Restaurant.

Eden Rock
St. Jean
6 rooms. Island's first hotel. Terrace bar.

The Hotel Carl Gustav
P.O. Box 6, 97133 Gustavia
Tel: 590 27 82 83

The Blue Marlin Hotel-Restaurant
Pointe Milou
Tel: 590 27 71 50

Other hotels on St. Barthelemy include La Banane Club at Lorient, Tel:
27.67.81, with nine bungalows in
lush, tropical gardens; Grand Cul de
Sac Beach Hotel, with 16 rooms on
the beach of the same name, Tel:
27.60.70; the 12 rooms of the Francois Plantation at Columbier, Tel:
27.61.98; the 25 cottages and studios
of the White Sand Beach Cottages at
Anse des Flamands, Tel: 27.63.66;
and Les Villas Castelle on St. Jean
Beach, Tel: 27.61.98. With villas in
mind, St. Barts boasts a wide range
of situations to suit every require-
ment. Rentals are generally by the
week: 26 one-bedroom villas, 65
two-bedroom, 39 three-bedroom and
7 four-bedroom villas all add up to a
grand total of 137 villas. Contact Sibarth Real Estate for full list at P.O.
Box 55 Gustavia, Tel: 011-590
27.62.38 Fax. 011-590 27.60.52.
Also available for a small charge is
the color brochure called the Vendome Guide, available from Sibarth.

Seventeen of St. Bart's hotels have
restaurants, some open to the public.
For those wishing to dine out or grab
a quick take-away snack, there are
more than sixty restaurants on the
island including hotel restaurants. For
relaxed atmosphere or prim formal
elegance, a cross-section of dining
rooms and terraced cafes await the
visitor. International cuisine is represented by the Italian eateries like Autour du Rocher in Lorient, or the
Dolphin in St. Jean. French crepes at
La Crêperie, or croissants and bur-
gers at La Bar de L'Oubli, both in
Gustavia. Local food is known as
Creole and many restaurants offer its
spicy specialities. Try Le Relais at
Petite Cul, New Borne in Flamands,
or La Case Creole in St. Jean.
Home-away-from-home is the authentic American cuisine at Chez Joe
in the capital, or a cheeseburger with
cold beer is offered at Le Select in
the town. There is even a top caterer
on the island called Taste Unlimited
and self-caterers can shop for international deleciacies at the Gourmet
Shop supermarket at Airport Termi-
nal, St. Jean.

Restaurants and Nightlife on Saint Barthélémy

It must be the balmy sparkling air that has induced so many restaurants and cafes, hotels and bars to provide facilities for diners out in the open. Both the breezes and unforgettable views make hillside and beach meals such a delight on this island of delights. Whether breakfast on a seaside patio while the sun wakes up the countless tiny singing birds, lunch on a quayside cafe pavement listening to the gentle clanking of a thousand halyards against a hundred yacht masts in Gustavia harbour or a hand-holding, sun-dipping, terrace dinner culminating in a starlit beguine, St. Barts has the setting. You bring the mood!

Almost any international dish, from pheasant to roast beef, is served at poolside restaurants like that at the Filao Beach Hotel or the garden at Hotel Normandie. The panoramic bar at Castelets, on a mountaintop,

or at the St. Barths Beach hotel with its magnificent views from the restaurant, or a shrubbery-surrounded lunch at Vieux Clocher in L'Hibiscus Hotel adds ambiance to the West Indian connoisseur's crab farcis or lobster thermidor. Gourmets the world over will not deny that the setting is an integral part of a meal and in St. Barts the chefs seem to try to rival nature's beauty spots with ravishing haute cuisine. Let's glance at a cross-section of the island's tempting dishes.

Can a Caribbean sunset compete with the rosy blush of snapper with salmon mousse, leg of lamb with pureed red peppers or the gold of brochette of grouper in saffron garnished with flambeed shrimp and chives? Poached egg and champagne sauce at La Toque Lyonnaise in Sereno Beach Hotel in Grand Cul de Sac, goose giblets with walnut salad and raspberry sauce at Castelets or lobster bisque and frog's legs at Taiwana on Anse des Flamards underline the magic that occurs when French cooking meets Antillian ingredients in West Indian island charm.

Could nouvelle cuisine at Le Pelican on St. Jean beach compete with the onion soup and souffleed pomme de terre overlooking the harbour at La Cremaillere in Gustavia? Could roast lamb with garlic sauce on quayside tables rival crab and christophene at Chez Tatie near the airport? Could Creole dishes like conch crepes override the attraction of beef filet with green peppercorns or a genuine St. Barts blaff distract from sliced breast of duck with pears and bananas? Take the exotic of the idyllic Caribbean and stir in the discipline of the French when they create their culinary masterpieces and you have the best in the west! There are more than sixty restaurants and beachside cafes on the island.

Try the hillside setting of L'Ananas overlooking the port of Gustavia or, just along Rue Sadi Carnot, an evening meal watching the twinkling harbor lights at Au Port. On Rue Jeanne d'Arc in the town, sample the exquisite fare at Le Brigantin or genuine Creole cooking at Presqu'ile on Place de Parade, Gustavia. Also on Rue Jeanne d'Arc is the terrace setting of La Marine or more authentic Creole preparations at La Langouste on Rue du Roi Oscar 11 in town. A "new age" Inn on St. Barts is known as "Hostellerie des Trois Forces."

Beachside temptations include Chez Jacki's terrace at Public, Le Bistro or Chez Francine on St. Jean Beach, Le Fore at Anse des Cayes or the Marigot Bay Club at Marigot. The hillside Le Flamboyant at Grand Cul de Sac or Le Sapotillier on Gustavia's harbor, Rotisserie Bertrand, or Le Tamarin at Saline, all present a wealth of island fruit, vegetables and herbs, the bountiful sea's fresh produce in shell or on the bone and a gamut of dishes piquant with the sauces made only from island spice recipes. Other excellent establishments include Au Bon Coin, Bartolomeo, Chez Tatie, Jardin Samba, L'Hibiscus, La Crêperie, Le Ouanalao and Le Pelican. The service and ambience are French, impeccably; the surroundings and weather are tropical, undoubtedly; and the two blend together, unmistakably St. Barts! Add the final ingredients of music and dancing at Le Must discotheque in Gustavia, La Frégate at Hotel PLM Saint-Jean, Le Jardin Samba-Flamands or Autour du Rocher at Lorient, a cognac at La Louisiane or the Maya in Public, a last coffee at La Banane Club or Le Fayette Club and one has the delicious combination of classic French or traditional Creole food, wine and dancing, brandy and breathtaking views. At last, these and the star-spangled sky together with amicable cosmpolitan company, lull the visitor into the arms of a tropical, velvet-skinned Morpheus.

Communications and Information

The telephone code for Saint Barthélémy is 27 and the island has two post offices in Gustavia and one in Lorient.

The town hospital lies on the corner of Rue Sadi Carnot and Rue Jean Bart, Tel: 27.60.00/27.60.35. The pharmacy telephone number is 27.61.82.

Police are on Tel: 27.66.66 and Gendarmerie on 12 or 27.60.12.

The nearest full Tourist Bureau is

on Guadeloupe but on Rue August-Nyman, Marie de Gustavia, there is the special Saint Barthélémy office, Tel: 27.60.88.

Taxis are best arranged from the airport as there are no taxi stands on the island. A Mini Moke or scooter can be hired from the center of Gustavia. Cars may be rented and service stations and garages can be found in the town or at the airport and at Lorient.

To and From the Island

Just 10 minutes flying time from St. Martin and one hour from Guadeloupe, there are many air links such as Air Guadeloupe and Windward Island Airways. Saint Barts has its own airline, Air St. Barthélémy, on Tel: 27.61.20. Air France links with services from Guadeloupe and Lufthansa links through San Juan with direct flights. Local flight arrivals are by Air Guadeloupe, American Airlines, Prinair, Crown Air, or Pan Am. St. Martin's airport is named

"Esperance," but Queen Juliana Airport in Dutch St. Maarten also serves the French "Quatier." Aeroport St. Jean is on Tel: 97 133.

CHAPTER XI

Martinique "Isle of Flowers"

Size and Location

Apart from its sister island, Guadeloupe, the isle of Martinique is the largest of all the Lesser Antilles islands. It has a total area of 417 square miles and is 50 miles long by about 21 miles wide.

Martinique is located in the Windward Islands and only Dominica separates it from the Leeward Islands and from Guadeloupe, 121 miles to the north. Its nearest neighbors are St. Lucia in the south and Dominica to the north, both about 50 miles away. Martinique is the farthest south of all the French islands of the West Indies and its capital is Fort-de-France, on the west coast.

Physical

Well in the tropics, at little farther north than 14 degrees latitude, Martinique consists of three groups of volcanoes. Gradually increasing in height from the south toward the north and gently sloping up from the coasts to the mountain peaks, Martinique's Mount Pelée, in the northwest, is the third highest summit in the Lesser Antilles. Pelée is 4,584 feet high and still an active volcano. The Carbet mountains peaking to nearly 4,000 feet lie northcenter of the island. In the south are the mountains of Vauclin at 1,654 feet and Diamant Peak at 1,400 feet high. The Plain of Lamentin is located in the middle of the island and all the foothills south of the plain are known locally as "mornes."

A number of rivers stream down from the steep mountain heights in the north. Most notable is the Lézarde River, 22 miles long, which emanates in the Pitons du Carbet and flows into the great Bay of Lamentin. Other rivers and streams cover the island's terrain and run either into the Atlantic Ocean on the east coast or the Caribbean Sea to the west. Many beautiful waterfalls are created by sheer mountain drops.

Other water sources, particularly in the Mount Pelée region, are sulphur and hot springs of volcanic origin.

The island of Martinique is shaped rather like an upraised boxing-glove with the "thumb" at its lowest point. The coast around the north and the west is quite regular except for the area around the Lamentin Bay, made up by the "thumb" and the "fist". From the large bay the rest of the island, especially the east coast, is indented and rugged. Many reefs and small islets lie off the island's southeast coast. Of great significance to this region are the trees of a petrified forest on the southernmost peninsula of the island.

Vegetation varies from tropical mountain rain forest to high cloud forest, from volcanic peaks and ravines with humid, dry forests and plains of scrub, thorn and cactus. Some coastal areas are swampy and ringed with mangroves, while others reach in to flat, agricultural plains or thick bamboo jungle. Generally green and verdant, with spectacular beaches and often luxuriant vegetation, it is no wonder that the Amer-Indians named this "The Land of Flowers."

Crater of Mount Pelé looms above shell of villa destroyed in 1902 eruption.

Climate

March is the driest month here, toward the end of the "Carême"—dry, January to April, season of Lent. The wettest month is November, toward the end of the wet period, from July to December—known locally as "Hivernage." Between 70 degrees F and 83 degrees F—21 degrees C–29 degrees C—almost year round, the rainy season consists mainly of short, violent showers that keep the air quite humid.

The trade winds cool the climate and refresh the hotter parts of the terrain running from the east and from the northeast alternately. These winds are known as "Les Alizes." The locals call the east coast the "Côte au Vent"—the Windy Coast—and the west, the "Côte sous le Vent." Tropical hurricanes can arrive between mid-July to mid-October.

Population

Approximately 345,000 people live on Martinique and these are divided by origin into six different mixes of races. The most important group to affect the island after the Amer-Indian Arawak and Carib races had been decimated were the white French colonists. Their descendants are now known as "Blanc-Pays" or "Békés"—whites born in Martinique. "Blancs-France" are the whites from the French mainland who are generally just visiting the island. The second major group is the black element, derived from slaves captured off the Benin Coast in Africa. Third, Chinese and Indian races are widespread due to the fact that their descendants replaced freed black slaves on the fields. The fourth group is made up of light-brown-skinned mulattoes—those of mixed blood. Fifth, a small number of Arab and Lebanese-derived races live on the island. The final group are those few remaining descendants of Carib and Arawak Indians, none of whom are considered of pure Amer-Indian blood. Martiniquaise, therefore, are a mixture of Negro, White, Indian, Chinese, Arab and, the largest group, Mulattoes—also known as Creole. Martinique is said to be home to some of the most beautiful women in the world—*c'est vrai*—judge for yourself!

Language

By far the largest ethnic group in Martinique is the Creole, or Mulattoes, and their dialect, a mixed language, is Creole, used quite extensively. French, however, is the official language of the island and English is understood in most of the more populous areas. Real Creole may be heard at folkloric performances and at those demonstrations of "Les Grands Ballets de la Martinique."

Holidays and Festivals

Carnival in Martinique is the culmination of many Saints' days and festivals. Starting on Sunday after Epiphany with a song competition and election of Carnival Queens, continuing into Monday with burlesque marriages, on Shrove Tuesday the Carnival reaches a climax with the burning of the effigy "Vaval," the Carnival King. This Mardi Gras is followed by Vendredi Saint, Good Friday; Pâques, Easter; and Fête du Travail, Labor Day (May 1). The local patron saint is commemorated be-

tween July and October, on Fêtes Patronales. Other holidays include: New Year's Day, Assumption (August 15), Armistice Day (November 11), Christmas Day and Easter Monday, Ascension and Whit Monday, Bastille Day (July 14), Schoelcher Day (July 21), All Saints' and All Souls' (November 1 and 2). Local events also include the "Tour de la Martinique" bicycle race of July; the semi-marathon in the first week in December; the Cultural Festival in July; the alternate "International Jazz and Popular Music Festival" in December with the "International Guitare Festival"; and the "Pro-Am International St. James Golf Tournament" in November.

History

"Madinina" was the Carib Indian name given to this green tropical island in the center of the Antilles. It meant "Isle of Flowers" and it was an apt word for such a colorful place. Some historians suggest that the name Martinique is a derivative of the Amer-Indian name. Certainly the tribes of both Arawak (180 A.D.) and Carib Indians (800 A.D.) were resident here for almost 1,500 years— first the sociable Saladoide-Arawaks and, much more recently, by the warlike cannibalistic Caribs. The Caribs slaughtered or drove out the Arawak settlers, retaining their women and fattening their male children for the pot. Indeed, one early map names the island "canibali." In the early

morning of November 3, 1493, just as he had sighted the island he named Dominica, Christopher Columbus noted, to south and west of his flagship, the Marie Galante, another large island. Although he may have had a choice on this, his second Caribbean voyage, as to which land to sail near, Columbus took the northernmost as he was anxious to reach his new colony in Hispaniola. He named the larger island after St. Martin, St. Martino, according to records. Some say it was named after Matins, the prayers that were being said on deck on that distant Sunday dawn.

For nine years Columbus was not to see the island again but, on an-

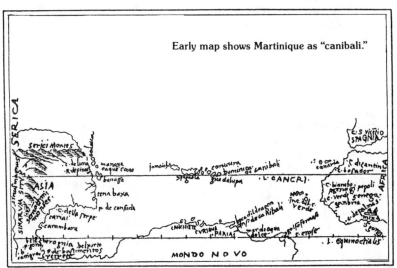

Early map shows Martinique as "canibali."

other Sunday, June 15, 1502, on his fourth voyage in the West Indies, he decided to make a landing. Both Columbus and the sailors of his large fleet were apprehensive. They had heard from Indians living in Santo Domingo, Hispaniola, that a fierce tribe of women-dominated Caribs lived on Madinina—a race of Amazons. The longboats pulled up on the beaches at Carbet on the northwest coast. Stunned by the scenery and clear air, Christopher Columbus wrote: ". . . the best, most fertile, sweetest and most charming land in all the world." No sooner had he written the words then a hail of Carib arrows drove his expedition party to their boats! They had spent only three days on the island.

Forgotten, except for the charts of Columbus's mapmaker, Juan de la Cosa, Martinique entertained few visitors, except Carib canoes for the next 120 years. During this time, maps showed the island variously as "Martinino" and "Martinique." Both Spanish and French sailors made use of the few coves around the island that were not plagued by Carib Indians, for replenishing supplies and evading detection by ships of enemy navies during these years. The enticing stories told by returning mariners about Martinique's attributes excited interest in the island.

In 1635, a party of 100 French settlers, under the leadership of Pierre Belain d'Esnambuc, arrived on the coast at the mouth of the Roxelane River. Here they built a fortress and began to plant crops. In the name of France and at the bidding of Cardinal Richelieu they claimed the island, even though they were forced to repel a band of 1,000 Carib warriors who attacked the encampment several months later. D'Esnambuc entreated the establishment of a full colony to his nephew, Jacques Dyel Du Parquet. Parquet governed the island of Martinique from January 20, 1637 until his death on January 3, 1658. During his period as governor, he had established Fort Royal in 1638 and introduced sugar cane to the island. At this time the Caribs occupied the east of Martinique while the colonists held the west. Dutch emigrées from Brazil tended the sugar cane fields and the island prospered for more than 100 years under French rule. All around was the sound of war between the French and the English, squabbling over colonies. In 1664, King Louis XIV assigned the island to Parquet's sons and in 1674 the land was annexed officially.

Wrecks, due to both hurricanes and ambush, occurred frequently around Martinique's coast. In 1636 a Spanish galleon, the "San Salvador," was wrecked on the way to Venezuela. In 1666 while pursuing five French vessels a great storm sank five British men o' war off the Bay of All Saintes. Another Spanish wreck occurred in the Baie du Galion and nearby Treasure Bay has its own tale to tell. English and French marine skirmishes rarely affected Martinique and both British and Dutch attempts to overrun the island right up to the beginning of the eighteenth century were repelled. The last, in the seventeenth century, was by the Dutch under the leadership of Ruyter, in 1674.

By 1667 Martinique had become the main French colony in the West Indies. For a while Guadeloupe was governed from St. Pierre, then the capital. Fort Royal became the official capital in 1680. Martinique soon became famous as one of the richest islands in the Lesser Antilles. The wealth came from extensive sugar plantations, initiated by the celebrated Dominican priest Père Labat. Coffee and cocoa also contributed to the economic boom. By the middle

Fort Royal today.

of the seventeenth century there was a total of 78,000 people living on Martinique, more than three-quarters of whom were black African slaves.

The age of pirates, privateers and corsairs brought its own colorful pattern of life to Martinique. Toward the end of the seventeenth century, Père Labat constructed a church at Macouba and in 1694 established the first distillery for rum on the island. Called "tafia" at the time, rum was a traditional attraction for seafarers of a type! Pirates such as the notorious

Captain Roberts made several forays on French shipping out of Martinique. In 1720 he captured a ship on which the governor of Martinique was taking passage. Without further ado, the pirate had the unfortunate governor strung up on the yard arm! Incensed by this outrage, the French took umbrage and declared war on the perpetrator. The following year, in defiance of the French navy, Roberts captured fourteen ships off the coast of Martinique, more or less blockading the port of Fort de France. To add insult to injury, Roberts flew a flag with the initials A.M.H. emblazoned across it. A. M. H. stood for "A Martiniquan's Head"! The full force of the French was brought to bear on the bands of sea-borne villians terrorizing Caribbean shipping. In 1723 the pirate Captain Edward Low was captured and he and his crew were executed in Fort Royal.

The legendary beauty of the Martinique women had not gone unnoticed by the French and particularly by King Louis XIV. A girl

named Françoise d'Aubigne, who spent part of her life in Le Prêcheur on Martinique's north coast, became Madame de Maintenon, Louis's second wife. Another woman, Aimée de Buc de Rivery, returning to her Martinique home from school in France, was captured by corsairs. Sold to the Grand Turk Abdul Hahmid, in Istanbul, she joined his harem and became the Sultana, giving birth to the future Emperor Mahmoud II.

Another Martinique claim to fame is that of Eugene de Beauharnis, who became Viceroy of Italy. Hortense, Queen of Holland, also came from the island.

Today a string of coastal fortress ruins bear testimony to the activities of the "brethren of the Coast." Throughout the eighteenth century the island was beleaguered by attacks if not from the pirates then from the English who attacked the capital in 1759 without success. A subsequent rally in 1762 gave Britain command of the city for nine months. Preferring the tropical climate of the West Indies to the cold of Canada, King Louis XV exchanged Martinique for the "Land of the Maple Leaf" at the Treaty of Paris in 1763.

By 1768 the government of the French Indies was established in Fort de France. The Company of the Indies, under Jean Baptiste Colbert, had quelled much of the privateering with his 30-strong fleet up until the War of American Independence. Insurgents of the war took refuge in Martinique and supplies from the island assisted the American forces. The French Revolution divided the allegiance of the islanders and the Count of Béhague took the Royalist side, while that of the Revolutionaries was led by the governor of Rochambeau. The Treaty of Whitehall by the Royalists, together with the English, put Britain once again in command of the island.

English occupation continued for eight years. In 1802, at the Treaty of Amiens, Martinique was returned to the French. Slavery, which had been abolished in 1794, was returned under the rule of Napoleon in the same year. Two years later Napoleon Bonaparte followed at least two influential admirers of the Martiniquaise beauty by marrying Marie Josephe Rose Tascher de la Pagerie, who had been born near Trois-Islets in 1763. The Creole girl became the Empress Josephine of France. In the Creole dialect the name of Fort Royal became "Fort Foyal," noting its mispronunciation, Napoleon changed it to Fort de France.

The battles between the English and French over Martinique and the French territories continued and in 1804 the English landed five cannon and 120 men on a pinnacle of rock off the island's southwest coast. From here, Commodore Sir Samuel Hood intended to blockade Fort de France and stop the passage of ships entering the harbor through the Fours Channel between the islet and the mainland. For nearly seventeen months the British held the 575-foot crag, known as Diamond Rock. The ship that supplied the islet was called H.M.S. Diamond Rock. Through the years the legend has been that the rock itself was given commission as a ship. Diamond Rock became known locally as H.M.S. Diamond Rock and the ships of the Royal Navy still salute the rock as they pass by. The French Commander Villeneuve, recaptured the rock for the French in a bloody battle in June 1805. He went on to lose one of Europe's most famous sea battles, Trafalgar.

Finally in 1815 Martinique was restored to the French and during the reign of Louis-Philip the preparations for abolition of slavery were drawn up. It was not until 1848 that Victor Schoelcher actively participated in

St. Pierre.

the enforcement of the bill and emancipation was finally attained. As a total of freed slaves exceeded 72,000, plantation owners resorted to taking on indentured workers from Asia to replace the workforce.

Always dogged by disasters, Martinique has suffered, during three-hundred-years of recorded history, thirty-three hurricanes, nine earthquakes and twelve tidal waves. The island has also survived three volcanic eruptions over the past three centuries. One of the worst earthquakes occurred in 1839 (the last hit the island in 1953). The cyclone of 1891 also devastated part of Martinique's coastal settlements but at the turn of the century it was the ominous peak of Mount Pelée (The Bald Mountain) which created one of the Caribbean's

worst natural catastrophies. On May 8 the volcanic plug in the 5,000-foot high mountain blew up in a series of explosions.

Apart from the island's subjection to a number of natural catastrophes, Martinique played no particularly significant role in world affairs. One-sixth of the population had been destroyed in the eruption of Mount Pelée and Fort-de-France remained as the island's largest city and its capital. In 1940 after the fall of France, Martinique became the depository for half-a-billion dollars' worth of Free French gold. On January 1, 1946, Martinique became a Départment of France and in 1974 the island became a fully fledged Region of France.

Trade, Industry and Economy

Although sugar production and the distilling of rum has been the traditional source of Martinique's income from the days of sugar cane introduction toward the end of the seven-

teenth century, tobacco, cotton, indigo, ginger and various spices had been cultivated there since 1635. Early in the eighteenth century, while sugar marched across the mountain

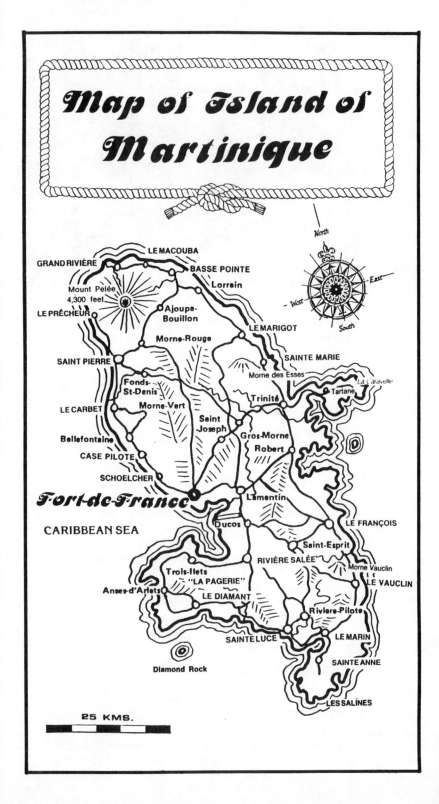

flanks of the island, an army captain was to be the first coffee planter in the Western Hemisphere. Captain Gabriel de Clieu brought to his Martinique home one coffee sapling from the greenhouse of King Louis XIV. From this experiment in the French West Indies, coffee spread through the New World. Cocoa was introduced at about the same time, but it was sugar that made Martinique's fortune.

The varied population of the island owes its mixture of races to the sugar trade. Up until the abolition of slavery in 1848, African laborers were shipped by the thousands to the French West Indies to work on the sugar plantations. No Caribbean island demonstrates more clearly the blending of races that the sugar industry brought to Martinique. In the north of the island where the majority of sugar plantations were located, the ratio of white "colons" to black slaves was minimal. Most of the white "Békés" lived in the south. Today, even though 90 percent of the population is black, one can still distinguish the trend toward a lighter skin and the evidence of more white people in the southern part of the island. The third and fourth elements in this melting pot of nationalities are the Indians and Chinese who were brought to work on the plantations when emancipation freed Martinique's 72,000 slaves.

The many political upheavals of the eighteenth and nineteenth centuries could not affect the firmly-rooted reliance of the country's economy in sugar. With Père Labat, the advent of "tafia" or local rum, made in Martinique's "Rhummeries," or distilleries, became a major by-product. In 1850 central sugar-processing factories were introduced by the small, family distilleries, like that at Beauséjour on the north coast, built in 1824. In 1958 there were 32 distilleries on the island. Today, sugar is the island's largest crop and more than 300,000 tons are produced annually. The majority of the sugar production goes into the making of Martinique's famous agricultural rum (more than two million gallons a year), three-quarters of which is exported. Famous brands of Martinique rum include Mauny Blanc and Vieux, named for a family that arrived from Normandy in 1749, and Clement, which produces Créole-Shrubb, Grappe Blanc Rum and a fifteen-year-old distillation. Because of the growing use of sugar beet as a European and North American source of sugar, the price of the commodity dropped drastically in the early part of this century. During the Second World War, because of the shortage of gasoline, many vehicles were run on rum! Production dwindled and the Martiniquaise sought an alternative export and another crop to keep the land-workers in employment. Bananas have become a mainstay in the island's economy since 1960 and today more than 150,000 tons are grown for export each year. Another important and indigenous crop, pineapples—or *ananas* to use the correct Carib Amerindian name for the fruit—take an important place in the agricultural production of Martinique. Approximately 15,000 tons are grown annually. Martinique has traditionally been a major source of pineapples for the European market and was one of the first fruits that the Spanish explorers presented at the Royal courts in the early sixteenth century.

Martinique has an essentially agricultural economy and its rich soil is no stranger to a variety of exotic and temperate fruits and vegetables. Most of the produce of the land—aubergines, avocadoes, tomatoes, green peppers and tropical flowers (115 tons)—go for export to the markets

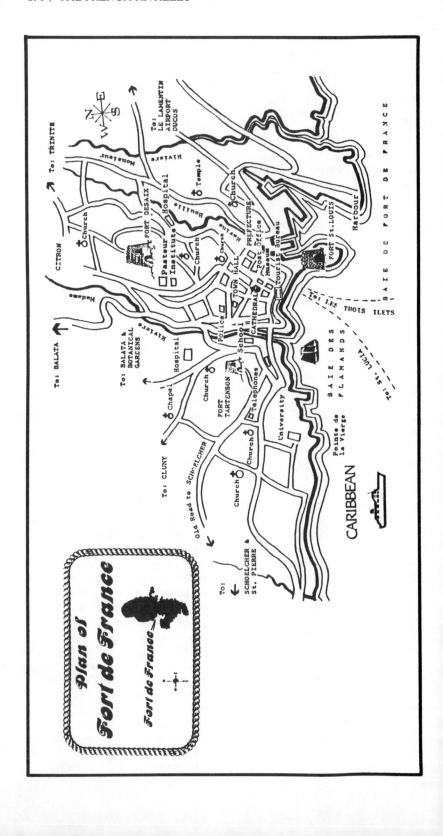

of Europe. Fishing is an important livelihood for a great number of Martiniquaise although beef, pork and chicken are raised for domestic consumption. Half of Martinique's population work on the land and many others work in the nine major distilleries or in administration, the oil refinery, the lumber industry, the cement factory or in the other dozen or so new projects being installed in the island to improve the economy.

Tourism is a major contributor toward the island's prosperity. Since the early 1960s Martinique has grown in leaps and bounds as one of the most popular destinations, not only in the Caribbean, but anywhere, as a tropical resort. With more than 50 hotels and over 2,000 rooms available, Martinique now attracts nearly a half million visitors a year from around the world.

Close-Up on Fort-de-France

Located on the north side of an excellent, wide bay of the same name, Fort-de-France commands its own deep harbor. Here, under the shadow of the Pitons du Carbet mountains, the sleepy, yet often bustling capital of Martinique, proudly flies the *Tricolore* flag of France against a tropical green backdrop.

This little corner of France was originally designed and laid out by the Count de Blénac as a commercial center in 1681. Named Fort Royal in 1638, this strategically-situated township evolved from the original fortified citadel now known as the Fort Saint-Louis, overlooking Carenage Bay. The fort had already withstood an attack by the Dutch in 1674 and its inhabitants also had survived the draining of mosquito-infested marshes close by the settlement.

Governor of the island, Jacques Dyel du Parquet, through perseverance got the Martinique colonists to accept the virtues of the outpost and from 1680 the official capital grew from its early Brazilian exiles to a town of more than 100,000. In 1681 the first Governor, Baas, moved his official residence to Fort Royal. Fort Boubon (Fort de la Convention or Fort Desaix) and Fort Tartenson were constructed to over-

look the town and protect it from marauders. From this date the town became the capital of the entire French Antilles and expanded rapidly.

Fort de France guards one of the best harbors in the entire Caribbean and for that reason soon became a center of trade. Notwithstanding constant attacks, hurricanes, earthquakes and fires, the town rapidly overspilled its borders, once delineated by the Rivière Madame, Rivière Monsieur and a former drainage ditch where General de Gale Boulevard runs. The earliest fire in Fort Royal occurred in 1671. In 1762 the British occupied the town and, during the Napoleonic era, Bonaparte renamed the township. Fort-de-France had variously been known as Fort-de-la-République, République-Ville and, during the French Revolution, the original name of Fort Royal was employed. Napoleon finally introduced the town's present name of Fort-de-France in 1801.

In 1839 a terrible earthquake damaged many houses and killed four hundred of the city's inhabitants. In 1890 a fire engulfed the entire settlement razing almost all the old wooden and stone buildings to the ground, followed by a hurricane the next year that brought down the cathedral's spire. Architect Henri Picq reconstructed the cathedral in 1895; its organ is a major attraction. By this time few old buildings were left in the city of Fort-de-France. Its sister town of Saint Pierre, with its classical architecture, fine theatres and boulevards, was Martinique's surviving example of grand French colonial buildings and public places.

Tragically, in 1902 when the total population of Martinique numbered just 178,000, the volcanic eruption of Mount Pelée destroyed Saint Pierre completely. At least 30,000 lives were lost in one of the worst natural disasters in history. Inside a few minutes Martinique lost what remained of its architectural heritage and also more than a sixth of its population. This dreadful calamity made Fort-de-France the country's only town of any significance. The population of Fort-de-France at the time of the eruption totalled just 10,000; in 35 years it had grown to four times the size.

By far the most central part of the city is La Savane, a large park shaded by royal palms, decorated with ornamental gardens and exotic flowerbeds. Near the ferry landing the park is a promenade, marketplace and center for events. La Savane is surrounded by cafés and hotels and has its own interesting sights. To the north of the square is the famous statue of Empress Josephine. Carved in white, Carrara marble, Napoleon's wife is depicted in the contemporary Empire dress which she wore at her wedding to the first Napoleon at the Notre Dame in Paris. Josephine faces out across the harbor to Trois Islets, where she was born; the statue was created by the sculptor Vital Dubray. Below her the green grass of La Savane rolls out like a verdant carpet across to the monument to the war dead on the south side and the bronze statue to

the city's founder, Belain d'Esnambuc. Esnambuc shades his eyes to look out across Fort St. Louis (special permission needed for visits to all Martinique's forts) and the sloops riding at anchor in the harbor. Around the square, police in khaki, instead of blue uniforms, direct the bustling rush-hour traffic.

Behind the green Savane, the Rue de la Liberté holds several sites of interest. Along Alfassa, fronting the Bay of Flamands, the corner building on Rue de la Liberté houses the Tourist Information Office and Air France. Walk along the street beside the park and one comes to the Musée Départmental de Martinique with its exhibits of early Arawak and Carib history, slavery, the costumes of the island and typical furniture. On past the post office the most notable building (and probably the most remarkable edifice in the Caribbean) is the Schoelcher Library. Named after the champion of emancipation, this structure was erected at the 1889 Exposition in Paris and then removed here. It contains relics from Martinique's history and was built by Henri Picq

La Pagerie, birthplace of Napoleon's wife, Josephine.

who also built the six-times-reconstructed cathedral, Saint Louis, just behind the post office on Place Labat.

Some of Martinique's finest shopping precincts are located near the cathedral which, with its earthquake-proof, steel-supported, 197-foot high spire, has recently been restored. Down on Pointe Simon, near the Rivière Madame, is the vegetable market with its bewildering variety of produce but, if you think the colors and selection here are breathtaking, try naming the varieties of tropical fish and shellfish at the fish market, north along the side of the canal. On the way to the fish market you will pass a bridge and then the footbridge made of stone over the Rivière Madame or, really, the Levassor River. This side of the canal is known as Boulevard Allègre and in this stretch of water the first design for the propeller, invented by Martiniquais Gilbert Canque, was tested. Note all the colorful fishing boats, now with their new outboard engines. These open boats are known as "gommiers," after the special type of wood. Once there were only black gondolas on the canal.

In front of the fish market is Place Cemenceau and, to the left, is Place Jose Martí (named after the famous Cuban hero) and farther on is the beautiful floral park. Although the city extends much farther north, also farther west from the canal, there is little of tourist interest except, with permission to visit, the two forts of Desaix and Gerbault, several small churches and the sports stadium. It is really in and around the port, the old city center and the canal that one views the city proper. Back toward the Savane one takes the pretty Boulevard du General de Gaulle past the Cultural and Administrative Center and the Hotel de Ville on the right to turn into the Rue de la République

and follow it down to the Palais de Justice on the left. Behind the law courts is a statue of Victor Schoelcher, the emancipation champion, in a neat garden. Continuing along past the law courts, the school on the right and the National Police Station on the left, one comes again to the front of the Schoelcher Library, the large building to the right of which, is the Prefecture.

Continue down Avenue des Caribes, alongside the Savane, past the residence of the consul general to the left, and one is again on the portside facing the yacht club and the quay. Just for the sheer exhilaration of the quarter-of-an-hour ferry-ride across from the city to Pointe du Bout, near Les Trois Ilets, one should take this regular service across Fort-de-France Bay. There are several small hotels and an 18-hole golf course, a tourist center and a marina at the Pointe.

One other excursion from Fort-de-France which is a must is to take the route to Didier, where one turns off up a road bounded by tropical woods and ferns, through Ravine Touza. Note the colonial-style mansions, colorful flowerbeds and fretwork verandas toward La Trace. Wonderful panoramic views of the city spread out behind as the road winds upwards. At Didier there is a mineral spring. You will see glimpses of your destination, tantalizingly through the luxuriant roadside growth. In a magical setting, surrounded by the palm-clad slopes of the Pitons de Carbet, Balata Church, modeled on Sacré Coeur in Paris, stunningly magnificent in its tropical environment, was built by Wulfleff in 1928. The Balata botanical park, Jardin de Balata, is named after the Carib word for a rare native tree. Here, after a breathtaking forest walk, one can purchase gifts of anthuriums and other spectacular tropical flowers.

Discovering the Island

The two contrasts of the island—the lush, green-forested north and the silver-gold of the southern savannah—are both set off by its turquoise seas. There are generally five suggested tours of the island of Martinique and, as all roads lead eventually to the capital, it is best to use the city as a departure and arrival point. Many organized tours can be joined in Fort-de-France or one can hire transport for any of the following seven suggested tours. It is recommended to take one's time and drink in the local ambience, the clean, fresh air, the tropical richness of Martinique's scenery and the overall *joie de vivre*. Just to listen to a conversation in the local market or cafe reveals the underlying and sometimes effervescent *bonhomie*. "Pa ni problem"—No problem—is as commonly overheard an expression as the words "mon cher" or "ma chère"—'my dear'—added to almost every conversation, demonstrating the happy, relaxed nature of a people who live in such idyllic surroundings.

On land, the island of Martinique is fascinating and crammed to its very nooks and crannies with serendipity—an unexpected delight, discovered purely by chance. Around the coast, the waters of this green and verdant island offer a host of unequalled experiences. Most ports, harbors and resorts are geared up for every waterborn and sub-marine enjoyment. Above the waves ketches of 14 metres, catamarans of up to 20 metres, sloops and the locally named *goelettes* can be hired from the main charter company at Port du Marin. Association Martinique Charter has about 25 sailing vessels for lease, rent, hire, with or without a crew.

Motorized launches, specialist deep-sea fishing craft, motor yachts, custom-designed 100-person cruise-party launches and fully-crewed sailboats are all available.

Why not experience the spectacular flora and fauna of the coral depths from the comfort of a glass-bottom boat or an unforgettable journey in an aquascope, right in among the fishes, sponges and corals?

Underwater provisions are also made for the amateur and professional diver, scuba, snorkeler or reef-drifter. Pro-trainers and guides are on call and most resort pools have an attendant diving instructor. Wreck diving, reef diving, night dives and fishing dives are a speciality of Martinique's ocean-orientated coastline. Is it any wonder that reviewers refer to Martinique as the St. Tropez of the West Indies and its capital as Paris in the Caribbean?

Route Excursion I. Fort-de-France to Basse-Pointe

The surroundings of Fort-de-France, as one takes the first tour out of the capital to the north, are quite breathtaking. Views from the plateau of Didier show the extent of the town and its large bay. The road sweeps around Fort-de-France to near the coastline at the Naval School, from where the built-up area continues on to the fishing village of Schoelcher, its university and nearby beach of Anse Collat. Fond-Lahaye is the next little settlement before Case Pilote, named for a chief of the Carib Indians who lived here. Case Pilote has an interesting Jesuit, Baroque-style, eighteenth-century church. The next village boasts an excellent viewing point in Panarame Verrier. Set on a cliff, Bellfontaine is a village of fishermen and is just around the point from Fond-Capot where the tomb of

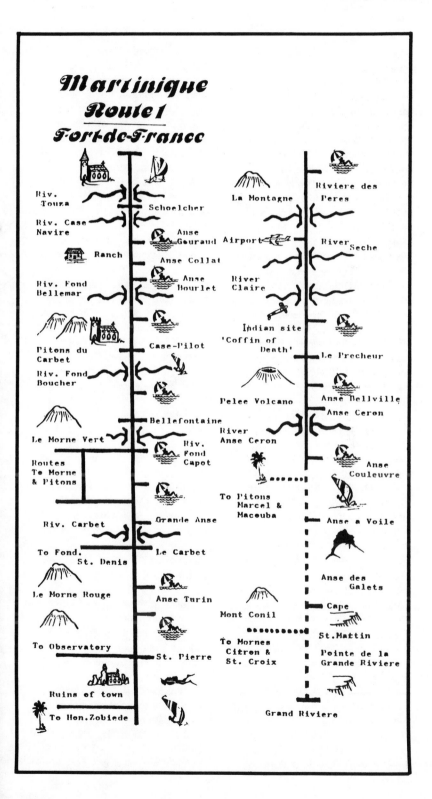

Martinique
Route 1
Fort-de-France

Riv. Touza

Schoelcher

Riv. Case Navire

Ranch

Anse Gouraud — Airport

Anse Collat

Riv. Fond Bellemar

Anse Bourlet — River Claire

Pitons du Carbet

Case-Pilot — Indian site 'Coffin of Death'

Riv. Fond Boucher

Pelee Volcano

Bellefontaine

Le Morne Vert

Riv. Fond Capot — River Anse Ceron

Routes To Morne & Pitons

To Pitons Marcel & Macouba

Grande Anse

Riv. Carbet

Le Carbet

To Fond. St. Denis

Le Morne Rouge

Anse Turin — Mont Conil

To Observatory — To Mornes Citron & St. Croix

St. Pierre

Ruins of town

To Hon. Zobiede

La Montagne — Riviere des Peres

River Seche

Le Precheur

Anse Bellville
Anse Ceron

Anse Couleuvre

Anse a Voile

Anse des Galets

Cape

St. Martin
Pointe de la Grande Riviere

Grand Riviere

Governor Bass lies.

Either from here or from Bellefontaine or from Le Carbet itself, farther on, one can take a short excursion into the Pitons du Carbet, the mountains that dominate the northern part of the island. Morne Vert (Green Mountain) is well worth a visit and it is not for nothing that the region is known as "Petite Suisse" (Little Switzerland). Plantation Lajus is to be seen en route. About 1,300 feet high, from Morne Vert one can see across to even higher peaks like Morne Rouge (Red Mountain). Down on the coast, Le Carbet has several attractions. First, it is the location of Christopher Columbus's first landing on the beaches here; second, the first settlers, under the command of Belain d'Esnambuc, landed here in 1635; third, the famous painter Gauguin spent about four months here developing his distinctive style of portraying vivid tropical hues. The Gauguin Museum here shows some paintings executed by the artist during his visit in 1887 to Anse Turin. A resort center, Latitude, is located toward one end of the village and the Bally Rhum distillery is nearby. Carbet has Martinique's only Olympic-size swimming pool, built on the hillside.

From Le Carbet one rounds the point to visit one of the island's major tourist attractions. Often referred to as the Pompeii of the Caribbean, Saint Pierre is the site of one of the world's most awful natural disasters. Erupting suddenly on May 8 (Ascension Day), 1902, at 2 minutes past 8, Mount Pelée hurled a fireball of gas and ashes down its slopes onto the lazing port town of St. Pierre. Once renowned worldwide as the Paris of the Antilles because of its spectacular architecture, classic public buildings and beautiful boulevards, the entire town was engulfed and razed within three minutes. The 30,000 inhabitants of the city (which was then the central township of the island) and its surrounds were destroyed in the holocaust. Several ships in the harbor were set on fire by the giant lumps of molten lava thrown high into the air and a pillar one thusand feet high of ash and rock rose as a monument to the disaster. The mountain had increased in size from about 5,000 feet to 6,000 feet. Subsequent eruptions occurred on a minor scale in 1929 and 1932. Today Mount Pelée is just 4,584 feet high. A tidal wave followed the explosion, sinking the remaining seventeen ships at anchor but the vessel "Roddam," a British cargo steamer, sailed like a fire ship to the nearby isle of St. Lucia. Just one survivor, Auguste Ciparis, was saved by the walls of his jail. The stevedore had been imprisoned for creating a disturbance and he went on to join Barnum's circus as a sideshow. The celebrated local poet, Lafcadio Hearn, describes the catastrophe thus: "Mount Pelée . . . the cloud-herder, lightning forger and rainmaker . . . drawing to itself all the white vapours of the land—robbing lesser eminences of their shoulder-wraps and head coverings." The Frank Perret Volcanological Museum, just near the rebuilt cathedral on Rue Victor Hugo, displays relics from the disaster including implements welded together by the super-heated firestorm. Perret studied the volcano from 1929–1943 and his statue stands near the entrance to the resurrected town. Other places of interest are the ruins of the grand theatre, built on the designs of that in Bordeaux; Ciparis's dungeon, the remains of the 1640 fort's church (Martinique's first church) and a monument to Belain d'Esnambuc, who constructed the fort in the late 1630s. On the outskirts of the Quatier du Fort is the 1766 stone bridge. Only just over 6,600 people now live in the once-proud city.

Skirting the lava-clad slopes of Mount Pelée and keeping along the coastal route, you cross two rivers, Sèche and Chaude. A little farther on is the group of limestone hills known as the Coffres-à-Morts (Coffin of Death) where Carib Indians in the seventeenth-century were supposed to have hurled themselves from cliffs in order to escape persecution by the colonists. They were supposed to have invoked the wrath of Mount Pelée on their attackers. From the "Tomb of the Caribs" the black, volcanic-sanded beach is called Anse Céron; this is the nearest beach to the westernmost village on the island, Le Prêcheur. It was from here that Francois d'Aubigne set out after many years as an island girl, to become Madame de Maintenon, second wife of Louis XIV. The first curate here, Father Dutertre, wrote his "General History of the Antilles" in the seventeenth century. From here on the track becomes narrow and almost impassable just after the village's eighteenth-century church, Anse Belleville, Anse Céron and many hot springs. Le Precheur is one of Martinique's oldest settlements and therefore displays a monument to Jacques Dyel du Parquet, one of the island's earliest colonizers. Without attempting the tortuous trail north to Grand Rivière one has to back-track to Saint Pierre and follow the south face of Mr. Pelee.

From St. Pierre one takes the road out to Morne Rouge. Keeping Pelee's peak to your left, the route leads up to the village of Morne Rouge which is the most accessible point from which to tackle the hour-long, tough climb to the volcano's summit. The village itself is not old as its original structures were destroyed in the volcanic eruption of 1902. Well-known for its pineapple cultivation, Morne Rouge also produces bottled mineral water from a hot spring. The village itself is 1,475 feet above sea level but it is another tiring 3,000 or-so feet to the fern-covered, twin domes inside the crater lip. Care should be taken scaling the peak and a guide is needed. Note the black snail shells underfoot and the great lumps of cooled lava rock scattered across the scree slopes. The smell of sulphur is ever-present reminder that this "lion" is just sleeping! An observatory on Morne des Cadets monitors its every snore. The road to the north continues through verdant tropical rain forest to Ajoupa Bouillon, a village noted for its nearby canyons known as the "Gorges de la Falaise" on the river of the same name. A spectacularly beautiful waterfall can be reached just up one of the mini-canyons. Ajoupa Bouillon dates back to the seventeenth century and it has a church still standing, built in 1848. Continuing from the tiny village, toward the coast, the right fork should be taken along the shoreline to the little settlement of Basse-Pointe.

A ruined sugar plantation house and factory, Habitation Capot, heralds fields of cane, banana groves and pineapple plots before the village of Basse-Pointe. Look for the lane leading to the Leyritz Plantation mansion, now a restaurant and doll museum, housing interesting objects made from sugar cane stalks and pineapple fibers. The next village is Macouba, surrounded by coffee, banana and tobacco plantations and noted for the tiny, clifftop church where Père Labat sojourned in the seventeenth century. Here also is the rum distillery of JM Crassous de Medeuil. Limestone caverns near here housed Carib Indians in pre-Columbian times.

The northernmost township on Martinique is Grand-Riviere. From here, on a clear day, one can see the island of Dominica in the far distance.

One of the prettiest of all the island's fishing villages, Grand-Riviere's beach is lined with colorful "gommieres," or fishing boats with their blade-like keels. These boats are made from the local gum tree, or gommier, and here the village boys emulate their elders by carving surfboards out of balsa trunks (langue de boeuf) and riding the waves where Atlantic waters meet those of the Caribbean. From Fort-de-France to Grande-Riviere, on this route, could take a full day.

Route Excursion 2. Fort-de-France to Caravelle

Running around the highlands of the Pitons du Carbet is the attractive route bisecting the island and linking Fort-de-France with the eastern coastline. Taking the Ravine Vilaine road out of the capital one is quickly submerged in a sea of green ferns and dense tropical foliage that tower over the winding road. The first small settlement to be reached is St. Joseph, a village noted for its fine agricultural produce. Gros Morne is the next township and, built on a hilltop, this is another noted agricultural center with its fields of pineapple looking like a spiny carpet. Just before Gros Morne one could take the left fork that leads up to Morne de Esses (known for its basket-weaving) and on to the northeast coast near Marigot. La Philippe Forest can be visited near here. However, continuing east, the road reaches the coast at Trinité, about halfway down the eastern flank of the island. It is here that one has a quandary, whether to travel north or south along this fine rugged coastline.

Route Excursion 3. Le Lorrain to Saint Anne

A guided tour on paper may probably solve the dilemma if one reads an account of what can be expected

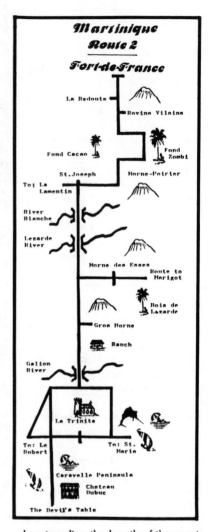

when traveling the length of the coast from Baie Grande Anse and Le Lorrain in the north to the Petrified Forest and Sainte Anne in the south. Noted for its spectacular scenery and being the site of pre-Columbian settlements, Le Lorrain is just south of the beautiful bay of Grande Anse and has its own expansive beach. Swimming is not recommended as the tide on the east coast can be most treacherous. At Le Marigot (town of flowers), a little farther around the point the bay of Anse Charpentier has a wide sandy beach and the township faces the sea on the hillside

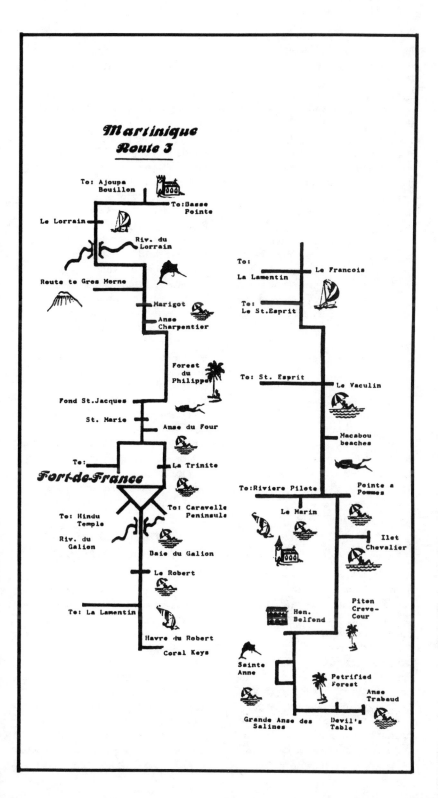

Martinique
Route 3

To: Ajoupa Bouillon
To: Basse Pointe
Le Lorrain
Riv. du Lorrain
Route to Gros Morne
Marigot
Anse Charpentier
Forest du Philippe
Fond St.Jacques
St. Marie
Anse du Four
Fort-de-France
To:
La Trinite
To: Hindu Temple
Riv. du Galion
To: Caravelle Peninsula
Baie du Galion
Le Robert
To: La Lamentin
Havre du Robert
Coral Keys

To: La Lamentin
Le Francois
To: Le St.Esprit
To: St. Esprit
Le Vaculin
Macabou beaches
To: Riviere Pilete
Pointe a Pommes
Le Marin
Ilet Chevalier
Hen. Belfend
Piten Creve-Cour
Sainte Anne
Petrified Forest
Anse Trabaud
Grande Anse des Salines
Devil's Table

like an amphitheatre. Farther south, the Center of Indian Studies is housed in an ancient sugar mill, part of the monastery of Fond St. Jacques. This old Dominican monastery (founded by Père Labat in 1658 and rebuilt in 1769) stands alone before you reach the town of Sainte Marie, site of the Rum Museum set up by the Saint James distillery. The church here was built in about 1850 and the island you will see in the bay can sometimes be reached by a causeway.

La Trinité stands at the root of the rugged eight-mile-long Caravelle Peninsula on the Bay of Havre de la Trinité. The town is one of the island's two "sous-prefectures" (political divisions) and guards the road out along the jutting peninsular to Tartane, Madras, Treasure Bay, Baie du Galion and Baie Grandjean. On Pointe du Diable (Devil's Point) there are marvelous views and an 1861 lighthouse. See Chateau Dubuc before returning to the mainland and continuing south to Robert. Famous for fish-breeding and stunning scenery, the little town of Le Robert commands an excellent site overlooking a bay full of tiny islets.

Cutting across a promontory, the road carries on south to the village of Le Francois, which is also a coastal community with tiny islands and a reputation for fishing and growing vegetables, in fields irrigated by water from the Manzo Dam, and the Clement distillery famed for its dark rum. Another agriculture center, Saint-Esprit, lies just inland from Francois.

Follow the route along the indented coastline and one can relax over a fresh fish dish at one of the restaurants at Vauclin. The fishing boats make excellent fodder for the photographer and the popularity of the nearby beach of Anse Macabou endorses Vauclin's claim to be the capital of the south. Try snorkeling over

"Josephine's Bath," a shallow, sandy sea pool. From here the road heads inland from the coast toward Marin on the south coast. The vegetation here is strikingly different from the lush tropical rain forests of the north, almost desert-like, the landscape is complemented by the south's gift of numerous attractive beaches. Le Marin is the other sous-prefecture and the site of an interesting (1766) Jesuit church with an altar taken from the wreck of a Spanish galleon. Farther along the Cap Chevalier (cape) and following the Cul-de-Sac du Marin (sea's dead end) one reaches Sainte Anne, the island's most southerly village. White beaches, the famous Les Salines resort and Les Boucaniers bay, all go to making Ste. Anne one of the most attractive areas on the whole of Martinique. Nearby is the Petrified Forest, an expanse of trees-turned-to-stone. Jasper and other semiprecious stones can be found among the stone tree trunks and calcified branches. The Savane des Petrifications is one of few anywhere in the world. There is a large lagoon worth visiting near Pointe des Salines. Sheltered by coco palms, the beaches around it are among the most delightful in the West Indies.

Route Excursion 4. Fort-de-France to Diamond Rock

All roads in Martinique lead to Fort-de-France and it is from the capital again that one takes the south coast route, which encompasses the southwest corner of the island. For many visitors the first section of the road will seem familiar as the auto route is the freeway to Lamentin Airport. Just under four miles from the city center, the town of Le Lamentin is more of an industrial area and sports its own race track. The refinery of California is located on the town's

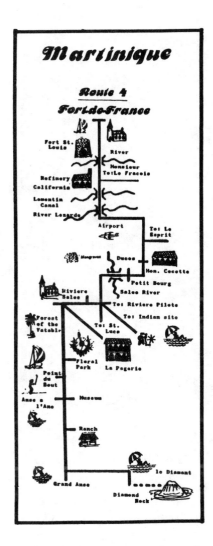

Martinique

Route 4

Fort-de-France

Fort St. Louis

Monsieur River
To: Le Francois

Refinery
California

Lamentin Canal

River Lezards

Airport

To: Le Esprit

Mangrove

Ducos

Hon. Cocotte

Petit Bourg

Salee River

Riviere Salee

To: Riviere Pilote

To: Indian site

Forest of the Vatable

To: St. Luce

Floral Park

La Pagerie

Point du Bout

Museum

Anse a l'Ane

Ranch

le Diamant

Grand Anse

Diamond Rock

After more sugar cane fields one comes to an attraction that has drawn many famous people to this part of this small Caribbean island. This is Trois Ilets, named after the isles in the bay off Pointe-aux-Pères. This is the birthplace of Napoleon Bonaparte's famous Josephine. Born at La Pagerie on the grounds of a sugar estate on June 23, 1763, her marriage to Napoleon in Paris on March 3, 1796, was predicted by her "quimbois" or local soothsayer. Named Marie-Joseph Rose Tacher de la Pagerie, she first married the island governor's son, Viscount Alexandre de Beau-harnais, in 1779; she later wedded the Emperor who, in 1809, divorced her as she produced no heir. The Martinique lass who rose to the highest of heights from such humble beginnings, sadly died at Malmaison in France in 1814. The Museum de la Pagerie contains many interesting antiques and artifacts including a love letter from Napoleon himself. The museum is Josephine's birthplace and the curator lives nearby. Nearby also are the ruins of the once-grand sugar estate house and factory. Maybe you would like to relax and play a round on the Empress Josephine Golf Course in the setting of Trois Ilet's Floral Gardens? Pointe du Bout resort, together with Trois Ilets, may be visited by boat from Fort-de-France harbor on day tours—a much more exciting and romantic method of glimpsing the intimacies of the eighteenth century at the Pagerie Museum and strolling in the beautiful grounds of the old sugar estate. Around the point from Trois Ilets is the pretty little fishing village of Les Anse d'Arlets. The Shell Museum with some fascinating exhibits near here should be visited as should its excellent beach.

Farther on past another point and up a steep narrow track, is the village of Le Diamant and for almost the

outskirts. Acres of sugar fields assail the eye after passing through Lamentin and the road continues on to the agricultural settlement of Ducos. Still quite a way inland, the country route crosses the plains of Riviere Salee toward the town of the same name. A bird sanctuary is located near the mouth of the River Salee where it enters the Baie de Genipa. From the little town the road cuts off due west if one avoids taking the turns to Riviere-Pilote or Sainte-Luce.

whole coastal route you will see the celebrated Diamond Rock standing lone and proud almost 600 feet high in the ocean bay. Just little more than two miles away the rock has a curious history, once having been officially dubbed "H.M.S. Diamond Rock" after the boat that supplied the 120 sailors who used the pinnacle as a fortress from which to lay siege to French trading ships. Today it is a haven for numerous varieties of sea birds. At Le Diamant itself, down in the cove, there is an ancient mill near the grand Gaoule Mansion.

Two other locations in the south of Martinique that should not be missed and can be reached after visiting Diamant or Rivière Salee are Sainte-Luce, on the south coast and Rivière-Pilote just a little way inland. Sainte-Luce is a fishing village known especially for its white sand beaches and the mahogany, locust and gum trees of the Montravail Forest nearby. Carib rock engravings, petrographs, can be seen here and the Saint Lucia canal is a popular resort spot. Rivière-Pilote is an agricultural township with rich soil surrounded by tropical vegetation similar to that found in the north of the island. The Mauny Rhum Distillery is situated near here and there is a private zoo at the Lescouet house. The giant rocks and slabs near the town are the result of ancient seismic action and, for a bit of action in more modern times, you might wish to visit one of the cock-fighting pits nearby. Both cock fights and mongoose/pit viper fights are very common in this area. Other well-known pits are at Morne Rouge and Quartier Bac

Route Excursion 5. "La Trace"

One of the most popular routes is that known as La Trace. This road cuts through the island from Fort-de-France in the South, up to Le Morne Rouge in the shadow of Mount Pelee. Running inland from the coastal Fort-de-France/St. Pierre route, this road crosses the beautiful Pitons du Carbet. Passing the domes of Balata Church and its botanical gardens, one climbs high into the rain-forested slopes of the mountains past the mineral springs of Absalom on to the woods of Donis. Here, giant ferns loom above the road, dwarfed only by the even taller branches of tropical trees of bewildering variety and color. The Maison de Foret stands on the edge of this thickly wooded region, just before the Floral Plantation of Nuages. Actually getting to the three-and-a-half thousand foot-high peaks of the Pitons du Trace means a stiff walk and one should beware of poisonous snakes, although the islanders imported the mongoose to eradicate the venomous pit viper, or Fer-de-Lance. Mongoose can often be seen darting across a road or disappearing into a gully or into the undergrowth like squirrels.

The peaks that can be scaled with the help of a guide are Piton Boucher, Piton de l'Alma, Piton Daumaze and the highest, at 3,924 feet, Piton Lacroix. These mountains lie to the left of the road, which rises to around 2,000 feet. Emerging at Deaux Choux (Two Cabbages), this is a crossroads where one can turn left to Fond-Saint-Denis on the road to St. Pierre or, to the right, one can take a scenic route to La Trinité, and the Atlantic coast. The Route de la Trace, however, continues through more rain forest to the very slopes of Mount Pelee at Morne Rouge.

Although divided here into about four day trips from Fort-de-France, it is popular to take six or seven shorter routes of a half-day duration each. Route maps may be obtained from the Tourist Bureau and car rental agencies. (Note: Information on Mount Pelee is best obtained from officials and guides.)

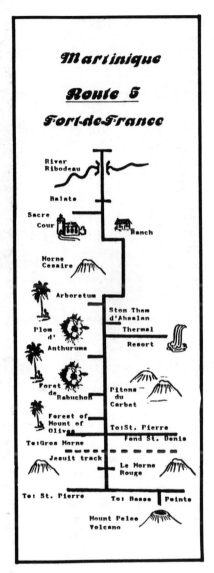

St. Pierre.

Wildlife

Martinique is first and foremost the island of flowers—Madanina. Its wildlife, however, has its own special interest and beauty. Apart from those islands where crocodile, alligator or cayman occur (Martinique has none of these) the only other dangerous species of the Caribbean is snakes. It is only in the Lesser Antilles where one finds venomous reptiles and then only on Martinique and St. Lucia. On Martinique, particularly in banana plantations and the sugar fields, the fer-de-lance or pit viper may be encountered. This snake has a bite that is highly toxic and undergrowth where the viper might roam should be avoided. In 1893, in order to reduce the number of snakes and protect the workers on the plantations, the government introduced the mongoose from the Asian continent. These furry creatures, rather like little racoons or squirrels, multiplied quickly; not all their meat was viper

steak—mongoose love hen's eggs! The mongoose is often seen in the country lanes and footpaths and has done much to cull the snake population. Viper fights, in a pit similar to that of a cockpit, where the serpents are set against the mongoose, are a common form of entertainment in rural areas.

The mongoose, however, is now considered something of a pest, especially with farmers, smallholders and wildlife conservationists. The small rodents have decimated some quite rare species of wildlife, particularly birdlife, lizards and the indigenous iguana. Manicous, a variety of opossum, are still to be seen in country regions as are some alarmingly large varieties of spiders.

In 1776, the British botanist Alexander Anderson, who did so much for the plant life of nearby St. Vincent, was captured by privateers as he was fleeing to Suriname. He was

A mongoose.

imprisoned for a while on this lush island, escaping eventually to St. Lucia.

The island's most prolific wildlife is its vegetation, ranging from dense, damp, tropical rain forest, to arid, cactus and scrub-covered limestone outcrops. The giant ferns and bamboo of the jungle regions are as spectacular as the towering cacti of the south or the stone forest where fossilized trunks lie as evidence of some geological action millions of years ago. Palms of numerous shapes and sizes, mahogany and gum trees, fruit trees and balsa-wood trees complement the stunning variety of lianas, bromeliads and creepers. Not for nothing has Martinique been known as the Island of Flowers ever since pre-Columbian days. The profusion of orchids, frangipani, oleanders, hibiscus and bougainvillea makes the countryside and little village roadsides a riot of color. Even the trees burst into the most magnificent blooms, such as the flame and tulip trees; if not, they are often laden with fruit like mango, paw-paw or avocado. Beware, however, not to stand under or touch any part of the mancineel tree, which may offer shelter during rainstorms. The sap, diluted in rainwater during a tropical shower, can burn the skin severely.

Under the seas around Martinique the color and profusion is even more abundant and corals, gorgonias, sea fans, sponges and marine plants offer shelter for a bewildering array of tropical fish, crustaceans and mammals such as the amphibious turtle and the dolphin. Game fish abound in both the waters of the Caribbean and the Atlantic. Kingfish, tuna, sailfish, marlin and barracuda are plentiful and fishing excursions can be organized from the many ports around Martinique's coast. A particularly popular region for discovering marine wildlife at ease and in a beautiful setting are the islets off the southeast coast, like at Le Robert. Seabird study could demand no better location than the Diamond Rock off the south coast and many cliffs on the Atlantic shores provide shelter for a variety of migratory birds. The Martinique parks and gardens system is organized through the Parc Naturel Régional de la Martinique in Fort-de-France. There are set areas of national parkland, botanical gardens and points of wildlife and natural interest that are overseen by this body and maps are provided through the Tourism Bureau.

Shopping

The rum of Martinique is held in high esteem by connoisseurs, from the light, young, variety known as Jeune Acajou, to the dark mahogany of Vieux Acajou. Bally and Clément distilleries make a fine twelve-year-old rum like a liquer and a clear, white version is made by Dillon. La Mauny is a favorite purchase, as are the rums made in the Saint James distillery at Sainte-Marie or that of Duquesne in Fort-de-France. In Sainte-Luce the Trois Rivières distillery makes an exceptional variety of Martinique "gold" rum; another is distilled at Gros-Morne (Saint Etienne) and yet another variety at Le Lamentin, known as La Favorite. In Fort-de-France there is another type distillery, Rhum Bernus. Together with this wide selection of spirits, the island's shops stock many of the world's liquors and the most exquisite of French perfumes and scents.

Duty-free stores sell a host of imported items from cameras to jewelry and from the high fashions of the European continent to fine porcelain. The best shops are to be found in Fort-de-France and especially in the streets Lamartine, Victor Hugo, Victor Schoelcher, Antoine Siger, Moreau de Jones and Rue Liberté. Although many stores stock international goods, many smaller boutiques and precincts display locally made items.

Handmade souvenirs include Carib basketware from Ste-Marie, Créole jewelry, tortoise-shell items (which some countries ban importing), printed head-scarves and wraps, conch shells and tapestry work, paintings in gaudy colors of local scenes, dolls dressed in the national Madras costume and music in the form of folk records. Sculptures in mahogany and other precious woods are very popular with visitors as are the ceramic articles, hand-turned and intricately decorated, bamboo and straw-work, as well as local flowers.

Banking

The banks on Martinique are all in the capital, Fort-de-France.

Banque Francaise Commerciale, 6–10 Rue Ernest Deproge, Tel: 63.82.57
Credit Agricole Mutuel, Rue Ernest Deproge, Tel: 70.01.92
Chase Manhattan Bank, Place Monseigneur Romero, Tel: 60.24.24

Banque National de Paris, Avenue des Caribes, Tel: 73.71.11
Societe General des Banques, Rue de la Liberté, Tel: 71.69.83
Banque des Antilles Francaise, 34 Rue Lamartine, Tel: 73.93.44
Credit Martiniquais, Rue de la Liberté, Tel: 70.12.40

Churches

Roman Catholicism is the official religion on Martinique and there are two cathedrals on the island. There are also two Benedictine monasteries, temples for the Indian community, a synagogue, churches of the Greek Orthodox and Baptist religions, and several Evangelical missions.

Hotels on Martinique

The period from late April to mid-December is known in Martinique as the "Season of Sweet Savings" and hotel prices can be as much as half the "high season" tarif. French hotels in the Antilles generally meet the high standards demanded by international travelers and service is often more than adequate. Five hotels offer meeting facilities and others are available at the Centre Martiniquais d'Animation Culturelle (culture center), the Salle de la Mutualite and La Meynard Conference Hall.

Les Abeilles
97216 Grand-Riviere. Tel: 75.56.72

7 rooms.

Airport Hotel
97224 Ducos. Tel: 56.29.82

7 rooms.

Alamanda
97229 Trois-Ilets. Tel: 66.03.19

20 air-conditioned rooms. Near beach, near airport.

Les Alizes
97280 Vauclin. Tel: 74.40.20

6 rooms.

Chez Andre
97229 Trois-Ilets. Tel: 66.01.55

11 rooms. Restaurant.

Chez Anna
97200 Fort-de-France. Tel: 71.55.62

12 rooms.

Anse Caritan
97200 Sainte-Anne. Tel: 76.74.12

94 rooms. Restaurant, bar, watersports, pool.

Auberge de L'Anse Mitan
97229 Trois-Ilets. Tel: 66.01.12

20 rooms. Beachfront, watersports, restaurant.

Auberge dE L'Atlantique
97280 Vauclin. Tel: 74.40.36

11 rooms.

Auberge dU Vare
97222 Case-Pilote. Tel: 78.80.56

7 rooms.

Au Reve Bleu
97200 Fort-de-France. Tel: 73.02.95

6 rooms.

Bakoua Beach
97229 Trois-Ilets. Tel: 66.02.02

140 rooms—one of the 'top 300 hotels in the world,' on Pointe du Bout.

Le Balisier
97200 Fort-de-France. Tel: 71.46.54

19 rooms in town hotel.

Bambou
97229 Trois-Ilets. Tel: 66.01.39

24 rooms. Restaurant, air-conditioned, golf, sea sports.

Bateliere—La Pagerie PLM
97200 Schoelcher. Tel: 71.90.41

215 rooms. Watersports, tennis, disco, casino.

Le Blenac
97200 Fort-de-France. Tel: 70.18.41

8 rooms.

Les Brisants
97240 Francois. Tel: 74.32.57
6 rooms.

Brise Marine
97228 Sainte-Luce. Tel: 62.46.94

18 rooms.

Bristol
97200 Fort-de-France. Tel: 71.31.80

10 rooms. Restaurant, bar.

Les Bungalows de la Prairie
97240 Francois. Tel: 51.34.16

10 rooms.

Calalou
97229 Sainte-Anne. Tel: 76.31.67

36 rooms. Beachfront, nearby golf
and tennis.

Caraibe Auberge
97229 Trois-Ilets. Tel: 66.03.19

14 rooms. Small, on beach.

La Caravelle Creperie-Studio
Anse l'Etang 97220 Tartane, Trinité.
Tel: 58.37.32

10 rooms.

Carayou PLM Azur
97229 Trois-Islets. Tel: 66.04.04

200 rooms. Restaurants, bars, disco,
pool, sports.

Chez Cecilia
97226 Morne-Vert. Tel: 77.12.83

4 rooms.

Club Mediterranee Buccaneers
Buccaneer's Creek, 97180 Sainte
Anne. Tel: 76.72.72

300 rooms. Air-conditioned, tennis,
sports, nightlife, bars, two restaurants.

Un Coin de Paris
97200 Fort-de-France. Tel: 70.08.52

14 rooms.

Courbaril Camping
97229 Anse-a-l'Ane. Tel: 76.32.30

Camping establishment.

Delices de la Mer
97228 Sainte-Luce. Tel: 62.50.12

5 rooms.

Diamant les Bains
97223 Diamant. Tel: 76.40.14

15 rooms.

Hotel du Diamant
Diamant.

180 rooms. Three restaurants, two
bars. Meridien Group facing Diamond Rock.

Douce Vague
97228 Sainte-Luce. Tel: 62.47.47

Dunette
97227 Sainte-Anne. Tel: 76.73.90

18 rooms. Restaurant, watersports.

Le Duparquet
97200 Fort-de-France. Tel: 70.28.36

20 rooms. Overlooking La Savane.

Eden Beach
Anse Mitan 97229 Trois-Ilets.
Tel: 66.01.19

Beach installation

Frantel
97229 Trois-Ilets. Tel: 66.04.04

200 rooms. Pool, watersports, golf,
disco, family hotel.

Le Gommier
97200 Fort-de-France. Tel: 71.88.55

10 rooms.

Grain D'Or
97221 Route de Saint-Pierre.
Tel: 78.02.27

7 rooms.

Imperatrice
97200 Fort-de-France. Tel: 63.06.82

24 rooms, overlooking La Savane.
Restaurant, cafe, bar.

Chez Julot
97280 Vauclin. Tel: 74.40.93

10 rooms.

Lafayette
97200 Fort-de-France. Tel: 73.80.50

24 rooms. Free beach, city-center
hotel.

Latitude
97221 Carbet. Tel:
78.08.08/78.01.64

90 rooms. Prefabs/bungalows, scuba,
sports, nightclub.

Madinina
97229 Trois-Ilets. Tel: 66.00.54

20 rooms, near marina. Creole restaurant, beaches, golf.

Madiana Motel
97223 Schoelcher. Tel: 61.28.78

17 rooms. Near beach.

Le Madras
97220 Tartane. Tel: 58.21.44

16 rooms. Nature reserve nearby,
watersports.

La Malmaison
97200 Fort-de-France. Tel: 63.90.85

19 rooms.

Manoir de Beauregard
97227 Sainte-Anne. Tel: 76.73.40

27 rooms in 18th century manor.
Restaurant.

Marina
97229 Trois-Ilets. Tel: 66.05.30

240 rooms. PLM hotel, marina,
beaches, pool.

Le Matador
97229 Trois-Ilets. Tel: 66.04.05

5 rooms. Various cuisines, near sea.

Meridien
97229 Trois-Ilets. Tel: 66.00.00

303 rooms. Like a cruise-ship. St.
Louis diner, casino.

Montauberge Pelee
97260 Morne-Rouge. Tel: 77.34.11

8 rooms.

La Nouvelle Vague
97250 Saint-Pierre. Tel: 77.14.34

5 rooms.

Novotel
97223 Diamant.
Tel: 76.42.42/73.66.15

183 rooms. Diamond Rock view,
beaches, restaurant, disco, nightclub.

La Pagerie PLM Azur
Tel: 66.05.30

98 rooms. Chinese and Creole restaurants, pool, sports.

Manoir de Beauregard.

Palasia
97200 Fort-de-France. Tel: 60.32.60

12 rooms.

Plantation de Leyritz
97218 Basse-Pointe.
Tel: 75.53.92/75.53.08

24 rooms. 18th-century manor on plantation, pool, Creole food.

Reflets de la Mer
97229 Anse-a-l'Ane. Tel: 76.32.14

6 rooms.

Residence Grand Large—Studios
97228 Sainte-Luce. Tel: 76.54.42

18 studio rooms.

Resitel
97200 Fort-de-France. Tel: 60.60.15

14 studios/bungalows

Rivage Hotel
Anse Mitan 97229 Trois-Ilets.
Tel: 66.00.53
Kitchenette rooms. Near beach, air-conditioned, pool, snack bar.

Saint-Aubin
97220 Trinite. Tel: 69.34.77

15 rooms. Near beaches.

Victo␣a
97200 Fort-de-France. Tel: 60.56.78

27 rooms. Hilltop Creole house-hotel, pool, solarium.

Martinique's 60 or so hotels and guest houses attract slightly more French visitors than those establishments on Guadeloupe and a percentage from the USA. Most installations are on or near the coast. From Club Bitaco, L'Hippopotamus and Vonvon, to le Zip and Topkapi, there are at least a dozen nightclubs on Martinique and, at La Bateliere and in the Méridien Hotel, one can play roulette or blackjack. Piano bars and jazz clubs are popular and there are at least seven cinemas on the island.

Restaurants and Nightlife on Martinique

The very fact that the island is a botanist's wonderland and its rich, fertile soil supports countless fruits and vegetables, makes Martinique particularly special when it comes to tropical foods. As the language evolved from French, Carib, African and mixed Asian into a peculiar patois called Creole, the dishes brought by the various races mingled into an exquisite Creole menu.

Creole cooking is exactly what you would expect from an exotic, tropical island—hot, spicy, peppery and, above all, interesting in its variety. Although some of the thirty-or-so main restaurants on the island and certainly most of the hotel restaurants serve international cuisine, it is the specialities of the island that bring the tastebuds to life in this short resumé.

The choice of Creole recipes varies with each restaurant but most meals commence with the traditional Ti Punch known as a "décollage"—a swift shot of aged or young Martinique rum followed by, maybe, a "planteurs" or planter's punch. Traditionally, after a meal the local coffee goes down so much better with the cognac-like 12-year-old vieux rhum. Naturally rum cocktails and fruit punch variations are practically unlimited.

Enough of the preliminaries, the starters might be awaiting in the form of the favorite soudins (sweet little clams in lemon juice or coquille de lambi (conch St. Jacques) at Le Caraibe restaurant. Maybe you will choose the Le d'Esnambuc for starters like escargot or frogs' legs but, for real creole appetizers, one could choose L'Escalier for crabes farcis (devilled land crabs) or accra (cod minced in batter). La Grande Voile at the Yacht Club serves classic langouste (a rock lobster) and other sea-

foods but the more exotic oursins (sea urchin) or chatrou (octopus) might be found in Le Tiffany. Cribiches (shrimp) are another delight but this time they are from the river and pike, also, particularly with crayfish sauce, might be fried at L'Arc en ciel. More Creole dishes could be found at Le Pigalle, like colombo, a curried stew with fish or goat's meat served on rice. You may plump (if that's the right word) for Blaff, an aromatic, Creole fish stew with pepper, garlic, chives, thyme and laurel seasoning.

Le Coq Hardi may serve you another excellent creole fish creation, Feroce, salt codfish salad served with avocado and manioc flour covered with a spicy, peppery sauce.

Apart from the many seafood delicacies on the Creole menu, a great number of restaurants serve various meat dishes cooked in the traditional local way. Why not try migan and salt pork; migan is a mash made of vegetables and created with the use of a "baton lélé"—a wooden, branched whisk. Perhaps you could try this in the Typic Bellevue restaurant or you might go for their Boucanier roast suckling pig. You might try the exquisite steaks at La Biguine or duckling in a delightful sauce La Belle Epoque. Pâté en Pot is a famous Creole dish made with vegetables in a thick soup with mutton chitterlings and could be tried at a table in L'Imperatrice or La Savane in the city.

Getting out into the countryside gives even more opportunity to enjoy dishes like turtle steak at Chateaubriand in Pointe du Bout or, just around the corner, at the Marina, a Creole red snapper at Chez Sidonie. More Creole cuisine can be savored at Le Matador and there are at least half a dozen more excellent places to dine nearby at Anse Mitan, not to speak of the tempting cuisine at Le Calalou, Anse-a-l'Ane. Mouthwatering fish or meat dishes can be enjoyed at L'Ecrévisse or a particularly special kingfish platter at La Villa Creole. Try naming some of the marine life in the tableside pool at Le Viver while you dine or listen to local music on the terrace at Le Bambou on the seaside. At Chez Andre, lambi and chatrous, turtle steak and langouste, are favorites. Back on the Pointe, Le Boucaut Restaurant serves sensational crepes and you can even get a taste of China at Le Cantonnais.

Just along the south coast, at Novotel Diamant Les Bains, Le Diamant, gaze out over Diamond Rock while feasting on matete de crabes—Creole prawns on rice. In the far south, at Sainte Anne, both Creole and French delicacies can be selected from the menus at the PLM eighteenth-century plantation house, Manoir de Beauregard—a most traditional setting—or at La Dunette on the beach at Salines. Also on the waterfront, but with the added attraction of a "vivier" or glass floor above live lobster pens from which one choose one's meal, is Les Filets Bleus. Grilled seafood in a rustic, thatched, native-style cafe is excellent at Poi et Virginie.

Another spectacular view while dining on soupe de tortue (turtle soup) is that over the shallow coral reefs from Club Nautique de Le Francois on the Atlantic coast. Just along the beach, try calalou aux crabes (fish stew) at Les Brisants, Dostaly, Le François. Farther up the west coast, at Robert, is the inexpensive Chinese establishment of Tong Yen and inland, at Le Morne Rouge, is L'Auberge de la Montagne Pelée. Glimpses of the awe-inspiring volcanic peak can be had while dining on pâté en pot (a Norman/Creole thick soup) on the terrace. With even

more ominous connections relating to the dread mountain, try dining in Saint Pierre itself at La Factorerie, a rural college; one can get the feel of the "Pelée proximity" over an aromatic Creole fish blaff or one of the excellent coconut desserts.

Right in the north, at Basse Pointe, a selection of restaurants serve varied menus like coconut chicken at the tiny Mme. Edjam's (Mally's). For a special Creole Columbo, try the splendid setting of the Leyritz Plantation, an ancient plantation house just outside town.

Dining out in Martinique, one has a varied choice of cuisine from the top in French table d'hote to Creole with a vengeance. The settings also are as varied as the menus and gingerbread mansions contrast with bamboo and palm thatch, columned colonial plantation halls offer elegance, while beach barbecue terraces lend an *al fresco* feel to the island's cuisine of which one could never tire. As with all French Caribbean islands, Martinique's excellence for its tropical cuisine has gone a long way before it and the world acknowledges its place in international superiority. There are now more than 150 restaurants on Martinique.

For nightlife and the fun of dance and excitement of the casino try Le Boabab, Le Sweety or Club 21. In Trinité is the Number One Club, at Carbet, the Trou Caraibe and L'Oeil at Ducos. In hotels there are clubs like the Vonvon in the Méridien, Le Vesou at the Carayou PLM and the Cabane at the Novotel. Try the Play-Back, another disco/cabaret, at Marin and Le Club Bitaco up in the ravine overlooking the capital. Ballets, local dance troupes, theatres, festivals of jazz and guitar traditionally offer alternative entertainment. Le Pelican, La Carafe, New Brummel's, Chez Gaston and Le Jardin Bresilien (the Brazilian Garden) are all jazz and piano bars—a delightful mix of entertainment and a relaxing tropical evening out. The casinos offer the chance to place your bets at the Méridien and La Bateliere to the north of Fort-de-France.

Communications and Information

The telephone code for Martinique is 19, then 596. The main Post and Telecommunications Office is located on Rue de la Liberté about halfway up, facing La Savane. Telegrams: dial 14. Radio Telephone: dial 10.

Hospitals include Meynard, Fort-de-France, Tel: 50.15.15. The Maternity Hospital on Route de Rédoute, Fort-de-France, Tel: 70.08.11. The hospital at Lamentin, Tel: 51.14.91. and the Clinic Sainte-Marie Cluny,- Tel: 63.39.40. Ambulance, Tel: 71.59.48.

The police are situated at the junctions of Rue Schoelcher, Victor Sévère, behind the Schoelcher Library, Tel: 17.

The Tourist Bureau is next to the Air France building on the Alfassa Quayside near La Savane, Tel: 63.79.60. The special Prefecture Delegation for Tourism is on Rue Victor Sévère, Tel: 60.18.61.

Taxis are either collective (always circulating and traveling in the island); private taxis especially for personal hire as a normal cab from the airport, most hotels and town centers; and the "véhicules populares," which are like an autobus, similar arrangements to the collective taxis in that you take potluck as to fellow passengers. Locals use both for everyday transport. Set tours are either in the north or the south of the island. Tours can always be arranged either with taxis or by minibus or by coach trip. There are at least 15 car hire companies including Hertz, Tel: 60.64.64, and Avis, Tel: 70.11.60. Ferries go on a regular basis to and from Fort-de-France-Pointe du Boute (Trois Ilets).

To and From the Island

Air France, Air Canada, American Airlines and several others now fly direct to Lamentin Airport, Martinique, from international destinations. Local Caribbean connections can be made with Air France, BWIA, LIAT, Air Martinique, etc. Fort-de-France is a popular stopover for many long-haul cruise liners and local shipping also uses the port at Sainte Pierre.

The telephone number for the airport is 51.51.51 and it is only a few miles from the center of the capital, Fort-de-France.

CHAPTER XII

Guyane (French Guyana) "Land of Many Rivers"

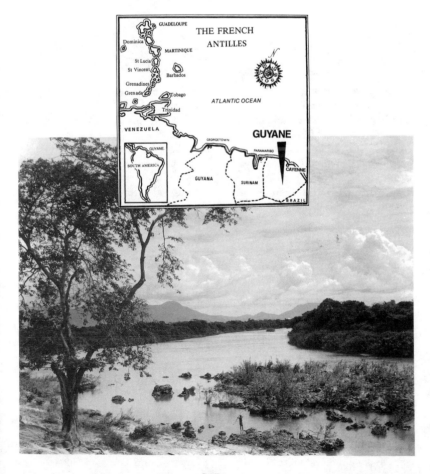

Size and Location

Guyane, otherwise known as French Guyana or French Guiana, is the smallest of the 13 countries on the South American continent and has a total area of 91,000 square kilometres (35,135 square miles). The country is basically heart-shaped and it lies just around 5 degrees north of the Equator which runs through the mouth of the Amazon River, not 250 miles to the south of Guyane.

As a French Overseas Department it is grouped together with the islands of the French Caribbean—the French Antilles—although it is not included in the Caricom States or as one of the ACP countries of the European Community. The country is sectioned into two arrondissements, Cayenne and St. Laurent.

One of the three divisions on the north-eastern "bulge" of South America which include Guyana and Surinam, Guyane is bordered to the east and south by Brazil, to the west by Dutch Surinam, and its northern coastline of some 200 miles faces the Atlantic Ocean. Its nearest French neighbour, Martinique, lies nearly a thousand miles to the north-west in the Caribbean. Guyane is the nearest American country to French Senegal on the West African coast.

Physical

Mangrove swamps line Guyane's coast, edging a dense blanket of tropical Amazonian forest. Equatorial jungle covers most of the country which is bordered to the west by the Maroni and Itany rivers and, to the east, by the Oyapock River. Only five other important rivers flow from the uplands to Guyane's coast. These are, from west to east, the Mana, the Sinnamary, the Kourou, the Comte and the Approugue rivers. Deep gorges, savannahs and low hills lie under the dense tropical forest in the interior. Guyane's highest point, in the south-western Tumucumaque Sierras, is Mount Mitraka at 2263 feet.

Climate

Guyane has an equatorial climate with a great deal of rainfall. It is hot, sticky and humid, relieved at times by cooling trade winds. The dry season is between August and December. From December to July it is rainy (up to 110 inches average per annum), damp and humid, with a maximum temperature of 82 degrees F (28 degrees C) in May. The rainy season in the south lasts from April to September.

Population

Some 85,000 people live in Guyane, 38,000 of whom live in the capital, Cayenne. Before the advent of foreigners the jungles of Guyane were

**19th Century engraving showing Amerindian and typical vege-
tation in French Guyane.**

inhabited by native Amerindians, mostly of the Inini tribe. Today the Inini account for only 10 percent of the total population, most of whom are of Creole descent, having infiltrated from neighbouring Surinam and Guyana. Twelve percent of the population are French and include some Chinese and Laotian settlers from Indo-China. The majority of the population is Roman Catholic.

Language

French is the official language in Guyane although a large part of the population also speaks English, especially in the business sector, and Creole pigeon-French is commonly heard. The native Amerindians speak Inini, an Amazonian tongue.

Holidays and Festivals

As with the French Antilles, Christmas and New Year's, Easter, Ascension and Assumption, Labour Day, Bastille Day (14 July), Armistice and All Saints' Day are observed. Roman Catholic holidays are also observed.

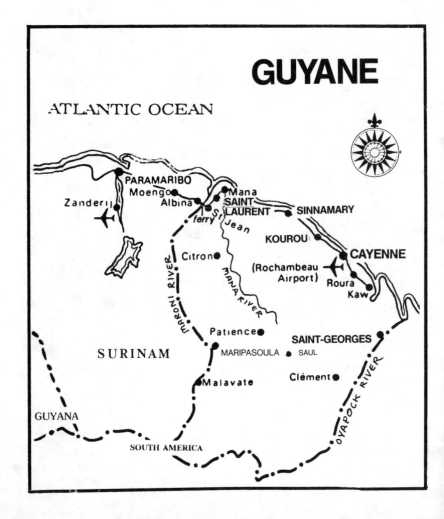

History

For millenia Amerindian tribes wandered undisturbed through the forests of Guyane, fishing its broad rivers, hunting and gathering in its deep undergrowth. Because of its numerous rivers the tribes gave the country the name of Guyana—"Land of Many Rivers," hence the French version, Guyane. Evidence of pre-Columbian occupation can be seen in several parts of the country and in the Musee de Cayenne.

Five hundred years ago Christopher Columbus just missed discovering the Guyane coastline, leaving that experience to Alonso de Ojeda and Amerigo Vespucci who sailed past the mouth of the Maroni River in 1499. A year later, Vincent Pinzon, Columbus' shipmate, noted the mangrove infested shore and the first chart of the coast was drawn up by Juan de la Cosa in the same year. Pizon sailed to this part of the South American continent again in 1508. Spain claimed the land until a group of French explorers settled near the estuaries of the Comte and Cayenne rivers in 1604, naming the country Cayenne. Eventually this name fell to the settlement which became the country's capital.

This part of the coast on the "shoulder" of South America, from the Venezuelan border in the west to the Oyapock River in the east, was divided intermittently between France, Holland and England during the early- and mid-1600s. French trading entrepreneurs set up a base in 1626 on the Sinnamary River and, in 1635, French Jesuits established a settlement at Cayenne Island.

An unsuccessful expedition of exploration, the Kourou Trip, followed the Jesuit lead. A little later, the Frenchman Malouet made an attempt to investigate the country's interior only to be met with a barrier of dense undergrowth and the specter of tropical fevers. A period of confused attempts at colonization followed, with slaves being imported from Africa and neighbouring countries to assist in clearing the coastal land for cultivation.

Just prior to the Empire Period of Napoleon Bonaparte in 1794, slavery was abolished in the French colonies, only to be reintroduced in 1802, after the Treaty of Amiens. The early settlement's population was increased during 1795 when political prisoners were deported from France to the colony. Napoleon unwisely invaded neighbouring Brazil in 1808, invoking Portuguese wrath and resulting in the occupation of Guyane by Portugal from 1809 until 1816. More slaves were imported to tend the sugar crops in the early nineteenth century until slavery was finally abolished in 1848.

During the second half of the nineteenth century gold was discovered in the highlands and in the rivers. Prospectors from Europe flocked to the fever-ridden country, followed by some of France's more desperate criminals who were imprisoned in penal colonies on the mainland and the offshore Isles du Salut. The most notorious of these colonies, Devil's Island, was established in 1852 and only closed in 1945. One of the island's famous inmates over its 93-year history of incarceration was Papillon, hero of book and film. In 1946 Guyane became a department of France and shrugged off its image of the "Land of Convicts."

More recently, in 1960, the rocket base of Kourou was established. More than 5,000 workers were subsequently imported to Kourou to man the space rocket station which

A map of 1530 indicates cannibals in the region of Guyane.

has been the site of many communication satellite launches using the Anglo-French Arienne rocket. The war in Indo-China resulted in many refugees being resettled in Guyane in the 1970s.

The advent of tourism and a newly restructured economy in the early 1980's began to give Guyane an identity in the world, although the country still remains poor. Known as French Guiana since 1816, it became Guyana in 1986. In the late 1980s another influx of French workers boosted the population and the government now hopes to exploit some of the country's mineral and natural wealth, in part through the promotion of tourism.

Trade and Industry

Guyane's successful sugar industry of the early nineteenth century fizzled out after the 1848 abolishment of slavery, and gold prospecting produced little wealth for the country. However, with Guyane's exposure after the establishment of the Kourou rocket base and the increased demand for tropical hardwoods in the early 1960s, the country began to build up an economic infrastructure.

Today the country still survives on imported goods exchanged for locally caught and processed shrimps, bauxite, precious woods and some gold mined in the hinterland. Sugar cane is still grown as is manioc, maize, rice, fruit and vegetables, like the bora bean, which form the nation's staple diet. Tourism, it is hoped, will swell Guyane's meager coffers.

Close-up on Cayenne

The pepper, cayenne, gets its name from Guyane's capital, located on what was once an island at the mouth of the Cayenne River. Facing the Atlantic Ocean and backing onto mangrove swamp and tropical forest, the town has a small port and fishing harbour and is built on a grid pattern around the Savannah Square on Avenue Leon G. Damas and Rue de Empire.

Cayenne, a town of some 38,000 inhabitants of mixed races, is typical of the many European colony settlements in northern South America which have struggled to survive almost 400 years of checkered history.

A number of attractive, "gingerbread style" French colonial houses still survive in the capital's center. These magnificient buildings sport wrought iron balconies and wooden verandas, contrasting with modern office buildings.

There are few items of interest to the tourist in Cayenne and its surroundings apart from the early French architecture in the Old Town, the house of Vidal, two little churches and the narrow canal on Avenue de la Liberte and the Boulevard de la Republique. This canal separates the town into the "left" and "right" banks. On Rue de Remire, near the

town square, is the interesting Museum of Cayenne and nearby is the Franconie Library. Cayenne boasts five cinemas, four discos and three art galleries.

In the hinterland around Cayenne are several attractions including the Fourgassier Waterfall and the Rorota footpath, an enjoyable jungle walk. There are also organized visits to the H'mong village of Cacao near the airport. The Gabrielle Creek walk involves taking the ferry from Stoupan, where the road east out of Cayenne meets the Mahury River, to the village of Roura. Further along the road, past Roura village, is the Kaw inlet, the town of Kaw, and the mountains of the same name which

are now being exploited for their bauxite deposits. The road east terminates at Kaw and another forest road leads south through Cacao to the settlement of Regina on the picturesque Approuague River.

The road west out of Cayenne crosses the Cayenne River and another skirts its little tributaries. This route from Guyane's capital heads west and north along the coast, linking the towns of Tonate, Kourou, Sinnamary, Iracoubo, Mana, the country's second largest settlement St. Laurent, and St. Jean. From St. Jean on the Maroni River, a ferry links the main road with the highway to Paramaribo, the capital of neighbouring Surinam.

Excursions

Driving is not the sole means of transport in Guyane although there are 10 car hire agencies in Cayenne and a good taxi service from the Central Hotel. Air transport and boat excursions are the only ways of reaching places south of the coast. Air Guyane

flies a light plane service to most major towns and villages including those on the coast, and boat services connect many of the coastal towns.

Excursions outside the capital can be arranged through one of the half-dozen tour operators like Takari

Land of Many Waters.

Tours, Club Transamazonia or Jacqueline Lassort in Cayenne. From Kourou the company Guyane Excursions arranges visits into the interior and to the offshore islands, as do Les Guides de Brosse from Roura, and Sinnarive Tours out of Sinnamary.

South of Cayenne a channel divides the island on which the town stands from the mainland, the Crique Fouillee. This creek runs from the Cayenne River to the Mahury River and, where the two join there are the remains of an ancient fort, Fort Trio. Another fort, Fort Diamant, is located on the eastern tip of Cayenne Island behind Mount Mahury, near the village of Remire. Nearby also, is the larger fishing village of Montjoy on the Atlantic coast. The airport, Rochambeau International, is located about 10 miles south of Cayenne, past the little village of Matoury.

Discovering the Country

If a visitor to Guyane wishes to visit an Amerindian native village it is essential to contact the Prefecture in Cayenne before traveling to Guyane. The Prefecture then issues a certificate of permission for an organized and supervised visit. Addresses for communications:

The Prefecture.
Delegation Regionale au Tourisme, 10 Rue L. Heder, 97307 Cayenne Cedex.

Tel: 318491. Tx. PREFGU 910532.

Other useful addresses for visitors include:

Agencie Regionale de Development du Tourisme et des Loisirs, Pavillion du Tourisme—Jardin Botanique, BP 801, 97338 Cayenne Cedex.
Tel: 300900. Tx. 910356 FG.

Several varieties of turtles are found in Guyane.

Bureau de Tourism de Saint Lorent du Maroni,
16 Rue du Colonel Chandon, 97320 St. Laurent.
Tel: 341086. Tx. NORBUR 910631 FG.

Office du Tourisme des Antilles et de la Guyane,
12 Rue Auber, 75009 Paris, France.
Tel: 42681107. Tx. TOURAG 215806 F.

There are regional tourist board representatives based in Cayenne, Remire and St. Laurent du Maroni who supply detailed information about excursions. It is recommended the visitor seeks the assistance and advice of either a reputable tour operator or the officials of the tourist board before embarking on any excursion in Guyane as much of the country is unexplored and cut off from the outside world.

Independent visits to the interior, Guyane's coastal settlements or neighbouring countries, by boat, car or plane can be arranged through Air France, Surinam Airways, Agence Sainte-Claire, Somarig or Havas Voyages in Cayenne; or Floreal Tours in Kourou. Any of the country's twenty-five hotels can advise on excursions and some even have their own arrangements for taking visitors on tours.

Kourou

Kourou is located on the coast about 50 miles, via the town of Tonate, north-west of Cayenne. It is from Kourou that excursions can be taken to the Iles du Salut, just off the coast. A 100-seater boat, booked at Carbet des Roches, takes visitors out to see the remains of the convict colony of Devil's Island and other remnants of the former French penal colonies. Also from Kourou excursions are organized to visit the Montagne des Signes a little way inland on the banks of the Kourou River. Kourou is famous for its rocket launching base

Kourou was a tiny village of a few hundred people before the base was founded in 1960 when 5,000 workers were installed there to operate the base. Today the population has dwindled due to cut-backs at the facility but the town is still the third largest in Guyane. The Centre Europeen d'Exposition Spatiale Guyanais (CSG) base can be visited on Tuesdays, Wednesdays and Thursdays by arrangement on Tel: 334919. established to put Anglo-French communications satellites into orbit.

Montsinnery, Sinnamary and Mana

These three towns are the bases for several popular excursions and are all located on the Atlantic coast. Montsinnery is a short drive south from Tonate, off the road to Kourou from Cayenne.

From both Montsinnery and Sinnamary photo-safari excursions can be made into the surrounding jungles. These trips and river excursions, including butterfly hunts, can be organized through Voyages de la

Place. The Route de Montsinnery is carefully arranged in order that the visitor can see the great variety of flora and fauna typical of this part of Amazonia. Another way to view the various species of animal, flower and birdlife is to visit the Botanical Gardens of the Zoo Eugene Bellony. For those interested in seeing some of the country's more exotic wildlife in its natural surroundings there is an ibis nesting ground near Sinnamary and another on the coast, north of Roura. Excursions along the Sinnamary River can be made by local boat or pirogue. A forest track leads from one of the river tributaries to the jungle village of St. Elie.

At Mana, about 150 miles north-west of Cayenne, past the towns of Kourou, Sinnamary, Tracoubo, and Organabo, there is the coastal breeding ground of the rare leatherback turtle. This fascinating sight can only be visited from April through July. Forest trips can also be taken from Mana up the river of the same name deep into the interior, almost as far as Saul.

Saint Laurent du Maroni

Located several miles up the wide estuary of the Maroni River on the Guyane bank, facing the country of Surinam, St. Laurent lies a good 160 miles north-west of Cayenne. From this, Guyane's second largest town with a population of around 8,000, visits can be made to the Camp de la Transportation, the early convict housings, and to the former leper colony on the Ile des Lepreux. Pirogue trips can be made on the Maroni River, visiting the settlements of St. Jean (from where a ferry connects with Albina on the Surinam side of the river) and Apatou, past rapids and islands overgrown with tropical vegetation, past Amerindian villages, as far as Maripasoula and Malavate, nearly two hundred miles upriver.

Wildlife

The wildlife of the Amazon region of South America is unique and still only partly discovered. So dense is the jungle in the interior of Guyane that none but the most intrepid explorers have ventured deep into its heart. The rivers and waterways are the sole means of communication and travel. Only a handful of excursions take the visitor more than a few yards from the safety of the long, wide rivers when journeying up-country. The coastal region, however, is easy to travel in and much of the typical fauna and flora of this part of the continent can be seen without going far inland. Airplane routes are the interior's only link with the coast apart from waterborne transport, as there are no roads into the region.

It is on the coast that Guyane's two famous ibis nesting grounds are located, one near Roura and another at Sinnamary. Also on the coast, at Mana, is the country's celebrated leatherback turtle breeding ground, a popular excursion for visitors between April and July. In the river

estuaries manatees, or sea-cows, can be seen as well as caiman, a type of alligator. The rivers are as rich with fish as the land is green with vegetation. It is in Guyane's rivers that the giant arapaima can be caught. This curious fish can grow to 12 feet in length and weigh up to 300 pounds! Among the numerous other fish, which the native Indians still hunt with bow and arrow, are the catfish, electric eel, sunfish, lukunani, hassar and patua. The notorious pirana, or perai, also inhabits the country's waters and an anaconda snake can sometimes be seen crossing the river in front of the only method of water transport, the native canoe, or pirogue.

The Amerindians, who still live a life comparatively unchanged in the heart of Guyane's jungles, hunt animals like the puma, ocelot or even the rare jaguars with blowpipe darts smeared with the deadly sap of the strychnos tree, curare. Other animals which can be seen in forest clearings include the giant anteater, tapir, small deer, capybara, the world's largest rodent, and wild pigs known as peccaries. In the high jungle canopies monkeys, like the sakiwinka, ukari and parauacu, or monk saki, and the rare sloth can sometimes be seen. Local guides will often point out to the unsuspecting tourist the

Guyanese bird-eating spider, the world's largest arachnid!

Insect and reptile life in the dark, humid forest is prolific and, because the malaria carrying mosquito is indigenous, innoculation is recommended before traveling in the interior. Malaria has been eradicated in the capital, Cayenne, but it is advisable to sleep under an insect net if the room is not air-conditioned. There is no vaccination, however, against the other fever-carrying creature, the notorious vampire bat which is also a native of this part of South America.

Birdlife fills the forest air with sound and vibrant colour. Toucans, parrots, hummingbirds feeding from orchids and hibiscus, brilliant cock-of-the-rock, bellbirds and screamers add to the jungle cacophany, and brightly painted kingfishers hunt in the thick lianas and tree roots which hem the rivers. Pelicans, herons and egrets also fish the estuaries and waterways of this virgin country. Dazzling butterflys, like the giant morphis and heliconi species, add to the exotic atmosphere of the Amazonian jungle and several tour operators organize butterfly hunts for tourists.

The variety of Guyane's jungle undergrowth is bewildering, from giant bromeliads, several types of palm trees, cannonball trees, brazil-nut

There are two important ibis nesting grounds on the coast of Guyane.

The strange Jacana darts across the giant leaves of the Victoria Regis water lilies.

trees reaching more than 150 feet in height, monkey-pot trees, and valuable hardwoods and commercial lumber trees like mahogany, balsa wood, greenheart, purple heart, mora, crabwood and locust trees; to the striking forest flowers, the orchid, the insect-eating pitcher plant and brilliant helicona. Lush tropical vege-

tation grows right down to the river's edge and giant tree buttresses, lianas and mangrove roots form an almost impenetrable barrier along its banks. Giant Victoria Regis water lilies sometimes choke small tributaries and cecropias drape across backwaters, often preventing navigation.

Early print of cayman which live in Guyane's many rivers.

Shopping

Several souvenirs made locally in Guyane are prohibited from export, including those made from turtle or tortoise shell, and the pelts of protected species like the ocelot, puma or jaguar. Gold ornaments and jewelry made from local precious stones, shells and animal teeth are popular keepsakes, native hardwood carvings make good gifts, and framed and boxed giant butterflies are decorative presents. A set of Amerindian bow and arrows makes an original souvenir—check the arrow tips are not dipped in the deadly curare!

There are fifteen art and craft shops and galleries in Cayenne, four in Kourou, and three in Sinnamary. Most hotels have a display of locally produced artifacts and souvenirs. Bargains can be found in the local marketplace and in the remote villages inland. A particular type of rum is also distilled and this is a liquor which should be treated with some respect!

Banking

The unit of currency, as in the other French Caribbean countries, is the French franc, divided into 100 centimes, and it is on a par with the French franc in France. Most major credit cards are accepted in the larger towns, shops, restaurants and hotels.

There are five banks in Cayenne, the Banque Francaise Commerciale, 2, Place des Palmistes; Bank Nationale de Paris-Guyane, 2, Place Victor-Schoelcher (branches in Kourou and St. Laurent); Credit Populaire de la Guyane, 93, Rue Lalouette. Banks generally open from about 7:30 a.m. until midday, and then from 3 p.m. until around 5 p.m.

Churches

Apart from two small Protestant communities, the majority of the population of Guyane is Roman Catholic although, up-country, there are pockets of Amerindian animists. Most churches in Guyane therefore, are Roman Catholic.

Health

Yellow fever shots should be taken by visitors who plan on staying in Guyane for more than two weeks, and both yellow fever and smallpox injections must be taken if arriving from an infected country. Malaria, the only other prevalent disease in Guyane, has been eradicated in Cayenne but is still a risk in the jungle regions of the interior. A preventative medicine is therefore recommended for travelers visiting locations outside the major towns, especialy between January and March. Salt tablets are

Colonial elegance graces Cayenne Old Town.

also a good precaution against the deficit caused by sweating in the humid climate, and a good supply of sun lotion is advised.

The water supply in the capital and in hotels throughout the country is fit to drink.

The main hospital, Centre Hospitalier de Cayenne, is located on Avenue d'Estrees, Tel: 303666. The St. Paul Clinic is at PK 2.5 Route de la Madeleine, Cayenne, Tel: 301580. Other medical facilities in the capital include the Clinique de Hibiscus on Rocade de Montabo, and the Clinique Veronique.

The Andre Bouron Hospital is located on Avenue du General de Gaulle in St. Laurent, Tel: 341037. There is also the C.M.C.K. at Kourou on Tel: 320045 and the Sauvetage en Mer on Tel: 304444.

Hotels in Guyane

As in most Francophone countries, the accommodations available to visitors varies considerably from the first class, air-conditioned rooms of the international-standard Novotel Cayenne, to rooms let by individuals in their own homes—Chambres chez l'Habitant—to Gites Ruraux, or rural lodges which offer basic facilities.

There are ten hotels in the capital, Cayenne.

Novotel Cayenne
Chemin Hilaire, Route de Montabo,
3 km. from Cayenne, 15 km. from
airport. Tel: 303888.
103 rooms with bath in attractive
forest setting, pool, restaurant, bar,
tennis, conference room, excursions.

Hotel Madeline
Route de Madeline
Tel: 301736
32 rooms.

Motel Beauregard
PK 9.5, Route de Remire.
Tel: 354100
30 rooms.

Guyane Studio
16 Rue Mole. Tel: 314400.
30 rooms.

Le Grillardin
PK 6, Route Matoury. Tel: 356390
16 rooms.

Chez Mathilde
42 Rue du General de Gaulle.
Tel: 312513
9 rooms.

Amazonia
28 Avenue du General de Gaulle.
Tel: 300302

Le Neptima
21 Rue Felix-Eboue. Tel: 301115

Le Polygone
Carrefour deu Larivot. Tel: 305400

Studios Baduel
Route de Baduel. Tel: 315058

Rooms in the home of a family or
individual in Cayenne include:

Mr. Eddy Sandot, 99 Rue du Lieu-
tenant Becker. Tel: 317020/314934.
Mrs. Izeros, Villa 'Les Manguiers'. Tel:
310655.
Mr. Pierre Baste, Route de Baduel.
Tel: 301099/311119.
Mrs. Armandine Marie-Josephe, 9
bis, Rue Rene Jadfard. Tel: 311168.
Mrs. Marie Jose Pepin, Route de
Matoury. Tel: 356884.
Mrs. Duclos, Residence Cogneau, 57,
Route de Matoury. Tel: 300091.

There are two hotels in Kourou and
one on the Iles du Salut.

Les Relais de Guyane
B.P. 814. Tel: 320066.
213 rooms.

Studio Sodexho
Place Newton. Tel: 320611.

Auberge des Iles du Salut
Iles du Salut. Tel: 324530.

The town of Sinnamary has two
hotels.

The Sinnarive Motel
Degrad Fontines. Tel: 345656.

Eldo Grill
7 Route Nationale 1.

Mr. Jaques Derain runs a country gite
at Pointe Combi in Sinnamary.
Tel: 345309.

Other hotels in Guyane include:

Hotel Star
Rue Thiers. St. Laurent. Tel: 341084
38 rooms.

Le Toucan
20, Avenue du General de Gaulle.
St. Laurent. Tel: 341005.

Le Relais de L'Acarounay
Route de Mana, Acarounay.
Tel: 341720.

Auberge Chez Dede
Bourg de Maripasoula, Maripasoula.
Tel: 372151/372150.

Auberge de Cacao
Bourg de Cacao, Cacao.
Tel: 318200.

Hotel Oyack
Bourg de Roura, Roura. Tel: 304193.

Chez Modestine
Bourg de Saint Georges, Saint
Georges. Tel: 370013.

Le Damas
Bourg de Saint Georges, Saint
Georges. Tel: 370010.

Rural gites include:

Mrs. Saibour, Bourg d'Iracoubo.
Tel: 346023.

Mrs. Syrianne Mangal, Bourg
d'Iracoubo. Tel: 346385.

Mr. Brunet, Plateau des Mines, Saint
Laurent. Tel: 341070.

Mangroves choke many of the river tributaries.

Mrs. Emile Hidair, Bourg de Mana.
Tel: 348062/311280.

Gite Rural du Syndicate d'Initiative,
Bourg de Saul.

Restaurants and Nightlife in Guyane

French, Chinese, Vietnamese, Moroccan and Creole restaurants are prevalent in the major towns.

There are twelve Creole restaurants in and around the capital, including Le Cric-Crac, Le Bambou, Le Grillardine, L'Acacia, Le Chat Noir, La Belle Cabresse, Le Palmier, Le Relais de la Plage (on the beach), Chez Roro, Le Broussailon Vert (on Savane Matiti), Le Montabo Grill and Le Snackbar Creole.

French cuisine restaurants in and around Cayenne include La Belle Epoque, La Bonne Casserole, La Croix de Sud, Snackbar des Palmistes, Auberge des Amandiers, Paris-Cayenne, Le Patriarche, Les Relais de Bourgogne, Cafe de la Gare, Le Guignolo, Le Relais de Gallion, Auberge du Vieux Chemin, Creperie Sarrazine and Le Montravel.

Two Moroccan restaurants are located in the center of Cayenne, Le Marrakech Terranga and Le Grand Atlas.

Chinese and Vietnamese restaurants in and around the capital include Le Cap Saint Jacques, La Pagode, Le Viet Nam, Le Cantonnais, Paradis des Amis, Les Invites, Le Chateau d'Asie, La Riviere des Parfums and Yun Lai La Pagode.

Snack bars in Cayenne include the Chez Kindou, Au Coin du Palmier and Comme Chez Soi.

Kourou, with its large French community associated with the rocket base, has fourteen French cuisine restaurants and just three restaurants which serve Creole food.

Saint Laurent also has a mixture of restaurants with four French cuisine centers including the restaurant of the Toucan Hotel. There are five Creole restaurants in St. Laurent. These include the Chez Philo, Chez Antoine, Chez Tintin, Chez Loe, and Le Relais de L'Acarouany Hotel on the Mana road north of St. Laurent. There is only one Moroccan restaurant, Le Casablanca, one Vietnamese restaurant, Le Viet Nam, and the Chang, the only Chinese restaurant in the town.

In Sinnamary there are four Creole restaurants, one French restaurant and the Li Hua Vietnamese restaurant.

There is a Creole restaurant, L'Iguane, between Tonate and Macouria, four French restaurants at Roura, seven between Montsinnery and Tonnegrande, one at Le Bourg de Regina, one French and one Chinese restaurant at Cacao, and two French restaurants each at Iracoubo and St. Georges.

Nightlife and Sports

Nightlife in Cayenne includes Club 106 on Avenue du General de Gaulle, Le Biguin on Place Schoelcher, Le Penitencier and Le Mega Hertz.

In Kourou the five disco clubs include the J.M. Club and the Lazar 2000 Club in the old town, Le Cachiri, Le Tropicana and Le Cercle des Roches. In St. Laurent entertainment is provided at the two hotels, Le Toucan and Le Star.

Sporting facilities are mostly located on the outskirts of Cayenne. Cayenne's municipal swimming pool is on Route de Baduel. The Breack Sporting Club is located on Route de Remire, east of Cayenne. The Stade Tennis Club of Cayenne is on Route de Suzini, and the Macouriana Ranch is located on the Route de Macouria. Another horse-riding club is situated just outside the town of Kourou, just west of Cayenne, the Club Hippique de Kourou. Also at Kourou there is an aeroclub, Tel: 334115. On Zephyr Beach outside Cayenne there is a Nautical Club and there is another club for sea sports at Saint Laurent du Maroni in the far west of the country. At the Novotel Hotel there is a pool and facilities for tennis both day and night. At the Relais du Gallion there is a miniature golf course and the Polygone Hotel on Carrifour du Larivot also has sporting facilities.

Communications and Information

Direct telephone lines link Guyane to France, and communications to other countries are relayed through Martinique. The country's only newspaper is La Presse de Guyane and Radiodiffusion Television Francaise (ORTF) broadcasts a limited service. There is one radio station in Cayenne. The electricity supply system operates on 127 and/or 220 volts AC (50 cycles). The metric system is used for weights and measures.

To and From Guyane

Rochambeau International Airport, Tel: 356046/356162, just ten miles south of Cayenne, is the only airport in Guyane capable of handling international air traffic.

Out of Cayenne, there are five Air France flights weekly to and from Paris, France. There is also the opportunity of making international connections through the islands of the French Antilles like Martinique or Guadeloupe, and occasional flights to Port of Spain, Trinidad.

Regional flights include five scheduled Air France flights per week to the islands of the French Antilles. The airline Cruzeiro do Sol flies once a week out of Cayenne to each of Surinam, Brazil, Peru, and Quito in Ecuador.

Guyane Air Transport (GAT) serves the interior of Guyane with regular connections to Kourou, Les Iles du Salut, Saul, Maripasoula, Regina, Cacao, St. Laurent and St. Georges. GAT also flies to Paramaribo in Surinam, and Macapa in Brazil. The GAT offices are at 2, Rue Lalouette, 97300 Cayenne. Tel: 317200.

Boat excursions are available to Les Iles du Salut, and from Carbet des Roches to Kourou. A ferry runs between Stoupan and Roura, linking the road from Cayenne to Roura across the Mahury River, another provides links with Mana, and another links Saint Laurent with Albina in Surinam.

A sign of friendship marks the border.

CHAPTER XIII

The French Connection

The French language needs no introduction to the average visitor and even those who have no knowledge of French whatsoever will find the basic words of "Good day"—*Bonjour;* "Good-bye"—*Au Revoir; "Please"*—S'il vous plâit; "Thank you"—*Merci;* "Yes"—*Oui;* "No"—*Non.* Very easy to pick up and rewarding to use. A small phrasebook or dictionary never goes amiss when traveling in the French West Indies as even the linguist may come across some unfamiliar words, particularly in these tropical isles.

The linguist may also find a completely new language awaiting on arrival in the French Antilles. Because of the curious mixture of creeds, colors, races, religions, faiths, tribes and sects, the island people in different parts of the region speak local dialects that differ vastly from the conventional French. Creole is the "Lingua Franca" of the everyday life, although French is the official language and English is not uncommon in resort areas.

Creole is an easy-come easy-go a language as one can come across anywhere. Its lack of grammar, its unorthodox pronunciation, its rythm and even its color add spice to the sound of daily life in the islands. Used mainly on Martinique and the main island and islets of Guadeloupe, Creole is one of the most laid-back languages anywhere in the world. Most often heard by the visitor in the local market places, on public transport or in native bars, cafes and eating-places, the lilt of this patois is truly Caribbean. Examples of Creole in basic speech demonstrate how the dialect has smoothed out the conventional French. Good day is *Bonjou;* Goodbye—*Au vouè;* Please—*Souplé,* Thank you—*Messi;* How are you?—*Ka ou fè?,* instead of Comment allez vous? and You're welcome—*Pa ni ayen adan ca,* instead of *Je vous en prie.* In special circumstances the language diverts dramatically from the basic French—a bird becomes a *zouézo* (a comical expression), a large woman might be called a *maman la baleine* (mother whale!) without any offense being taken. Certain sayings and proverbs have evolved in the Creole language and it is especially in the tribal-like traditions and local ceremonies where exotic deviations from French exist and the language takes on its own syncopation. The tradition of keeping wake at the graveside is ancient and mysterious and involves the Creole "Cric-Crac" chants. Fêtes such as Toussaint, Indienne and Carnival also include sophisticated Creole liturgies. The tender and expressive tones of this patois are reflected in the almost obligatory use of *mon cher* or *ma chère* whenever addressing another person.

CHAPTER XIV

Tourism Details

Although all the measurements of distance in this guide are in statute miles, the French West Indies, similar to several other Caribbean islands, operate in kilometers. One kilometer is equivalent to 0.62 of a mile, just over a half mile for rough judgment. Twenty kms would equal about twelve-and-a-half miles. For smaller measurements, the centimeter is in use. The centimeter equals 0.39 of an inch and one foot is equal to 30.48 cms. One yard is just under 100 cms. in 91.44 cms.

With measurements for temperatures, the C degree = Celsius calculations are in use on the islands. The translation from C degree to F degree = Farenheit is by multiplying the Celsius figure by 1.8 and then adding 32 degrees. This will give you an accurate reading in Farenheit and provide something for you or the children to do with the pocket calculator!

Money, as previously stated, is in French Francs everywhere in the islands and this is divided into 100 centimes. The exchange rate, which varies, is something else to calculate. Coins come in 5, 10, 20 and 50 centimes (cts.) and 1, 2, 5 and 10 francs (F). The notes are in denominations of 10, 20, 50, 100, 200 and 500 F. Postage stamps are the same as in use in European France but, with some foresight, the islands are slowly introducing their own more exotic covers. Most credit cards are acceptable throughout the islands and it is wise to take traveller's cheques in U.S. dollar denominations. One useful question is "C'est combien?"—How much is that?

Conversion Charts

As the metric system is used in the French Antilles, it may be useful to refer to the following scales for distance, speeds, weights and temperatures.

Distance			Weights (Imperial)		
kilometres (km)	km or miles	miles	kilograms (kg)	kg or lb	pounds (lb)
1.609	1	0.621	0.454	1	2.205
3.219	2	1.243	0.907	2	4.409
4.828	3	1.864	1.361	3	6.614
6.437	4	2.485	1.814	4	8.819
8.047	5	3.107	2.268	5	11.023
9.656	6	3.728	2.722	6	13.228
11.265	7	4.350	3.175	7	15.432
12.875	8	4.971	3.629	8	17.637
14.484	9	5.592	4.082	9	19-842
16.093	10	6.214	4.536	10	22.046
32.187	20	12.427	9.072	20	44.092
48.280	30	18.641	13.608	30	66.139
64.374	40	24.855	18.144	40	88.185
80.467	50	31.069	22.680	50	110.231
96.561	60	37.282	27.216	60	132.277
112.654	70	43.496	31.752	70	154.324
128.748	80	49.710	36.287	80	176.370
144.841	90	55.923	40.823	90	198.416
160.934	100	62.137	45.359	100	220.462

Speed

```
mph  20 30 40 50 60  70   80   90  100
    +--+--+--+--+--+---+----+----+---+
km/h 32 48 64 80 96 112 128 144 160
```

Temperature

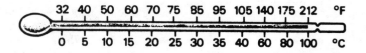

```
      32  40  50  60  70  75  85  95 105 140 175 212  °F
      0   5   10  15  20  25  30  35  40  60  80  100  °C
```

litres	litres or UK gallons	UK gallons (UK gal)
Volume (Imperial)		
4.546	1	0.220
9.092	2	0.440
13.638	3	0.660
18.184	4	0.880
22.730	5	1.100
27.276	6	1.320
31.822	7	1.540
36.368	8	1.760
40.914	9	1.980
45.460	10	2.200
90.919	20	4.399
136.379	30	6.599
181.839	40	8.799
227.298	50	10.998
272.758	60	13.198
318.217	70	15.398
363.677	80	17.598
409.137	90	19.797
454.596	100	21,997

Distance

Kilometers are used on the islands instead of miles and a quick guide to converting kilometers to miles is to half the number of kilometers and add the leading digit. An example of this rough method is: 50 kilometers is approximately equal to 30 miles, 50kms. ÷ 2 = 25 + 5 = 30 miles.

Useful Addresses

GUADELOUPE
POINTE-A-PITRE
Tourist Information Department
Place de la Victoire, B.P. 1099,
F-97159, Pointe-à-Pitre.
Tel: 82.09.30
Tourist Office
5 Square de la Banque, B.P. 1099,
F-97181, Pointe-à-Pitre.
Tel: 82.09.30

BASSE-TERRE
Maison du Port, 97100.
Tel: 81.24.83

SAINT-FRANÇOIS
Route du Méridien, 97118.
Tel: 88.59.95

USA
French Government Tourist Office
610 Fifth Avenue, New York, NY
10020. Tel: (212) 757-1125
111 North Wabash Avenue, Chicago,
IL 60602. Tel: (312) 726-6661
323 Geary Street, San Francisco, CA
94102. Tel: (415) 986-4161

CANADA
Services Officiels Francais de
Tourisme
1840 Ouest rue Sherbrooke,
Montreal, Quebec, H3H 1E4.
Tel: (514) 931-3855
372 Bay Street, Suite 610, Toronto,
Ontario, M5H 2W9.
Tel: (416) 361-1605

GREAT BRITAIN
French Government Tourist Board
178 Piccadilly, London, W1V OAL.
Tel: (01) 493-3171
      0906 824 4123

FRANCE
Office Tourisme du des Antilles et de
la Guyane Françaises
12 rue Auber, 75009 Paris.
Tel: 42.68.11.07

MARIE-GALANTE, LA DESIRADE
& ISLES DES SAINTES
(All through the Guadeloupe Tourist
Board)

MARTINIQUE
FORT-DE-FRANCE
Tourist Information Office
Boulevard Alfassa, B.P. 520.
F-97206, Fort-de-France.
Tel: 71.79.60
Tourist Office of St. François
Route du Meridien, 97118 Saint-
François. Tel: 88.59.95

SAINT MARTIN
MARIGOT
Mairie de St. Martin, Port de Marigot,
F-97150, Marigot. Tel: 97.50.04

SAINT BARTHELEMY
GUSTAVIA
Mairie de St. Barthélémy, Rue Au-
guste-Nyman, F-97133.
Tel: 87.60.08

**Chamber of Commerce &
Industry**
B.P. 64-97142, 6 Rue Victor Hugues,
Point-à-Pitre, Cedex,
GUADELOUPE.
Tel: 82.51.15/81.16.56

**Regional Tourism Development
Agency**
Anse Gouraud, 97233 Schoelcher,
MARTINIQUE.
Tel: (16-596) 61.61.17

**Office National des Forets Jardin
Botanique Basse-Terre**
Guadeloupe. Tel: 80.05.53

**Parc Naturel Regional de la
Martinique**
Caserne Bouille, Rue Redoute du
Matouba, F-97200 Fort-de-France,
MARTINIQUE.
Tel: 72.19.30

**Agencie Regionale de
Development du Tourisme et des
Loisirs,**
Pavillon du Tourisme—Jardin
Botanique, BP 801, 97338 Cayenne
Cedex.
Tel: 300900. Tx. 910356 FG.

**Bureau de Tourism de Saint
Lorent du Maroni,**
16 Rue du Colonel Chandon, 97320
St. Laurent.
Tel: 341086. Tx. NORBUR 910631
FG.

**Office du Tourisme des Antilles
et de la Guyane,**
12 Rue Auber, 75009 Paris, France.
Tel: 42681107. Tx. TOURAG
215806 F.

ADDITIONAL INFORMATION

Since the success of the first edition many enthusiastic readers have contacted the author and publishers with additional information both for this revised guide to the French Antilles and for its sister guide book—*The Netherlands Antilles.*

Among these contributors are Air France's Jet Tours Holidays which offer vacations in the French Caribbean in Guadeloupe, Martinique, St. Martin and St. Barthelemy. Air France particularly recommend the Meridien St. Francois, the Auberge de la Vielle Tour PLM-Azur, Gosier, the Marissol-Bas-du-Fort PLM-Azur and the Relais du Moulin, St. Anne, hotels on Guadeloupe; the Novotel Le Diamant and the Meridien—Trois Ilets hotels on Martinique; the Habitation de Lonvillers on St. Martin and the El Sereno Beach Superior hotel on St. Barthelemy.

The luxury sailing cruise ship company, Windstar, which operates its 440-foot, 148-passenger yacht *Windstar* in the Caribbean between Antigua and Barbados, have also contacted us about its new tours which began shortly after our first edition was published in 1990. *Windstar,* one of the company's three ships, makes seven-day cruises to Martinique (Fort-de-France), the Iles des Saintes and St. Barthelemy (Gustavia), among other ports of call.

We have also been notified that the Sonesta Beach Resort hotel on Bonaire, which opened in January 1990, has now changed its name to Harbour Village Beach Resort. We are also informed that this resort complex consists of 30 luxury suites and 40 first class room accommodations plus 44 villas. The Harbour Village operates in connection with Great Adventures Bonaire, a local sport diving organization. From the U.S.A. contact is on Tel: 1 800 424 0004, or Bonaire 599 7 7500.

Places of Interest to Visit on Guadeloupe.

Pointe-a-Pitre
Schoelcher Museum, 24, rue Peynier
Exhibition of artifacts and objects connected with the famous champion of the blacks, Victor Schoelcher.
Open: 9:15 am.–12:30 pm. Mon. Thurs. Sat.; 2:00 pm.–5:00 pm. Wed. Fri.; Closed Sun.
Tel: 82 08 04

Le Moule
Edgar Clerc Museum, 'La Rosette', 97 160
Museum of exhibits from Pre-Columbian times and displays of contemporary arts.

Open: 9:30 am.–12:30 pm. and 2:30 pm.–5:30 pm. Mon. Wed. Thurs. Fri.; Closed Tues. and Sun.
Tel: 23 57 57

Basse-Terre
Fort St. Charles History Museum
Exhibits of archives, ancient documents and maps.
Open: 9:00 am.–12:00 and 2:00 pm.–5:00 pm.
Tel: 81 37 48

Vieux-Habitants

Griveliere Plantation
Restored ancient plantation house.
Restaurant by reservation.
Tel: 98 48 42

Places of Interest to Visit on Martinique.

Fort-de-France

The Departmental Museum, 9, rue de la Liberte, 97200
One of the most fascinating and well presented archeological museums dedicated to the Arawak and Carib civilizations which inhabited the island in Pre-Columbian times.
Housed in an attractive, typical 19th century townhouse.
Open: 9:00 am.–1:00 pm. and 2:00 pm.–5:00 pm.; Sat. 9:00 am.–Noon.
Tel: 71 57 05

Fort Saint Louis
Dating from around 1640, this dramatic fort contains examples of cannon and ancient anchors within its massive battlements.
Open: Contact the Public Relations Officer for admission.
Tel: 63 72 07 ext. 109

The Transport and Commerce Museum, 53, rue Victor Hugo
Documents, models and displays trace the development of transportation from the dugout canoe to the most modern jet plane, tropical island produce and other interesting aspects of Martinique trade.
Open: 8:00 am.–1:00 pm. and 2:00 pm.–5:00 pm. Mon.–Thurs.
From 9:00 am. on Fri.

The Geological Gallery, Place Jose Marti
Documents, specimens and exhibits connected with the region of the Caribbean and particularly Martinique itself.
Open: 9:00 am.–12:30 pm. and 3:00 pm.–6:00 pm. Tues.–Sat.
Closed Aug.
Tel: 70 68 41

The Schoelcher Library, rue de la Liberte
Housed in a fantastic structure created by architect Pick, this is a repository for the black champion Schoelcher's 9,000 volume library. Many of the other books and documents here can be borrowed by the public.
Open: 8:30 am.–12:00 and 2:30 pm.–6:00 pm. daily; 8:30 am.–12:00 Sat.
Tel: 72 45 55

The Botanical Gallery, Place Jose Marti
Exhibits refer to the known 2,800 species of plants on the island in specimen and photographic displays.
Open: 9:00 am.–12:30 pm. and 3:00 pm.–6:00 pm. Tues.–Sat.
Closed Aug.
Tel: 70 68 41

Tartenson

Martinique Archival Services, rue Saint John Parse, 97263
Housed in a modern building, this museum displays ancient maps, old documents and engravings depicting the life and times of the island throughout the centuries.

Open: 7:30 am.–1:00 pm. Mon. and Thurs. and also 3:00 pm.–6:30 pm. Tues. Wed. Fri.

Balata

Balata Botanical Gardens
Rivalling any similar gardens in the Caribbean, Balata's 1,000 species of flora are not only a magnificent tribute to Mother Nature but a haven for tropical birdlife. A Creole house in the grounds exhibits choice flower and fruit displays.
Open: 9:00 am.–6:00 pm. Daily.
Tel: 64 48 73

Saint-Esprit

Museum of Popular Arts and Traditions
Examples of the island's arts, crafts, furniture and domestic utensils trace the development of the island and the islanders across the ages.
Open: 9:00 am.–12:00 and 3:00 pm.–5:00 pm. except Tues.; 9:00 am.–Midday on Sun.

Les Trois Ilets

The Pagerie Museum
Once the birthplace of Marie Joseph Rose Tascher de la Pagerie, Napoleon Bonaparte's Empress Josephine, this quaint old house now contains exhibits relating to the celebrated islander and her Emperor and artifacts of Pre-Columbian occupation.
Open: 9:00 am.–5:00 pm. Daily except Mon.
Tel: 68 34 55

Parc des Florales
Inaugurated by the wife of President Valery Giscard D'Estaing, this beautiful botanical park is set in 3 hectares of idyllic tropical landscaping managed by the Regional Nature Park authorities.

The Sugar Cane Museum
A complete set of exhibits, models and artifacts from the sugar cane industry of the island through the centuries housed in the restored 'Vatable' distillery.
Open: 9:00 am.–5:30 pm. Daily except Mon.
Tel: 68 32 04

Anse a L'Ane, Les Trois Ilets

Seashell Art Museum
Created by local artist Madame Heloise Ten-Sio-Po, who demonstrates this art in her unique exhibition, this museum consists of models made entirely with seashells indigenous to the island.
Open: 9:00 am.–12:00 and from 3:00 pm.–5:00 pm. Daily except Tues.
Tel: 68 34 97

Saint-Pierre

The Vulcano Museum
Memorabilia and artifacts discovered in the ruins of Saint-Pierre after the eruption of Mount Pelee on May 8, 1902.
Open: 9:00 am.–12:00 and 3:00 pm.–5:00 pm. Daily.
Tel: 77 15 16

Anse Turin Le Carbet

Paul Gaugin Memorial Art Centre
The French painter lived here during 1887. Martiniquais paintings and reproductions celebrate Gaugin's life. Exhibits also include local costumes and artifacts from Saint-Pierre.
Open: 10:00 am.–5:00 pm. Daily.
Tel: 72 52 49

Le Coin Le Carbet

'Amazonia' Zoological Gardens
Located on the probable site of Columbus' landing, June 15, 1502 the

zoo houses more than 80 exotic species of animals, reptiles and birds.
Open: 9:00 am.–6 pm. Daily.
Tel: 78 00 64

Leyritz Plantation, Basse Pointe

'Poupees Vegetables' Doll Museum
Made entirely from plants and vegetable fabrics by a local artist, the exhibits here celebrate national and historic costumes of the island.
Open: 7:00 am.–5:00 pm. Daily.
Tel: 78 53 92

Sainte-Marie

Saint James Rum Museum
This magnificent Creole mansion houses industrial artifacts and objects of interest from the rum industry from 1654 to the present day.
Open: 9:00 am.–5:00 pm. Mon.–Fri.; 9:00 am.–1:00 pm. Sat.–Sun.
Tel: 75 30 02

Saint Jaques Plantation and Pere Labat Museum
Once a monastery and Pere Labat's residence, built in 1658, this site includes the ruins of an ancient chapel and houses remnants and artifacts pertaining to the rum industry and its history. Pere Labat Museum exhibits celebrate the famous friar's life and achievements and the island's history.
Open: Tours daily between 9:00 am.–6:00 pm.

Tartane, The Caravelle Peninsula

Chateau Dubuc
Built in the latter half of the 16th century, the ruins of this country house are now part of the Regional Nature Park and an airy exhibition hall contains references to the turbulent era of this part of the island.
Open: 8:30 am.–12:30 pm. and 2:30 pm.–5:30 pm. Daily; Sun. 8:00 am.–Midday.

Index

TRAVEL THE WORLD
WITH HIPPOCRENE BOOKS!

HIPPOCRENE INSIDER'S GUIDES:
The series which takes you beyond the tourist track
to give you an insider's view:

NEPAL
PRAKASH A. RAJ
0091 ISBN 0-87052-026-1 $9.95 paper

HUNGARY
NICHOLAS T. PARSONS
0921 ISBN 0-87052-976-5 $16.95 paper

ROME
FRANCES D'EMILIO
0520 ISBN 0-87052-027-X $14.95 paper

MOSCOW, LENINGRAD AND KIEV (Revised)
YURI FEDOSYUK
0024 ISBN 0-87052-881-5 $11.95 paper

PARIS
ELAINE KLEIN
0012 ISBN 0-87052-876-9 $14.95 paper

POLAND (Third Revised Edition)
ALEXANDER T. JORDAN
0029 ISBN 0-87052-880-7 $9.95 paper

TAHITI (Revised)
VICKI POGGIOLI
0084 ISBN 0-87052-794-0 $9.95 paper

THE NETHERLANDS ANTILLES:
A TRAVELER'S GUIDE
ANDY GERALD GRAVETTE
The Caribbean islands of Aruba, Bonaire, Curacao, St. Maarten,
St. Eustatius, and Saba.
0240 ISBN 0-87052-581-6 $9.95 paper

HIPPOCRENE LANGUAGE AND TRAVEL GUIDES:
Because traveling is twice as much fun if you can meet new people as well as new places!

MEXICO
ILA WARNER
An inside look at verbal and non-verbal communication, with suggestions for sightseeing on and off the beaten track.
0503 ISBN 0-87052-622-7 $14.95 paper

HIPPOCRENE COMPANION GUIDES:
Written by American professors for North Americans who wish to enrich their travel experience with an understanding of local history and culture.

SOUTHERN INDIA
JACK ADLER
Covers the peninsular states of Tamil Nadu, Andhra Pradesh, and Karnataka, and highlights Goa, a natural gateway to the south.
0632 ISBN 0-87052-030-X $14.95 paper

AUSTRALIA
GRAEME and TAMSIN NEWMAN
0671 ISBN 0-87052-034-2 $16.95 paper

IRELAND
HENRY WEISSER
0348 ISBN 0-87052-633-2 $14.95 paper

POLAND
JILL STEPHENSON and ALFRED BLOCH
"An appealing amalgam of practical information, historical curiosities, and romantic forays into Polish culture"--*Library Journal*
0894 ISBN 0-87052-636-7 $11.95 paper

PORTUGAL
T. J. KUBIAK
2305 ISBN 0-87052-739-8 $14.95 paper

ROMANIA
LYDLE BRINKLE
0351 ISBN 0-87052-634-0 $14.95 paper

THE SOVIET UNION
LYDLE BRINKLE
0357 ISBN 0-87052-635-9 $14.95 paper

THE CEMETERY BOOK
TOM WEIL
The ultimate guide to spirited travel describes burial grounds, catacombs, and similar travel haunts the world over (or under).
0106 ISBN 0-87052-916-1 $22.50 cloth

GUIDE TO EAST AFRICA:
KENYA, TANZANIA, AND THE SEYCHELLES (Revised)
NINA CASIMATI
0043 ISBN 0-87052-883-1 $14.95 paper

TRAVEL SAFETY:
SECURITY AND SAFEGUARDS AT HOME AND ABROAD
JACK ADLER and THOMAS C. TOMPKINS
0034 ISBN 0-87052-884-X $8.95 paper

And three books by GEORGE BLAGOWIDOW to keep you on your toes:

TRAVELER'S TRIVIA TEST:
1,101 QUESTIONS AND ANSWERS FOR THE SOPHSTICATED GLOBETROTTER
0087 ISBN 0-87052-915-3 $6.95 paper

TRAVELER'S I.Q. TEST:
RATE YOUR GLOBETROTTING KNOWLEDGE
0103 ISBN 0-87052-307-4 $6.95 paper

TRAVELER'S CHALLENGE:
SOPHISTICATED GLOBETROTTER'S RECORD BOOK
0398 ISBN 0-87052-248-5 $6.95 paper

TO PURCHASE HIPPOCRENE'S BOOKS contact your local bookstore, or write to Hippocrene Books, 171 Madison Avenue, New York, NY 10016. Please enclose a check or money order, adding $3 shipping (UPS) for the first book, and 50 cents for each of the others.
Write also for our full catalog of maps and foreign language dictionaries and phrasebooks.